The Wisdom of the Living L

Gaiasophy

Kees Zoeteman

The Wisdom of the Living Earth

Gaiasophy

An Approach to Ecology

Lindisfarne Press

This book is a translation of *Gaiasofie* published by
Uigeverji Ankh-Hermes bv, Deventer, Stuttgart.
© 1989 Verlag Uitgeverji Ankh-Hermes, Deventer.

Translated by Tony Langham and Plym Peters

Translation © Floris Books, Edinburgh, 1991.
This edition © Lindisfarne Press, 1991.

Published by Lindisfarne Press
RR4 Box 94 A1, Hudson, NY 12534

Library of Congress Cataloging-in-Publication Data
is available: L.C.#91-21-866

ISBN 0-940262-43-6

Printed in the United States of America

Contents

CONTENTS

Foreword

This work was originally written as a diary, a collection of brief excursions which, to my surprise, ultimately led me to a valuable goal. The final result is what matters, and I hope many readers will see it as a source of inspiration for their own personal life-styles and their work; a source of inspiration for achieving a new and lasting relationship with Mother Earth, who bears life and tolerates our many social activities.

However, in addition to the end result — which is by no means a static goal, but is constantly developing and moving — the path by which this goal was reached is also of importance. Not that there is only one path; on the contrary, there are many. However, every path is an example of the struggle to find the truth. A struggle which everyone must undergo for himself. A struggle in which we only see the truth in the external world around us after we have touched upon the truth in our inner selves. That is why this book contains a reflection of my own spiritual quest. In my search for new insights I was strongly influenced by theosophy and anthroposophy. There are also other ways of learning about the essence of the Earth. I ask for the forbearance of those who see an element of one–sidedness in the literature which I consulted. No doubt a great deal more has been written, and I would be grateful for any suggestions and comments. But doesn't everything ultimately come from the same source? On the basis of the literature consulted here we can take an important step forward in our view of the organization of the Earth organism. The fruition of the insights described here is the primary goal of this book. I hope that many people will wish to continue this work.

Chapters 2 and 4 contain a brief summary of the spiritual teachings about the spiritual world and the creation of man and the Earth. Anyone who is already familiar with these ideas can leave out these chapters, and anyone who is only interested in the way in which the Earth organism functions can take up the thread of the discussion in chapter 8.

My wife Marianne and dozens of friends encouraged me directly and indirectly to complete this work. While I was writing I was given books and magazines by Marianne Carolus, Robert Hogervorst, Jan Zee, Maria Brouwer and Anita van den Berg. I had some valuable discussions with them and with Marius Enthoven, Gerard Wolters, Klaas van Egmond, Hans de Kruijf, Rien de Jong and Jan Diek van Mansvelt. Their comments encouraged me to translate my ideas into day–to–day practical terms. The text was typed with the enthusiastic co–operation of Lenie Oostwouder and Marga van Oostrom, the many diagrams were designed by André Berends, all devoted members of the Dutch National Institute of Public Health and Environmental Protection in Bilthoven. Without their support, and of course the inspiration of those who support us in the spiritual world, this book could not have been written. Now that it is finished, I hope it will serve as a reference work to mark the way, and as an encouragement to further exploration.

1. The wall

The Soul of the Earth raised its voice to heaven in com-
plaint:
   "Why was I created? What is the purpose of my exis-
tence? I am exploited and exhausted. The gifts of my
fertility are being squandered. Tyranny and extravagant
human whims use me as a target. No one comes to my aid.
I cannot count on any mercy.
   Therefore I turn to you, O God, as my last refuge.
Have mercy on me and my fertile fields. "

Zarathustra, Yasna 29:1

1.1   The search

The idea of writing a book about the Earth organism arose when
I saw the relationship between fragments of information which
I have been collecting for many years.

This started more than thirty years ago. As a child I would fall
into a trance looking at the fast whirling beetles on the mirror
surface of the pond behind our house in Dordrecht. They made
their circles so effortlessly, as though they dwelt in a completely
different reality. My heart would beat faster when I saw the dark
hollows in the thick trunks of the oak trees in the park in the
town. What would I meet if I were really to penetrate those
hollows? I remember a summer afternoon, sitting on the win-
dowsill of my parents' house, dreamily looking out. I saw the
white and dark blue sky, threatening thunder, over the railway
crossing which my father would soon pass on his way home. The
sky reminded me of a related but unattainable distant reality.
Even more intriguing was the pitch black muddy ditch alongside
the railway, where salamanders, leeches and tadpoles swarmed
in the mud, and where you would suddenly see the bright red

poppies or the delicate lilac of campion. I would run from flower to flower in delight, until I had picked a fistful.

Years later, when I was at secondary school in Vlaardingen, I crawled on to the roof of the block of flats where we lived in Schiedam to look at the Milky Way through some opera glasses, behind the reflection of the eternal flames of the Shell Refinery in Pernis. Breathlessly, I peered at the Moon, Venus, the Signs of the Zodiac, sought out the Andromeda Nebula, and finally felt myself almost floating off towards the cool starry mists.

Sometimes I would get off my bike on my way to school and stop to look into the fresh mud at the bottom of a clear pool on the road, as though the evolutionary process would unfold itself once more before my spiritual eye in this rust–brown murky mass. It was because of this expectation of getting closer to the miracle of creation that I decided to study chemistry at the Polytechnic in Delft in 1962. For four years I was a member of the Christian student union, Societas Studiosorium Reformatorum, and of a fraternity with the ominous name "Tartaros." The concepts from Greek mythology which were used as a matter of course were foreign to me with my technical secondary school background. During my years at university, my feelings of curiosity and a sense of wonder were increasingly obscured by layers of logic and analytical thinking. In one examination in biochemistry, Professor Berends accused me of viewing the life of a cell as a sack of enzymes, yet he was unable to present me with a more comprehensive view of life. What he heard from me was what I had heard in his lectures.

In this way the process of dissection continued. A chasm developed between those things that could be scientifically investigated and the intuitions about a reality behind all this. In the 1970s I started work as a scientist for the National Institute for Drinking Water in Scheveningen. In 1984 this Institute was amalgamated into the National Institute for Public Health and Environmental Protection (RIVM) in Bilthoven. First, I studied the consequences for drinking water of the pollution of rivers and the soil. Later on I studied the cycles of substances in the environment and the ecological consequences. During these years my thinking became more practical, to fit in with the scientific circles where I hoped to be accepted and valued. When this actually started to happen after about ten years, when I was thirty-five years old, a time came when all my work seemed increasingly repetitive: organizing conferences with the same experts, referring in publications to your own work and that of friends as far as possible, defending subjects for all you're worth because you have invested so much in it and your identity has started to depend on it. All this began to make me feel constricted. In my research I was forced into ever-increasing specialization. In these conditions, who is still capable of a broad perspective on things? No one any longer seems to aim at a synthesis, an overall view, for fear of losing a new idea because of a detail and of unpredictable progress. Was I still working on something important for the future? In one of the rare moments that I took some time off to think about myself, usually during holidays, I heard the echo of the words of Rabbi Yehuda Ashkenazy from Amsterdam, whose lectures I had attended at the University of Utrecht in 1981: "You must only do that which is *lebenswichtig.*" I asked myself what was of importance to life, not in general, but for myself.

Slowly, after years of self-analysis and listening to religious leaders, once again reading books by others seeking an answer to the question of what is of vital importance, and those who purported to have found an answer, I started to discover that there is great agreement in what they all say: Plato, Goethe, Jung, Steiner, Buber — all have a common starting point. Eastern religions, transcendental yoga, Bhagwan, holistic religion and the New Age movement are also all based on the suspicion, or the inner certainty, that the natural sciences provide a description of a more comprehensive underlying reality. Learning about that reality and entering into a relationship with it finally seemed to me to be the only thing that could really be considered *lebens-wichtig.* Thus I embarked on a quest which, after twenty-five years, brought me back to the question about the beginnings of life, the beginnings of Earth, the beginnings of myself. I had to relearn what I had unlearned; to ask myself questions, no matter how comprehensive. In addition, I learned to unpeel arbitrarily and put back together the layers of knowledge which I had built up as a scientist. Although it is essential to be open to intuition, you soon lose the way without logical thinking to guide you.

This book is intended as a description of the road I want to follow between the factual discoveries of natural science, and what others have to say which is based on myths, esoteric writings, or extra–sensory perceptions. In itself this book is not alive, but hopefully it will witness a real meeting of disciplines, like a work of art. It must be possible to find the relationship between them. I am starting out on this quest in the hope that a road will appear in this context, coming from the past and leading to the future, in which man, as a conscious being, will have a decisive influence on his own development and that of the Earth. Is it possible to point the way towards a harmonious development of man and Earth?

This book scratches away at the horizons of time to establish beacons for those who wish to follow the same path. Even more, it serves to feed my desire to seek the surmised goal behind that horizon.

1.2   Two worlds

My attempts at looking back at the creation of man and Earth, and forward to future developments, are based on what has been revealed by an analytical scientific approach. However, I also wish to be as open as possible to everything that comes to us from earlier cultures, and that is told us by the initiated and by clairvoyants. If scientists and those initiated into spiritual science are both right — and this is my basic assumption — it is only shortsightedness and a lack of perseverance on my part that makes it impossible for me to discover the relationship between these two types of insight. By using both types of knowledge as a basis, by being open to both worlds, it may be possible to break through the wall which stands between the intellect and intuition, between mind and matter, between the mechanical and the spiritual, the egocentric and the universal, fragmentation and the whole. Before I take the plunge into scientific views on the development of the Earth and man, as expounded in Darwin's theory of evolution, I would like to have a better understanding of how this division originated in the world of experience.

In the first instance, I shall try to stand on top of the wall dividing "the realm of reason" from the "realm of the imagination." Without coming up with value judgments straightaway, I would like, for this purpose, to make an inventory of contributions from the realm of the imagination. Later I will discuss these critically and compare them with scientific theories. I cannot yet speak directly from the imagination; at best I might succeed in doing so a few times *en route*. But I can listen to those who say they have stood on both sides and to those who are trying, like me, to find a way of looking over the wall between the physical and the spiritual.

1.3   The aims of the New Age movement

In my attempts I soon came across the views of the New Age movement, as expressed during the first half of the 1980s. This movement is an expression of the desire to be liberated from the clockwork life of modern society. The dominance of the machine is the consequence of the mechanistic view of man and society that has been propounded since Descartes and Newton.

René Descartes (1596–1650) wrote his most famous work, *The Discourse on Method,* in 1637. From 1628 to 1649 he lived in the Netherlands. This French philosopher and mathematician viewed nature as a machine made by God. This machine is governed by mathematical laws. He thought of mind and matter as being completely separate. Since the seventeenth century his view that the human body is essentially no different from a machine has dominated all natural science. It is the precursor to the idea that all living organisms are merely machines which can be analysed and exploited. With these concepts, Descartes was elaborating the philosophy propounded by the English philosopher and statesman, Francis Bacon (1561–1626). Bacon introduced the inductive method of thinking, in which general laws are derived from precise observations of natural phenomena. General conclusions follow from the study of the particular. The law of gravity was deduced from the observation of a stone falling. Up to that

time deductive thinking had been predominant; deductive thinking develops the particular from the general on the basis of
reason. The starting point is an idea, for example, the concept
hand, which appears in reality to exist in as many different forms
of hands as there are people. This type of philosophy goes back
to Aristotle (384–322 BC). In his best–known work, *Novum
Organon,* Bacon deliberately emphasized the contrast between
Aristotle and his own ideas. The Italian philosopher and theologian, Thomas Aquinas (1225–74) elaborated Aristotelian philosophy and developed a general framework of concepts which led
the way throughout the Middle Ages. In this world view the
organic relationship of mind and matter was central. However,
after Bacon and Descartes, this relationship became less clear.

In the same century in which Descartes formulated his vision
of nature as a machine made by God, the notion was translated
into real terms by Newton. Isaac Newton (1642–1727) saw matter as being composed of solid, indestructible spheres, created by
God for all eternity. The existence of these spheres or atoms had
already been postulated at a much earlier date. Even before
Aristotle's time, the Greek philosopher and natural scientist,
Democritos (*c.*460–370 BC), had conceived of atoms as being the
eternally unchanging smallest particles of which all matter is
composed. Aristotle successfully challenged this mechanistic
view, but in the seventeenth century the theory of atoms resur-
faced. In *Principia* (1687), Newton's most important work, he
described how all physical phenomena can be reduced by mechanical laws to the movement of material points in space. These
movements are governed by gravity. In this way the orbits of
planets and comets, the movement of the tides, and of a stone
falling could all be explained by the same principle. It was not
surprising that his theory met with general enthusiasm. In the
following centuries the religious awe of nature increasingly
disappeared under the influence of this analytical way of thinking. The spirituality which was still alive in the above–mentioned
great thinkers has been lost since then. The New Age movement
wishes to cast aside the numbness which resulted from mechanistic thinking.

Marilyn Ferguson, an American scientific journalist, is an

important advocate of the New Age movement. In her book, *The Aquarian Conspiracy* (1980), she describes the characteristics of a new age. According to Ferguson, this new age will dispense with the duality between science and religion, the external and the internal, and materialism and spiritualism. Man will become his own guru by a process of interiorization, and by being open to the timeless and the spaceless with the help of yoga or other consciousness expanding methods, such as transcendental meditation. The New Age movement considers that it operates in the form of an invisible network of people seeking the holistic principle behind visible reality which makes all things whole. Mankind has started on a process of changing the inner self to expand his consciousness. This process sprang from a sense that the balance had been lost. In this context, the Dalai Lama calls modern man an intellectual giant and spiritual dwarf. In his book, *The Turning Point* (1982), the nuclear physicist Fritjof Capra, who was born in Austria and works in California, showed how the mechanistic view of nature has not only started to dominate natural science, but also the social sciences. A physical cause is sought for every illness. Disease is supposedly only the result of chemical poisoning, an infection of bacteria and viruses, or, for example, a nutritional deficiency. The importance of harmony between body and mind as a precondition of the healing process is increasingly ignored by doctors. Even in psychology the human mind is considered as though it is a machine in the tradition of Sigmund Freud (1856–1938). Freud viewed the human mind as a psychological space in which the components of the personality (Id, Ego and Superego) are located rather like objects. As in mechanics, these objects are characterized by their dimensions, location and movement. The driving forces include instinctive drives, especially the sexual drive. In this way mind and body were divided to an even greater extent than in Descartes' work. This is what the New Age movement is opposed to.

1.4   The mechanical conquers the biological

Obviously, mechanistic thinking has had an effect on insights about the origins of life. In the first instance, following Descartes, nature was seen as a material mechanism which operates according to strict laws of cause and effect. In this view matter has no goal or spirituality. The different species in the chain of already existing organisms were determined from the day of their creation.

A fundamental change in this view was introduced in the nineteenth century by the French biologist, Jean–Baptiste Lamarck (1744–1829), who stated that life had started with single cell organisms (ciliates), from which the higher species had gradually developed separately. His theory was overshadowed by the theory of evolution of Charles Darwin (1809–82), published in *On the Origin of Species by Natural Selection* (1859). The concept of evolution meant that the Cartesian view of nature as a perfect machine had to be replaced by a universe that is considered as a constantly changing system developing towards higher levels of complexity. At the same time, the concept of evolution was grist to the mill of the real materialists, who saw all of reality as being composed of matter without it being based on any spiritual initiative. Thus analytical thinking also assumed a dominant place in biology. The initially rather simple clockwork mechanism was successfully elaborated to become increasingly sophisticated. In the eighteenth century the French father of chemistry, Antoine Lavoisier (1743–94) had already demonstrated that respiration involves a special type of chemical oxidation. This showed that the mechanism of chemical processes is important for the functioning of living organisms. The Italian Luigi Galvani (1737–98) discovered that the transmission of nerve impulses is accompanied by electrical currents. All of this confirmed the view that living organisms are complicated mechanisms based on physical and chemical interactions.

In addition to the theory of evolution, it was accepted that the cells observed at an earlier date by Robert Hooke (1635–1703) under his microscope were the building blocks of all plants and animals. Louis Pasteur (1822–95) was the founder of bacteriology, which established the connection between micro–organisms and disease. Gregor Mendel (1822–84) discovered the existence of genes, the carriers of hereditary characteristics, which are passed on in reproduction without changing their identity. In the twentieth century the science of genetics was developed on the basis of Mendel's work, showing that genes are arranged in a cell in the chromosomes. These are large molecules in the nucleus of the cell, sometimes called the atoms of heredity. The changes which can occur in species in the course of time can be traced back to the small changes, mutations, in the composition of the genes, which are passed on to the next generation as an inherited characteristic during cell division. These changes can be brought about by radiation, or carcinogenic substances. This idea stimulated the French geneticist, Jacques Monod (1910–76) to state in *Le hasard et la necéssité* (1970) that chance is the sole source of every change, of every creation in the biosphere. During the last century the attention of biologists has shifted from cells to chromosomes in an attempt to determine the molecular structure of genes. James Watson and Francis Crick succeeded in doing this for DNA, of which the hereditary material in chromosomes is composed. Together with Maurice Wilkins, they received the Nobel Prize for Medicine for their work in 1962.

Chromosomes consist of a double helix of DNA molecules. Each gene is a particular piece of this double helix. The special quality of a gene is that it contains a code which lays down the structure of certain protein molecules known as enzymes. Enzymes regulate the chemical processes in a cell. Cancer appears to be related to errors in the reproduction of certain genes. As stated above, these errors may be caused by certain substances or by radioactive radiation, and are comparable to a damaged magnetic tape on which a computer program is recorded. The same error is then constantly repeated. In this way biologists penetrated the mechanisms underlying the processes of life in ever more precise detail. They discovered that for all living organisms the characteristics in their chromosomes are coded by the same chemical substances. Biologists have discovered the alphabet of the universal language of life. This is the crown of mechanistic thinking, and for many it confirms the view that materialistic philosophy is correct.

1.5   Holism and systematic thinking

In *The Turning Point*, Capra described that the triumph of mech-anistic thinking also heralded the end of the hegemony of this paradigm. This had already started at the beginning of the century with the pioneering work of nuclear physicists such as Max Planck (1858–1947), Albert Einstein (1879–1953), Niels Bohr (1885–1962), Erwin Schrödinger (1887–1961) and Werner Heisenberg (1901–76). Their work forms the basis of the insights propounded by the New Age movement, which is best summar-ized in the concept of holism. Holism is a discipline in biology which explains the parts of the whole in terms of the whole, and in which the individual parts are determined by the whole.

The term was first used by Jan Christiaan Smuts (1870–1950) in *Holism and Evolution.* This South African statesman and philosopher saw in nature an attempt at unity through synthesis. His holism attempted to establish unity in Darwin's theory of evolution, Einstein's atomic physics, and his own ideas about the evolution of mind and matter, to form a whole. He argued that evolution went deeper and deeper, and acquired an increasingly inner spiritual quality. This view was taken up in modern systems theory. Some well-known systems theoreticians include Ervin Laszlo and Erich Jantsch. The systems approach does not con-sider the universe as a machine, but as an indivisible dynamic whole, of which the parts can only be understood as the patterns of a cosmic process. Systems are integrated wholes of which the characteristics cannot be reduced to smaller units. All living organisms can be viewed as self-regulating systems, intercon-nected by networks of reciprocal relationships, and thus forming larger ecosystems. Laszko and Jantsch view evolution as a dyna-mic process of self-regulation, or in other words, a dynamic process of self-transcendence. Evolution is an adventure which always goes further and is open-ended, creating its own goal in a process of which the exact outcome is essentially undetermined. Nevertheless, one can discern a progression from multiplicity and chaos to unity and order.

In order to understand how this leap from mechanistic to holistic thinking occurred, we need to look in more detail at the events which have taken place in science in this century. Again and again researchers have scaled the wall which stands between intellect and intuition, so that the new intuitive insights could be fitted into the adapting materialistic world view with the help of logic.

At the beginning of this century it was shown that atoms do not consist of Newton's hard solid particles, but of extremely small electrons which are believed by some to move with great speed around the nucleus consisting of protons and neutrons. Moreover, atomic particles, which subsequently turned out to be made up of even smaller components, have a twofold character. Depending on the way in which they are observed, they behave like particles which have mass, or as an electro–magnetic wave pattern. In addition, Einstein showed in his quantum theory that light can be described as a current of particles (quanta). This means that the characteristics of an object composed of atoms are not essential, but depend on the way in which man interacts with the object with the help of his equipment and his senses. Matter is not something that really exists, but reveals tendencies to exist. The observer determines what he observes, and not the object.

As scientists penetrated more deeply into matter, they did not discover any fundamental building blocks, but according to Heisenberg, an intricate web of events appeared. At the atomic level, matter is a collection of reciprocal relationships which can only be expressed in terms of probabilities.[1] In nuclear physics, the Cartesian distinction between mind and matter, the observer and the observed, could no longer be made.

This led to the radical change in the understanding of space and time, as expressed in Einstein's theory of relativity (1916), which described the dynamic character of matter. Events were related to the observer's sense of time, as well as in a spatial sense. It is never possible to discuss space without also discussing time. The most important result of this theory was that mass can be considered as a spatial and temporal manifestation of energy; its spatial aspect is manifest in the form of objects with a particular mass, the temporal aspect as processes in which the corresponding amount of energy is involved. Everything is part of the same space/time reality. On this basis, the English nuclear physicist, David Bohm, developed a theory of the uninterrupted whole, which can be characterized as holistic.[2] Everything we observe with our eyes, telescopes or microscopes, is an experience of the external order of nature, determined by space and time. However, behind this he conceives of an inner order which is encapsulated at an unperceived level in the cosmic web of relationships. The whole, the inner core, is contained in each one of the parts of the observed world, as in a hologram.

Holography was a photographic technique invented by Dennis Gabor in 1947, which made it possible to create three-dimensional images by means of projection in space. This projection is based on interference patterns of light with the same wavelength as that of laser beams. The hologram is the photographically fixed light interference pattern of an object. When the photographic plate on which the hologram is fixed is broken, the complete original image, the inner order, can be created in space from each piece.

In 1977 the American, Karl Pribram, also made a holographic model in the field of neuropsychology to explain the functioning of the brain.[3] He believed that by means of complex mathematical calculations, visual perceptions are analysed in the brain for frequency patterns, and the visual memory is organized like a hologram. This gave rise to the idea that our brain builds up reality as we perceive it in a mathematical way by interpreting the frequencies of a dimension which transcends space and time. The brain is like a hologram, and interprets the universe which presents itself holographically. The reality around it is like a continuous rhythmical dance. Ordered structures are produced from these rhythmical patterns. In the new holistic world view, object and structure are replaced by vibrations and rhythms. On this subject Capra wrote: "Atoms are patterns of probability waves, molecules are vibrating structures, and organisms are multi–dimensional interdependent patterns of fluctuations. Plants, animals and human beings undergo cycles of activity and rest, and all their physiological functions oscillate in rhythms of various periodicities. The components of ecosystems are inter-linked through cyclical exchanges of matter and energy; civilizations rise and fall in evolutionary cycles, and the planet as a whole itself has its rhythms and recurrences as it spins around its axis and moves around the sun."[4]

Every event is influenced by the whole universe. The universe is present and encapsulated in each lower order of matter. Bohm described this dynamic phenomenon as a "holostream" from which all forms of the material universe flow. He believed that this higher reality comprises both mind and matter, although they are not causally connected.[5]

1.6 Mind and matter in natural science

The holistic world view also acted as an impetus for the elaboration of ideas about the relationship between mind and matter with the help of logic. The American anthropologist Gregory Bateson stated that life and the mind were expressions of the dynamics of a system's way of organizing itself. Mind is the essence of the life process. Mind and matter are both expressions of the same universal process, and are not essentially divided. Mind is not something that interacts with matter. On this subject, Jantsch wrote: "God is not the creator, but the mind of the universe."[6]

The deity was considered to be equivalent to the self-organizing dynamics of the whole cosmos. It is the highest level in an order of nature which begins with cells and bacteria. Higher spiritual layers encompass animal minds and individual human minds. These in turn are embedded in the greater minds of social and ecological systems, which are finally integrated into the planetary and cosmic minds. Capra concluded that this new insight produced harmony between the views of scientists and mystics.[7] He referred to the ideas of the French Jesuit scientist, Pierre Teilhard de Chardin (1889–1955), in *The Phenomenon of Man* (1955). Chardin's theory was that evolution progresses towards an ever–increasing complexity of growing consciousness, and he defined consciousness as the specific result of organized complexity. This definition is close to the concept of the mind as developed by Bateson and Jantsch. Teilhard de Chardin, who saw God as the source of all existence, was popular with the New Age thinkers, provided that God was defined as the universal dynamic of self–organization.

Various modern scientists have a more direct mystical connection with Eastern traditions such as Buddhism and Taoism. Ancient Chinese Taoism, as laid down in the *Tao Te Ching,* ascribed to Lao Tse and probably written in the sixth century BC, bears great similarity to holistic thinking. Works inspired by it include Paolo Soleri's *Matter Becoming Spirit* (1973) and Henryk Skolimowski's *Ecophilosophy* (1981), in which the starting point is the spiritualization of matter. The dynamic character of the Taoist world view is expressed in the duality of male/female, light/dark, active/passive, yang/yin, creation/dissolution. Tao manifests itself in the alternating dominance of one of the two aspects. Tao is the path which transcends all description, which is without beginning or end, is not bound by space or time, and does everything through non–activity. Tao, Bohm's holostream, and Teilhard de Chardin's and Bateson's concept of mind are indisputably very closely related.

1.7 On the borders of natural science

I have now arrived at the point where science cannot take someone searching for the meaning of existence any further. I have come to the wall, and sometimes I can look over it, though without being able to see anything behind it. For a while I thought that holism would carry me over the wall, but now I wonder whether it is actually any more than a very sophisticated form of materialism. It does provide us with ways of flying over the wall, but it does not give any answers to really fundamental questions. It shows me that the universe is a cohesive whole in the space/ time continuum, that it is built up of self–regulating living systems, the smallest parts of which consist of vibrations which manifest themselves as mind and matter with a certain degree of probability. It has also inspired me with the conviction that nature is developing in the direction of greater complexity and higher consciousness. But the question of the origin of nature and the goal towards which nature is developing has remained completely unanswered. By contrast, the scientific answer is that the direction of the development is clear, but that it nevertheless has no goal. Unconscious chance is lord and master on this side of the wall.

I must therefore conclude that we are still dealing with a more sophisticated version of mechanistic thinking, except that the clockwork mechanism has been replaced by the cybernetic mechanism of the self-regulating cistern in the toilet or of the thermostat in the fridge. This self-regulation is then equated with a new definition of the concept of mind. However, no stopcock is able to change the volume of water in the cistern, any more than a computer is able to carry out operations which were not programmed in by an external mind. It is true that holism takes a leap from the clockwork mechanism to the mechanisms of cybernetics and holography. It touches on the probable presence of a spaceless and timeless dimension, but does not provide any real information about this. What is the essence of gravity or of the sexual drive? What determines the shape of a crystal or a leaf on a tree? How does an organism spring from a fertilized egg? Can the universe develop in a certain direction without the initiative for this being taken at a higher level? Can something regulate itself without the capacity to do so being given from outside? For the objects in our immediate environment the answer is clear. No building is built without an architect's plans, no car without the designer's initiative, no well-ordered card index is compiled without someone who has decided to arrange the cards alphabetically. Holism is a final attempt, on the borders of materialism and spiritualism, to recognize the mind, but at the same time explain it on the basis of matter. This is done by placing matter in a larger conceptual framework, so that the mind is produced at the origin, as it were, at the same time as matter. As Capra states, holism seeks to incorporate the paranormal in a scientific framework.[8] Thus it seems that holism is intended — consciously or unconsciously — to deny the mind the primacy of the origin of creation. It sees the spiritual footprints, but seeks to explain the origins of this spirituality in material terms. However, I am not satisfied with this; I have the feeling that science is denying me something, and consequently my consciousness remains clouded.

It is time to leave this side of the wall and explore the area on the other side.

2. The spiritual world

> *Then the Soul of the Earth turned to He who carries the*
> *cosmic order, and asked:*
> *"Where is your justice? My body seems to have been*
> *created only to be trampled upon. Where is there a heart*
> *beating for me? Where the power which can come to my*
> *aid?"*
>
> Zarathustra, Yasna 29:2

2.1 Spiritualism versus materialism

Spiritualism, which ascribes true reality only to the spiritual, is
often set against the materialism of science. In order to describe
this reality in any way at all, I will have to master a range of
new concepts which were in many cases dispensed with long ago
in the world of science. To begin with, I will have to ignore the
scientific contempt for this approach.

The spiritual, the other side of what I perceive with my senses
of the time/space continuum, cannot be directly observed by
scientific methods, for I am entering the field of the so-called
extra-sensory perceptions, or spiritual world. As the scientific
method, which is always based on observation by the senses,
such as the eye or the ear, cannot penetrate this extra-sensory
world, the scientist *a priori* denies the existence of this side of
reality. The recognition of this reality weakens the universal
validity of the scientific method. Nevertheless, without denying
materialism to be part of reality, I wish to take this step, and not
to deny *a priori* the spiritual side of reality as a possibility.

Arguments can be put forward to support this standpoint. After
all, how is a scientific discovery made? Not simply by observing
nature, as many scientific geniuses will confirm. After experimenting for a long time — apparently hopelessly — in the search

for causal relationships, there is usually a moment of enlightenment, and the scientist is struck by a liberating idea, a flash of
light, the certainty of truth. Subsequently this idea is elaborated
and described with logic and reason, on the basis of observed
facts, creating the illusion that it arose spontaneously from the
calculations made. In this way scientists project an illusory world.
Not that logic is unnecessary; every idea has to be tested in the
light of logic to see whether it is consistent with data already
available, so that incorrect fantasies can be distinguished from
fundamental truths. Logic is used for analysis, comparison and
assessment, but it is not creative. For new insights, something
which has been described as imagination, inspiration or intuition
is needed. It is possible to be open to this influence, but it cannot
be forced. Nowadays all sorts of attempts are made to maximize
the conditions for being open to new ideas. This has resulted in
brainstorm techniques in industry, conferences in natural surroundings, quality groups, creativity training, courses in the use
of the right half of the brain, and in the most extreme case, the
use of drugs and so on.

According to esoteric literature, in seeking the spiritual world
it is essential to be prepared to enter into a process of internal-
ization. It is only in the inner self that one can find the entrance
to the spiritual reality concealed behind visible reality. In my
inner self I have to develop new senses with which to observe
the spiritual world, with which to see behind the wall. A precondition for this is to put a stop to the ideas which autono-
mously arise in our consciousness. If the pool of our soul is still,
with no ripples, the heavens can be reflected in it, clearly outlined. Inner peace and presence of mind are preconditions for
observing the extra-sensory world. In doing this the first step is
to learn to observe one's own thoughts. In the spiritual world
thoughts or images have as much reality as objects do in the
sensory world. After perusing these signposts in esoteric literature, the question arises as to what the mind really is. It is clear
to me that Freud's definition of a psychological space in which
the components of the personality are located like objects, is too
limited. This also applies to Bateson's description of the mind as
the dynamics of a self-regulating system, or the essence of the

27

life process which comprises thinking, learning and remembering. In a dialogue with Bohm, Krishnamurti described the mind as everything we have, think, feel, hate and love. He concluded that what we normally call the mind is no different from the body.[1] However, the end of the material process is the vacuum within the mind, and in this vacuum there is the movement of timeless energy.

Seen in this light, the mind is independent of time. However, I am seeking further characteristics of the mind which rise above the material plane. I will base a more detailed description in the first instance on what has been written on this subject in esoteric literature, particularly by theosophists and anthroposophists, because this is still closest to the scientific experiential world. In elaborating this, I will also make use of other roads to understand the mind or spirit and the spiritual world. In this respect ancient myths and fairy–tales play an important role. Although Greek and Germanic mythology are still fairly well–known on a superficial level in Europe, the deeper meaning of these myths has often been lost. Yet for a careful interpreter, mythology, like the Bible, contains a wealth of clues about the spiritual world.

2.2   Theosophy, anthroposophy and the Sufi movement

The work of the Russian Helena Blavatsky (1831–91), who founded the Theosophical Society in New York in 1875, together with Henry Olcott and William Judge, is an important source which expounds the insights of the theosophists. One of her most important works, *The Secret Doctrine* (1885–89), had a great influence. Apart from modern theosophy there was also a historical theosophy, which is embodied, in, *inter alia,* Brahmanism, Buddhism, Neo–Platonism, and the Christian theosophy of Jacob Böhme. At the beginning of the twentieth century the Rosicrucians and the anthroposophists broke away from the Theosophical Society. The Rosicrucians had played a role as an esoteric movement since the Middle Ages. Their most important work is *The Chemical Wedding of Christian Rosenkreuz* (1616), which described the initiation of Christian Rosenkreuz (1378–1484). It was most probably written down by the German theologian,

Johann Valentin Andreae (1586–1654), though he later repeatedly distanced himself from the Rosicrucians.

The Austrian Rudolf Steiner (1861–1925) has left us several hundred books, mainly consisting of transcribed lectures, first as a theosophist, and after founding the Anthroposophical Society in 1913, as an anthroposophist. In this way a wealth of material about the spiritual world has become generally accessible. In anthroposophical circles, Steiner is considered to have been initiated at a high level, with direct access to spiritual worlds. He studied many of life's questions with the help of what he called "spiritual science." Steiner maintained that all his insights were based on his own spiritual scientific research[2] and in the body of knowledge he acquired in this way he recognized the ideas of Wolfgang van Goethe (1749–1812). His views also correspond with the scriptures, the works of Aristotle and Plato, and traditions of even more ancient cultural epochs. Many of my discoveries about the spiritual world are derived from Steiner's work. Moreover, there is clearly a large degree of correspondence between the esoteric sources on the most important events in the developmental history of the Earth and man. The work of the theosophist Alice Bailey was published in the 1930s. She wrote many books, which she claimed were inspired by a great Tibetan mystic who was an abbot in a Lama monastery. The books invite the reader to judge their truth for himself, and to follow the road of initiation into the secrets of the spiritual world as a disciple. Anyone who feels an emotional impulse to embark on this task is invited to do so in the form of unselfish service for the development of mankind.

The Sufi movement was founded by the Indian mystic, Hazrat Inayat Khan (1882–1927), and follows on from Sufism, a collection of mystical sects in Islam. The emphasis on the universal aspect in all religions is characteristic of the Sufi movement. A recent Dutch movement, related to the Sufi movement, is psychosophy, inspired by Zohra Bertrand–Noach.

Of course, many works have been published in the last fifty years on related themes and by individuals who are inspired. Examples of these many works include the Hindu–oriented movement centred on Sri Sathya Sai Baba and the movement which was inspired by the work of the American medium Edgar Cayce (1877–1945). In the Netherlands Jozef Rulof, a powerful medium who died in 1952, became well known as a result of his paintings and books. However, I get the impression that the impulse to disseminate esoteric wisdom more widely took place in the most original way at the turn of the twentieth century.

2.3   Observing the spiritual world

Before exploring the concept of mind or spirit, I would like to devote some more attention to the ability of people to experience the spiritual world, because everything which comes from this reality otherwise seems completely improbable to me. By the spiritual world, I mean the domain which cannot be observed physically, and which is said to contain the origin of all the effects on the world observed through the senses. For the rest of my study of the spiritual world I must assume that it does exist, though I am not able to observe it myself. I have decided to take this giant step, and in this I am by no means the first to do so. One interesting precursor is the English biologist Rupert Sheldrake who took science on to another plane with his hypothesis of morphogenetic fields which are the causes of the forms in our material reality beyond our spatial dimension. He pioneered the idea that the physical world we know is influenced by forces originating in a different reality, a non–physical reality which can offer a better explanation for our evolution than the operation of blind chance.[3]

For an understanding of the methods of entering this different reality I began to study Rudolf Steiner's work. Steiner describes how in earlier times man was able to make direct contact with the spiritual world, and how this ability has been temporarily lost in our own time. In his lectures on *The Gospel of St John,* Steiner shows how this division arose between the experience of the spiritual and the physical, between heaven and earth.[4] For this purpose he returns to the time known in theosophical literature as the Age of Atlantis. With the concept of Atlantis I am truly entering the world on the other side of the wall. I do not wish to reject this sort of concept as nonsense, but first I would

like to gather information which is necessary for a better understanding of the esoteric literature. Later on, I will have to make
judgments.

The Age of Atlantis is believed to have existed about fifteen
thousand years ago, that is, before the start of the recorded history of mankind. The character of man and nature were different
from now. Remnants of this age are preserved in Germanic
myths and sagas, which refer to Atlantis as "Niflheim," because
it was shrouded in thick mist. The ancestors of modern man lived
on this Atlantic continent (which was later submerged). This was
the area that now forms the bed of the Atlantic Ocean, and disappeared under the waters following the catastrophe. Reminders
of this catastrophe can be found, for example, in the biblical
story of the Flood. At night, in their sleep, the inhabitants of
Atlantis still "saw" a part of the spiritual world, because they
were endowed with a misty clairvoyance. Clairvoyance is the
ability to perceive images in the spiritual world comparable to
some extent with the imagery of dreams. The experience of a
clairvoyant is different from that of a medium. A medium makes
his or her body available to other spirits; a clairvoyant does not
do this. Clairvoyants retain their own consciousness.

Steiner explained the clairvoyance of the inhabitants of
Atlantis in terms of man's structure, comprising four organizations or bodies.[5] For the sake of clarity, I will discuss this in
greater detail.

The outer body is the tangible body which can be perceived
with the senses. It has a solid form filled with chemical elements,
and contains the organs and senses. The physical body has volume and gives us a spatial presence. According to theosophy,
man has an ethereal body, or growing force, as well as a physical
body. The ethereal organization, which is responsible for growth
and reproduction, ensures that the chemical substances are combined in such a way that they assume the characteristic shape of
the organs and of the body as a whole, of every living creature.
Plants in particular reveal the effect of what is described as the
growing force, form force, or ethereal body. However, animals
and humans also have an ethereal body. Rupert Sheldrake's
hypothesis, already mentioned, that all forms originate in

morphogenetic fields situated beyond our spatial world, can be seen as a modern variation of what is known as the ethereal body in esoteric literature. When the ethereal body leaves the physical body in death, the latter irrevocably passes on to the decomposing forces of nature. The ethereal forces are responsible for the transformation and building processes in every living organism. They control the fluid streams in the living organism, just as the seas and oceans flow around the earth; it is the ethereal body which places a living organism in the stream of time.

The ethereal body is permeated with an even higher organization which is denoted by the name, "the astral body." The astral body is the bearer of the feelings and drives of animals and humans. The growth and formative forces are influenced by the feeling or astral body, and in turn influence the physical body. The way in which a dog joyfully wags its tail is an example of the influence of the astral body and ethereal body on the physical body. The astral body stands at the threshold of time and space, and in a sense it merely overshadows our lives. The astral body is also expressed in air currents, or respiration. The physical and ethereal bodies are cut off from their surroundings: the astral body, the "air" body, is open and reaches out to the stars and the signs of the zodiac. The word *astra* (star) is contained in the name, the astral body.

Finally, man is the only living creature with a fourth organization: the Self. The Self is the bearer of man's spiritual individuality; man's self-consciousness is expressed through the Self. It permeates and monitors the three lower organizations. The Self is even further distanced from time and space than the astral body. The Self is expressed in man's warmth system and extends to the end of the cosmos. The four organizations of which man is composed reflect the four elements of which — according to the Greeks — the world was composed: earth, water, fire and air.

In summary, man is said to have a physical body, an ethereal body, an astral body of desires, and finally, highest of all, the Self, as demonstrated in Table 2.1.

We have seen that man is the only living creature on Earth with an individual Self. Man shares an astral body, which reflects

Type of organization	Function	Area of effect	Highest organ- ization of:
Physical	bearer of organs and senses	solid	minerals
Ethereal	responsible for metabolism, growth, repro- duction	liquid	plants
Astral	bearer of feelings and drives	gas	animals
Self	bearer of spiritual individuality	heat	human beings

Table 2.1. The characteristics of man's fourfold organization.

the feelings of joy and sorrow, with animals. In common with plants, men and animals have a formative growth body or ethe-real body, which is responsible for reproduction, growth and the organism's form. All organisms, like minerals, have a physical body, the only one which can be perceived with the senses. Hazrat Inayat Khan describes this beautifully, quoting a Dervish proverb: "God slept in the realm of minerals. He dreamed in the realm of plants. He awoke in the animal kingdom, and became aware of himself in man."[6]

In death the ethereal body, the astral body and the Self, leave the physical body, so that the latter immediately falls prey to the decomposing forces of nature, as stated above (see Tables 2.2 and 2.4). If the ethereal body stops functioning, the physical body dies. Similarly, when the astral body ceases to affect the ethereal body, man has no consciousness. Clairvoyants are able to per-ceive the higher bodies of man and other organisms in their auras and energy fields, and from the colours and shape of the moving auras they are also able to tell a great deal about an organism's health and mood. During sleep there is also a separation of the bodies, though in a different way from in death. The Self and the astral body leave the resting physical body, and only the ethereal body remains connected to the physical body at night. Thus while we are asleep our bodies are like the bodies of plants. Because the astral body and the ethereal body are completely separated at night, the experiences which man has at night in the spiritual world through the astral body do not enter his consciousness (see Tables 2.3 and 2.4). However, in order to become conscious in thinking, the experiences of the Self and the astral body must become imprinted on the ethereal body, as Steiner explained in *Anthroposophy as Cosmosophy*.[7] Fragments of spiritual experi-

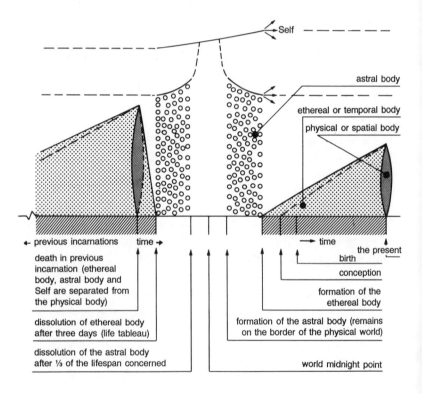

Table 2.2. A schematic survey of the formation and dissolution of the physical body, ethereal body and astral body in time.

ences may be recorded in the conscious mind in dreams which occur at the moment that the Self and the astral body re–enter the ethereal and physical body, just before waking up. The Self has to make a special effort to remember the dream.

In modern man the ethereal body virtually coincides with the outlines of the physical body. During the Age of Atlantis, particularly in the early stages, the head of the ethereal body still protruded above the physical head. This meant that when the astral body left the physical body at night, it still remained partly connected to the ethereal body. In this way reflections of the infinite distances of the spiritual world were constantly received by the protruding ethereal body through the astral body. At night the inhabitants of Atlantis were in the presence of the gods at a level of consciousness comparable to our consciousness in dreams. In fact, compared to us, they were spiritually awake at night and rather unconscious in the day. Dreams give modern man a last memory of the former contact with the spiritual world. After the waning of Atlantis this contact was gradually lost.

Steiner described how man in the Ancient Indian culture (7200–5100 BC), the first after the Age of Atlantis, still dominated the nostalgia for this link with the world of the gods.[8] Reality was seen to be full of spiritual creatures. A small number of exceptional people tried to flee the illusory material world by means of yoga and to retain the link which started to be lost to the rest of mankind. In the subsequent Ancient Persian culture (5100–2900 BC), man still considered the physical world as something repellent, as the domain of the God of darkness, but in this world he hoped to muster the forces of good and of light by building temples and by tilling the soil. Work on the material world from the spiritual world had begun. During the Egyptian–Chaldean culture (2900–750 BC), man no longer saw external reality as being misleading, but as a manifestation of divine spiritual creatures which could be controlled if it could be understood scientifically. At the same time it became more difficult to be initiated into making direct contact with the spiritual world. The further man descended into the material world, the longer the path upwards. Thus during the initiation into the mystical temples the novice had to spend three and a half

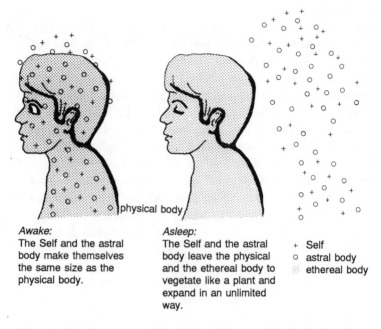

Awake:
The Self and the astral body make themselves the same size as the physical body.

Asleep:
The Self and the astral body leave the physical and the ethereal body to vegetate like a plant and expand in an unlimited way.

+ Self
o astral body
▒ ethereal body

Table 2.3. The departure of the Self and the astral body during sleep.

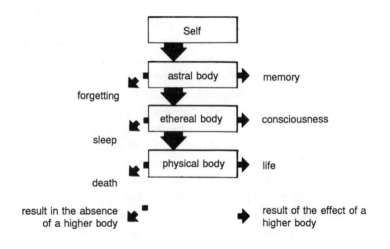

Table 2.4. Memory, consciousness and life as the result of the effect of a higher body on a lower body.

36

days in a sort of deathlike trance, following a period of preparation. A recent description of this was given by Elisabeth Haich in her book, *Initiation*. During this deathly sleep the ethereal body departed from the physical body by artificial means. What was consciously experienced by the astral body in the spiritual world could therefore be imprinted on the ethereal body. Upon returning to a normal condition, the initiate would know what he or she had experienced in the spiritual world. In this way an enlightened consciousness arose.

In the Graeco–Roman culture which followed (750 BC – AD 1410), the marriage between mind and matter took place in Greek art, which created a world of gods in the image of man. The Romans went even further, seeing themselves as the image of the gods, although the Romans experienced the forces of nature as the works of the gods. The world of the gods became ever more obscured.

Present and future cultures will have to rediscover the way to the spiritual world step by step. In this process the world is no longer available to man as a completed work. Man will have to start acting as a creator himself, instead of merely being an image of the Creator. According to Steiner, man will be able to work at this by consciously following a path of learning based on critical self–reflection.[9] This path aims to develop the astral body in such a way that it forms higher organs of perception; the process is also described as a process of purification or cleansing. Subsequently these organs are imprinted on the ethereal body during the process of the enlightenment of the ethereal body which is often referred to. The purification of selflessness and enlightenment together form the initiation by which the arbitrary observation of spiritual worlds is possible with the newly developed senses. As the astral body can only develop these higher senses when it is free, during sleep, at a time of unconsciousness, the conditions for this must be established in the daytime. The impressions received by the physical body during the day must remain in the astral body when it departs at night. This is possible after a process of spiritual training in the daytime based on concentration and meditation. The discipline of yoga works mainly through thinking. The Christian discipline, which can barely be achieved by modern man because of the isolation that is required, is aimed at feeling. The discipline of the Rosicrucians is more closely attuned to modern man, and is aimed at exercising feeling and the will to achieve inner security, inner strength, control over the emotions, a positive attitude, and candour. Moreover, Hazrat Inayat Khan has shown that man, who is more self-centred than any other creature, can only develop these spiritual senses if he succeeds in eradicating selfishness from his heart, so that the power of love can fully develop.[10]

Here we must conclude this necessarily brief account of the direct access that man formerly had to the spiritual world, the time when this ceased to be possible, and how the way can be rediscovered through training of the Self.

2.4   The cosmic spirit and the individual spirit

I will now explore in greater detail the concept of the spirit on which the reality on the other side of the wall is based. The concept of the spirit or mind cannot be separated from the concept of the soul, and from concepts such as thoughts and ideas. The spirit contains the essence of anything. The spirit leads me from the wall into the cosmic distances of the spiritual world in which there is no space or time, and which is full of "essences." Space and time are created where the spiritual world seems to hold back.

Bateson calls the spirit "the essence of the life process," and Krishnamurti "that which transcends time," while in *Perception and Thinking,* Steiner describes the spirit as that which "introduces necessity into chance," or in his commentary to *The Chemical Wedding of Christian Rosenkreuz,* as "the purpose of the will of nature." Where there is mind, there is consciousness. In his work on the spiritual foundations for education, Steiner made a clear distinction between mind (often translated as "spirit") and intellect. The mind is the active, creative, absolute productive element, while the intellect is absolutely passive, the passive image of the mind with which we understand the world around us. Bailey describes the spirit in *White Magic* as "the cause of all manifestation."[11] These descriptions are not mutually exclusive. For the moment I will merely describe the mind or spirit as the purpose of the will of nature and the cause of all manifestation.

Steiner uses the term "mind" in another sense as well, closer to the scientific sense. He explicitly states[12] that the mind is not the capacity to produce thought, but the capacity to perceive ideas. Thus in his eyes it is a human organ for capturing thought, just as the eyes catch images. If the first all–embracing concept could be described as "the cosmic mind," the essential aspect behind the nature surrounding us, the organ with which man per-ceives expressions of the cosmic mind in the form of thoughts and ideas can be described by the term "individual mind" or individual consciousness. The mind is a cosmic entity composed of innumerable facets, which forms the basis for everything that exists in the spiritual world, and which is revealed so that it can be perceived by the senses. Apart from the human mind, or the mind of mankind, higher or divine beings can be discerned with-in the cosmic mind, as well as lower creatures or creatures of nature. The latter do not have a Self, as man has.

The organ with which man perceives thoughts, which is able to watch the stage on which thoughts present themselves, is this Self, the individual mind, the individual consciousness. Inayat Khan names five aspects in which the functioning of the indi-vidual mind is revealed.[13] These are the capacity for thinking, the memory, the control of thought or powers of concentration, reason and feeling. Reason is the most valuable thing there is, but it is worthless if it is a slave to the mind. Reason can come up with arguments for anything, but it only has any value when it is based on a knowledge of morality, and it is only perfect in conjunction with feeling. The mind only starts to come alive at the moment that feeling has been woken. In man's initiation process exercises are carried out to develop these powers.

2.5   The soul as intermediary between body and spirit

I will also have to decide what is meant by the concept of soul, as well as the concept of mind or spirit. In theosophy the soul is described as the intermediary between the body and the spirit. I

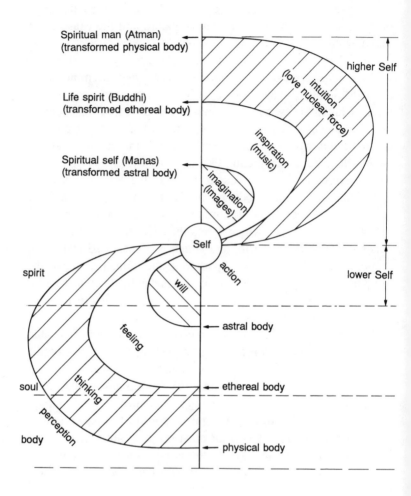

Table 2.5. The physical and spiritual composition of present and future man and the transformational task of the Self.

find this concept of the soul the most difficult to grasp. In *White Magic,* Bailey describes the soul as the relation between spirit and matter, the foundation of consciousness.[14] According to Steiner, the soul essentially comprises the astral body as the intermediary between the living physical body and the Self. In a sense the ethereal body is a transitional form between the material body and the soul.[15] The description given by Inayat Khan of the concept of spirit shows how the spirit has an effect on aspects of the soul. The soul itself is described by him as a stream which connects the physical body with its origin. In this context, he quotes Rumi as saying that Man is a prisoner on earth. His body and his mind are the bars of his prison, and his soul unconsciously yearns to experience once again the freedom which it enjoyed originally.[16] The soul is served by thought, feeling and the will, as shown schematically in the bottom half of Table 2.5.

Bailey characterizes this threefold division as knowledge, love and will.[17] The centre of these three functions of the soul is located in the head for thinking, in the heart for feeling, and in the belly and limbs of the physical body for the will. Man is most conscious of the thoughts of his physical body which are bound to perception. In his feeling he is conscious, as in his dreams, and in his will his consciousness is subdued, as in sleep. Inayat Khan describes it on the basis of three functions: "We are ministers when we are thinking, we are servants when our body is functioning, and we are king when the will is functioning."[18] Another view of the three functions of the soul reveals that it can have an external as well as an internal aspect. Externally in the head there is the sensory system, and internally, the nervous system, which is the vehicle for perception and thought. The chest contains the lungs and the heart, respiration and circulation as expressions of feeling and intuition. The metabolism and limbs (legs) are found in the abdomen, where internal forces and external actions are manifest. Thus the centre of the soul is reflected in the chest and in feeling, which can be summarized together as the conscience. Feelings are to the soul what food is to the body. Anyone who wishes to be initiated must start to feed his thoughts with ideas, his conscience with feelings and his will with ideals.

2.6 Thoughts, ideas and the higher Self

Thus the world perceived by the mind consists of thoughts and ideas. By observing natural phenomena, the scientist transforms perceptions of the outside world into thoughts, or concepts in the internal world, describing the perceptions. In *Phaedo,* Plato wrote that the characteristic of every concept distinguished by the intellect is that it is single, stays the same, unchanging and invisible.[19] In this way spiritual reality comes towards us from scientific observation. Reason then distinguishes the unity which can be discerned in the multiplicity of intellectual concepts. Goethe called this unity "the idea," the eternal and unique manifest in what can be perceived. In this way, seeing an object fall can lead to an encounter with the inner idea of the law of gravity. Steiner showed that the sciences can only penetrate ideas which have been revealed in inorganic nature. For organic nature and man, another approach is needed. In inorganic nature it is possible to penetrate the active force from what is perceived by the senses, but for organic nature this is only possible by using another method of investigation which Steiner called the method of observing thought.[20] For example, by thinking oneself into the form of an organism such as a plant, it is possible to discover the idea of the essence of the plant. This would have roots, a stem with leaves and a flower. It is present in every manifestation of a plant. However, to understand man it is not a matter of the general idea expressed in members of the species, but it is a matter of the separate individual person. Each person is a conscious and responsible being. Each person is not a single product of the original idea, for example, in his shape and organization, but is the only possible end result of this idea.

The subject of what Steiner called "spiritual science" is the idea, the spirituality which can only be known by the immediate perception of the reality of ideas from the point of view of a higher consciousness. Only spiritual science does justice to man as an individual organism, while science can only describe the dead exterior, man's mineral quality. It is only possible to understand the true significance of man if one has been initiated into the senses which perceive the world of ideas. Thus spiritual science has a further–reaching perceptual method than natural science, although the results relate to the same reality as manifest in material phenomena. The spiritual scientist will have greater understanding as his consciousness penetrates the higher levels of

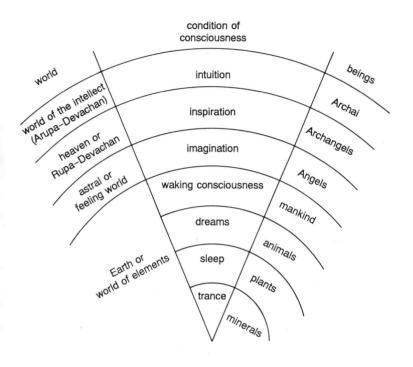

Table 2.6. Characteristics of the Earth and the higher spiritual world with their levels of consciousness and characteristic higher beings.

the spiritual world. Someone who does not have these organs of perception at their disposal must be satisfied with what is handed down to them by others who do have these powers. Obviously it must be possible to compare the results with logic and the phenomena encountered in the physical world. With the increase of the new organs of the astral body, described in Buddhism as lotus flowers or *chakras,* the capacity for an understanding of the spiritual world increases. In his book, *Knowledge of the Higher Worlds,* Steiner describes how a clairvoyant's consciousness of images, or the imagination, first arises. It is possible to "see" into

43

the so-called astral or feeling world by means of images (see Table 2.6).[21]

The next step is that of inspirational consciousness, which provides contact with the "inner word," the word of revelation, the source from which pure truth flows, according to Bailey. This consciousness expresses itself fully in musical inspiration, and with this it is possible to step into the world of the heavens, also described as the world of thoughts or "Rupa-Devachan."[22] This is followed by intuitive consciousness, which gives rise to the concept of the world of ideas. Intuitive consciousness is the harbinger of omniscience. This world in which spiritual beings are encountered is also known as the world of the intellect or "Arupa-Devachan." In future, with the help of the imagination, inspiration and intuition, man will transform his three lower bodies from the Self step by step to three higher bodies, respectively called the spiritual self (Manas), the life spirit (Buddhi), and spiritual man (Atman), as shown schematically in Table 2.5. In this process the astral body is transformed into the spiritual self. Man, initially dominated by selfish drives, is transformed into someone who wishes to serve the spirit of mankind as a whole, and mankind itself. Next, the ethereal body is transformed into the life spirit and, at an even later stage, the body which is most difficult to reach from consciousness, the physical body, is transformed into spiritual man or divine man. In this future age, the physical body must be imagined in a much less concrete form than we know it today. This produces the image of man with seven aspects, with a physical body, ethereal body, astral body, Self, spiritual self, life spirit and spiritual man. In some circles the three higher bodies are known as the vital body, the mental body and the spiritual body and together they form the higher Self. This higher Self has continuous consciousness, is as awake at night as in the day and is also known as the Monad.[23]

2.7   The higher hierarchies

I have given a first impression of the historical development of man's capacity for perceiving in the spiritual world, and of some of the esoteric movements in Europe. In addition, I touched upon the effect of initiation, the characteristics of the concept of the cosmic mind and the individual mind, and the role of the present four organizations in man involved in the ability to perceive in the spiritual world. Finally, there was some elucidation of the higher capacities of future man, consisting of imagination, inspiration, and intuition.

The question remains regarding what the initiate actually perceives in the world on the other side of visible reality. Steiner pointed out that in the spiritual world feelings, thoughts and ideas are hierarchical realities which interact in their own particular way, just as material entities do in the physical world.[24] So far, this does not conflict with the teachings of Freud. However, Steiner describes how these active realities should be viewed as living spiritual entities which are at different stages of development, and, more or less recently, went through a developmental stage comparable to present–day man. In addition, these spiritual entities actively influence developments on earth and in the cosmos. They formed man and guided his development in the same way as this is done at a lower level, for example, by teachers, managers, clerics or conductors. Just as the animal kingdom, the plant kingdom and the mineral kingdom are at a lower stage of development than man, there are also nine hierarchies of spiritual entities above man. Steiner describes these hierarchies in various places. In *Die himmlischen Hierarchien,* Hans W. Schroeder lists the Bible references to these hierarchies.

In order of ascendancy the first three higher spiritual entities are the Angels, the Archangels, and the Archai or Primeval Forces (see Table 2.6). These are closest to man. The Angels (Angeloi), also known as Sons of life, guide individuals like guardian angels, and instil guiding ideas in the astral body to develop brotherly love and spiritual freedom in man.[25] In other words, the Angels affect man's thinking. As they are at the highest level of consciousness, they themselves have imagination, and as the lowest body, they have an ethereal body. In addition, they gave man the ability to feel joy and sorrow in the ethereal body. In the process of incarnation they help man to find parents which suit his life plan. Moolenburgh has recorded the many encounters which people of our time claim to have had with angels.[26] The

Archangels (Archangeloi), also known as the Spirits of fire, act as the soul of groups of people, such as nations, and are the inspiration for the linguistic and cultural characteristics of those groups of people. They help man in the process of incarnation to find a nation suited to his life plan. They gave man the capacity to feel love and hate in the astral body. Just as we can perceive what appears to our senses, the Archangels perceive what takes place in inner consciousness in the soul of the people of a nation. The world of the Archangels ends with the astral body of man, and is not aware of the lower realms of nature of animals, plants and minerals. Man and the Archangels have in common the laws of grammar, mathematics and so on. However, their most important influence on man is related to feeling. In addition to the imagination, the Archangels also have inspirational consciousness, which is as awake in them as our consciousness of the physical world is in us during our waking consciousness.

The Primeval Forces (Archai) are also known as the Spirits of Personality. They perform a task for mankind as a whole and join impulses from nations together, so that this can give rise to a higher unity for the benefit of all mankind. Their activities are unfolded in cultures with a rhythm of about 2100 years. Temporarily, seven of the highly developed Archangels can also rise to the level of Primeval Forces, and they then act as regents and leading temporal spirits of the age for a short period of about three hundred and fifty years. In this way the leading temporal spirit at the moment is the Archangel Michael who took over from Gabriel in the second half of the last century. As the Archangel of the portal of birth, Gabriel acted as a stimulus to the voyages of discovery, and the development of materialistic science and technology. Michael stands at the portal of death, and as a guide he leads man away from his earthly existence after a life filled with experience, back to the spiritual world. Michael acts as a stimulus for new spirituality. The Primeval Forces gave man his own personality in the astral body. In addition, the primeval forces determine the time and place of birth when man is incarnated. They influence man's will and determine his individuality. Their highest level of consciousness is that of intuition.

The second triad of higher entities consists of the Powers, the

Higher hierarchy	Effect in the earlier development of mankind	Present effects

1st hierarchy

Seraphim	outpouring of love	(have dis–appeared from
Cherubim	outpouring of intellect	the human sphere)
Thrones	the seed of the physical body	

2nd hierarchy

Dominions (Kyriotetes)	structure of physical body ethereal body	
Forces (Dynameis)	capacity for movement astral body capacity for consciousness	
Powers (Exousiai)	delimited form of the body own Self capacity for remembering	

3rd hierarchy

Primeval Forces (Archai)	own personality in astral body	leaders of cultures
Archangels (Archangeloi)	capacity for love and hate in astral body	spirits of nations, temporal spirits
Angels (Angeloi)	capacity for joy and sorrow in ethereal body	guardian angels pro–vide leading ideas in astral body

Table 2.7. Composition of the higher hierarchies.

Forces and the Dominions (see Table 2.7). These are even further developed than the Angels, Archangels and Primeval Forces.

The Powers, or Spirits of the form, are also known as the Revealers or *Exousiai*. In Hebrew they are called by the name *Elohim*. In the present stage of development of mankind the Powers have played an important role because they gave man the creation of the Self, the capacity for remembering. In even earlier times they first gave man a delimited — though still plastic — form.

The Forces, which are one step higher, are also known as the Spirits of movement or *Dynameis*. They granted man the astral body, and with this, the capacity for consciousness. They also gave man the capacity for movement.

The Dominions, or *Kyriotetes,* are also known as the Spirits of wisdom. They placed their wisdom in building man's physical body, and also formed man's ethereal body.

Finally, there is the highest or first hierarchy of higher entities, consisting of the *Thrones,* or Spirits of the will, the Cherubim, or Spirits of harmony, and the Seraphim, or Spirits of love (see Table 2.7).

They planted the seed for the physical body, and made the intellect and love flow out towards man as an offer and a gift at the beginning of his creation. They have now left for higher spheres which are no longer in direct contact with man. These Creators withdrew so that man would be free.

According to Steiner, this hierarchy of spiritual entities, more highly developed than man, takes us to the horizon seen by the clairvoyant of our time who looks into the spiritual world.

2.8   Man as a spiritual entity

In addition to these higher spiritual entities which have all contributed to the development of man, and at the same time develop themselves through man, human souls can be discerned in the spiritual world. Apart from the people who populate the spiritual world while they are asleep, the dead inhabit a spiritual life between death and rebirth. Steiner described this in many ways. After death, man makes conscious contact with his Angel in the astral world, and then with the Archangel belonging to his people. A well documented account of the first experiences of people who had died and who returned shortly afterwards, is given by R.A. Moody Jr. in *Life after Life*. When man starts to prepare for his next incarnation at the end of the journey through the spiritual spheres — which happens for most people at least once every thousand years — alternating between man and woman and different nations, he first enters the field of the Primeval Forces (Archai). These carry man back from being dissolved in cosmic space and timelessness to the earthly definition of his essence. Man becomes increasingly condensed, meets the regions of the signs of the zodiac, develops the basis for the new organs of his body, and then traverses the areas of the planets and finally that of the Moon. During this descent the higher spiritual entities determine the time, the place, the nation and other characteristics of the life to come. What man experiences during his physical existence as the outside world is experienced by him between death and rebirth as his cosmic inner being (see also Table 2.2).

2.9   The essence of animals, plants and minerals

It is not only human souls and higher spiritual entities that can be found in the spiritual world. The souls of the lower realms on Earth are also present in the spiritual world, as shown in Table 2.8. Later on I will explain how, from the point of view of spiritual science, the lower realms on Earth are closely related to man. At this point I will merely say that spiritual science considers animals, plants and minerals as human seeds which have been retarded in their development and have fallen behind. Animals were the last to fall behind; minerals the first. Every species has a group soul, a group Self, just as man has an individual Self. This group Self of every species can meet the human soul in the astral world and communicate with it, just as people on Earth talk to each other. Sometimes the group Self becomes visible in the collective wheeling movement of a flock of birds in the air, a herd of cattle on land, or a shoal of fish in the sea. Plants which render pure ethereal forces visible, have their astral bodies in the

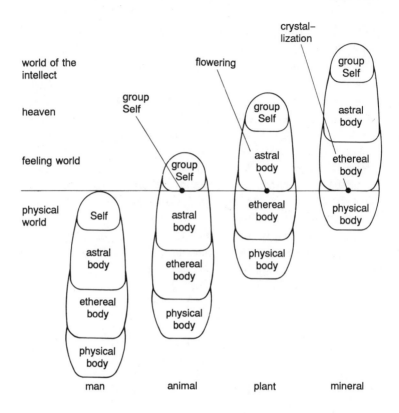

Table 2.8. The place of the four bodies of minerals, plants, animals and man and phenomena on the border of the astral and physical world.

astral world. The astral body momentarily touches the plants in the physical world when they flower. Their group self is on a higher sphere, which was described earlier as the heavens or world of thoughts, the sphere of inspiration. In minerals and gems the ethereal powers only operate in the process of crystal-lization. In fact, the ethereal body of minerals is in the astral world, the astral body in the world of ideas, and the group Self in the even higher world of the intellect. Thus, behind the lower realms on Earth there are spiritual entities, of which the Self is less profoundly incarnated because it belongs to a lower realm.

This is also the reason why the development of these lower realms is behind that of man. On the other hand, they are a manifestation of spiritual entities active at higher levels, with greater purity, though without their "own wisdom."

In spiritual science the falling behind of these realms is viewed as a sacrifice of the entities in these lower realms, allowing the development of the higher realms. At the same time, in future it will be the duty of the higher realms to liberate the entities from the lower realms from falling behind.

This is a short outline of some of the important sorts of entities which can be met in the spiritual world, according to the literature that was quoted. As they achieve a higher level of initiation, initiates can enter into more direct contact with these entities.

2.10 The Akasha Chronicle

Yet another characteristic of the spiritual world is important, because much of the information which follows is based on this. It is sometimes called the Akasha Chronicle. The Akasha Chronicle is on the border of the physical world and stores the spiritual essence of everything brought about in the world by conscious beings in the form of images. In his book on the Akasha Chronicle, Steiner wrote that the initiate learns to understand the eternal character of events which have passed by means of a considerably increased memory capacity.[27] These stand before him not as dead witnesses of history, but full of life. Anyone who is initiated into reading this sort of living script can see much further back into the past than what was recorded in external history. In addition, he pointed out that even in spiritual perception, there may be errors and inaccuracies. For this reason, one should not be surprised when the theories of different occult schools which basically concur, do not always correspond completely. Thus in the Akasha Chronicle the initiate can inwardly experience history as far as the distant prehistoric era in all its aspects and emotions. However, what is experienced is not perceived through the normal physical senses, which make it difficult to express in language. Messages from the realm the timeless and the spaceless have to be expressed in terms of time and space.

When we come up against these differences between our physical world and the world on the other side of the wall, we confront the difficulty — already mentioned — of the different terminology used to describe that other sphere of reality. Irksome though it is, this difficulty must be patiently faced.

3. The origins of the physical Earth

3.1 The Earth in the universe

At this point, I would like to take a closer look at the origins of
the Earth and the biosphere. Without analysing the precise eras,
I will begin by drawing up a plan of the creation of the Earth
according to scientific knowledge. This will be based on the
current theories of the creation of the universe and the disciplines
of geology and palaeontology. The next step will be to compare
this with the findings of spiritual science, in the hope that a
synthesis of the two will provide us with new insights into the
origins of the Earth and man's role in this. In the following
chapters I will discuss the origins of the biosphere as viewed in
terms of natural science and spiritual science, and the time
differences which are given for the developmental stages.

In scientific terms, the Earth is a tiny speck of matter in the
universe. According to Albert Einstein, the universe is a curved
time–space continuum with four dimensions and a finite content.
The universe consists of numerous stars, grouped in a large
number of galaxies, of which the Milky Way is just one. The
well–known Andromeda Nebula is another galaxy like the Milky
Way which is close to us and visible with the naked eye. Like
stars, Milky Way galaxies can be grouped together. These groups
are called clusters, and contain hundreds or thousands of galaxies. Our Milky Way contains an estimated ten billion stars, and

is shaped like a flattened disc in which the stars are arranged along spiral–shaped arms. In contrast, the centre of the Milky Way galaxy is composed of a gigantic spherical collection of stars in which gaseous masses are in turbulent movement and moving outwards. All the stars of the Milky Way galaxy move around this centre, each at its own speed. The Sun takes about 230 million years to orbit once round the centre of our Milky Way galaxy. The diameter of the Milky Way is at least 100000 light years. A light year is approximately 9500 billion kilometres, the distance travelled by light in one year.

The scientific picture can be filled out with a number of other well–known facts. The Sun is situated at approximately 30000 light years from the centre of the Milky Way galaxy, and has a surface temperature of about 6000°C. Energy is produced in the Sun by internal nuclear fusion reactions in which helium atoms, light, heat and so on, are created from hydrogen atoms. The internal temperature of the Sun is estimated to be approximately 15 million degrees C.

The Earth is one of the nine known planets of the solar system. The Earth's mass is 0.0003% of that of the Sun and 81 times that of the Moon. Table 3.1 shows a comparison of the Earth with the other planets of our solar system. The middle planet Jupiter is the largest, while the inner planet Mercury and the outer planet Pluto are the smallest. The time it takes for bright Venus, slightly closer to the Sun than Earth, and red Mars, slightly further from the Sun, to orbit the Sun is not very different from that of Earth, so that these two planets can be seen in the sky at night in the same place for a long time.

3.2   The creation of the universe

Research into astronomy carried out by the American Edwin Hubble (1889–1953) showed that the universe expands at a rate of approximately 25 km per second for every million light years of distance. Thus the rate increases at a greater distance from the centre. By calculating back to the starting point on the basis of the rate of expansion of the universe, we arrive at the moment that all the galaxies coincided, in other words, when the universe

Planet	Diameter compared to Earth	Distance to the Sun in AU*	Orbit in years
Mercury	0.38	0.39	0.24
Venus	0.95	0.72	0.62
Earth	1.0	1.0	1.0
Mars	0.53	1.5	1.9
Jupiter	11.0	5.2	12.0
Saturn	9.5	9.5	30.0
Uranus	3.7	19.0	84.0
Neptune	3.9	30.0	170.0
Pluto	0.39	39.0	250.0

* 1 astronomical unit (AU) is the distance between the Sun and the Earth, approximately 150 million km.

Table 3.1. Characteristics of the planets of our solar system.

must have been created. This was 10 or 20 billion years ago. At this point the cosmos was created with a huge explosion. At the moment that the universe was created, matter must have been very compactly compressed, creating enormous pressures and very high temperatures of billions of degrees.

There is a large question mark about how things ever went so far, and what happened between the Big Bang and what preceded it is shrouded in mystery. This is the point at which the familiar laws of science no longer have any validity.[1] In 1965, Robert Wilson and Arno Penzias showed that there is still some radiation remaining from the background radiation released by the Big Bang, and this is the greatest argument for the Big Bang theory of the creation of the universe. Following the Big Bang, which lasted only a few seconds, the extreme heat began to cool down and space rapidly expanded, and then there was a period of tens of thousands of years when light ruled supreme and dominated over matter. After approximately a million years the expanding space became sufficiently rarefied to allow the creation of galaxies. These were initially spherical clouds of gas in which spherical collections of stars formed. Subsequently most galaxies compacted into a flat disc and in this way the spiralling arms with their collections of stars developed. In this view of the creation of the universe there was first a very short stage of heat radiation, followed by a longer period in which light was dominant. This was followed in turn by an even longer period in which clouds of gas formed, and finally this condensed to allow the formation of liquid and solid matter. This view corresponds closely to the view presented below, which is based on spiritual science.

Natural science still has no answer to the question whether the universe will continue to expand for ever, and will develop to an empty cosmos, or whether gravitation will eventually put a stop to this expansion so that it will give way to a process of contraction. On the basis of the quantity of matter known to exist in 1985, there is believed to be too little mass to make it possible for gravitation to put the brakes on the expansion, and start the process of contraction. On the other hand, it is recognized that a great deal of matter is still "invisible" in the forms of gas clouds and stars which emit virtually no light, in the form of "black holes," or even more complicated phenomena, such as unidimensional "ribbons" which coil in space on the borders of time and space, and exert huge gravitational force. These ribbons are believed to be remnants of the pre–Big Bang situation. It is assumed that such a ribbon is responsible for the large forces of attraction which are exerted by our Milky Way galaxy together with the neighbouring galaxies towards a place behind the Southern Cross constellation, with a speed of approximately 700 km per second. Thus, in addition to expansion, there is also localized concentration of forces in the universe.

3.3   The creation of the solar system and Earth

By dating rocks on the basis of their content of radioactive isotopes, it is estimated that the solar system was formed between four and six billion years ago. On the basis of the same method of dating, iron meteorites are up to six billion years old and some lunar rocks are also between approximately four and six billion years old. An age of four billion years has also been calculated for some of the oldest groups of rocks on Earth.

There are a number of different views regarding the creation of the solar system in the expanding universe. Two centuries ago Pierre Simon Laplace (1749–1827), a French mathematician and astronomer, had already put forward the idea that there was a gradual process of condensation of the Sun and the planets from a primeval nebula which consisted of interstellar particles of matter and gases. Elaborating on his hypothesis, the Sun was assumed to be composed of a slowly rotating cloud of gas which, under the influence of gravitation, started to spin on its own axis with increasing speed as it contracted. Then mists were dispelled by centrifugal force, which initially condensed to form mini–planets. These mini–planets gradually grew in size as a result of collisions to form the present system of planets around the Sun. This fusion to form planets did not occur in the asteroids which orbit around the Sun between Mars and Jupiter. During the process of contraction of matter the Sun itself became hotter and hotter. It was calculated that this process was completed in a very short time, only several hundred days, and in this time the temperature suddenly rose steeply to millions of degrees. In this way the Sun, like other stars, became a source of light, and the Sun's source of energy, the nuclear fusion reaction of hydrogen atoms into helium atoms, was unleashed. In the centre of the Sun, 657 million tonnes of hydrogen are converted every second into 652.5 million tonnes of helium. The 4.5 million tonnes which are lost in this process are converted into energy, and approximately one billionth of this energy reaches the Earth. The planets are arranged in such a way that the Sun's gravitational force and the centrifugal force of the rotating movement around the Sun are in balance. The Sun comprises more than 98% of the matter in the entire solar system.

It is estimated that the Sun will have used up its hydrogen in the nuclear fusion reaction to form helium in about five billion years. As a result, the internal production of energy will decline and therefore also the internal pressure of gas. Gravity will gain the upper hand, and as a result of the contraction of the centre, the temperature will rise again. At a nuclear temperature of over 100 million degrees, there will be another ignition temperature resulting in another nuclear fusion reaction. Helium atoms react together, producing carbon. In this second stage of the Sun's life, the internal pressure of gas will be higher, so that the Sun will expand and the planets Mercury and Venus, and possibly also the Earth and Mars, will be swallowed up. During this stage the Sun will burn ten thousand times more brightly than it does now, until it reaches the age of 20 billion years. By this time the helium will be burned up and the core will contract even further, producing nuclear reactions at even higher temperatures. This will take a relatively short time, until neon, oxygen, silicon and iron have been formed in the nucleus, one after the other. After this, no more energy will be released in the core. The Sun will then collapse because of gravitation and end, first as a white dwarf, and then, after cooling, as a black dwarf.

For stars which are more than one and a half times as heavy as the Sun, the contraction is even greater, followed by an enormous explosion in which the star explodes as brightly lit "supernova." When this happens, atoms are split by the shock wave and propelled outwards. A small proportion of the atomic nuclei are converted into heavier elements, such as calcium, uranium and lead. In the remaining core of the star, protons and electrons are compressed as neutrons, releasing so-called neutrinos, particles which pass through virtually anything. The remaining neutron star can be considered as a single huge atomic nucleus. In stars which have more than thirty times the mass of our Sun, this produces a "black hole." In a black hole, matter has assumed the unimaginable compactness of hundreds of millions of tonnes per cubic centimetre, and is still continuing to condense. Matter moves in spirals towards the centre at a speed of more than 100000 km per second, and a large part of the energy is emitted as X-rays. This is a phenomenon of the destruction of matter in which the gravitational force is so strong that it even captures light. Hence the name "black hole"; the area sucks up everything, even rays of light. The concentration of ribbons in galaxies referred to above is a smaller scale version of these black holes in the solar system.[2]

There are other hypotheses for the creation of the planets in our solar system apart from the above-mentioned explanation of Laplace. These presuppose catastrophes, such as the explosion of

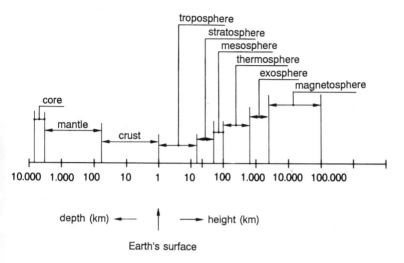

Table 3.2. Composition of the physical Earth on the basis of a logarithmic scale of distances.

a binary star which supposedly occurred with the Sun. Other possible causes include near collisions of foreign celestial bodies with the Sun. This is cited as an explanation for the dispersal of the planets and their moons.

It has been suggested that the Moon was created and expelled by the Earth at a later stage, leaving behind the scar of the Pacific Ocean. Other theories maintain that the Earth did not rotate on its axis fast enough to be able to explain this expulsion of solid matter.

As yet, there is no conclusive theory regarding the creation of the solar system. However, it is generally agreed that the Earth's separate existence must have started approximately 4600 million years ago.

First of all it was a spherical mass of sold particles and gas, which heated up under the influence of gravity during the process of contraction. The chemical composition of the Earth with the elements we now know was already determined at that point. Because of the increase in temperature inside the planet to approximately 1000°C, the iron in the outer layers of the Earth is believed to have melted and moved to the centre to form a liquid core.

Nowadays the Earth, which has a diameter of about 6400 km, can be subdivided into an inner core 1200 km thick, which may be solid because of the high pressure, and a liquid outer core with a thickness of 2300 km (see Table 3.2). The inner core consists of nickel and iron, and has a density 10.7 times that of water. Although the core comprises 16% of the Earth's volume, it accounts for 32% of its mass. The liquid outer core consists of iron, and has a temperature presumed to be between approximately 3000° and 4000°C. The outer core is surrounded by the mantle, which is 2900 km thick. The mantle consists of olivine rock up to approximately 400 km below the Earth's surface. The upper 350 km is soft or molten, and is known as the asthenosphere. Cells which rise from this layer cause the rigid crust of the Earth, which is between 5 and 50 km thick, to bend and break, which results in earthquakes and volcanic eruptions.

Above the surface of the Earth, 71% of which consists of water, the troposphere rises up 11 km, as indicated in Table 3.2. This is where clouds are formed and the weather is created. Above this the stratosphere and ozone layer stretch up 47 km. The mesosphere above this demarcates the area in which the circulation of air ceases. As far as the upper border of the mesosphere the composition of the air is the same as that on the surface of the Earth, with 78% nitrogen and 21% oxygen, although the pressure is greatly reduced and the temperature is down to −90°C. In the thermosphere above, which stretches from 90–550 km, the pressure drops to 10^{-11} atmospheres, but as a result of radiation the temperature rises to approximately 1200°C. At the same time there is a greater proportion of oxygen to nitrogen. Above 550 km there is the exosphere, which contains only the simplest elements, helium and hydrogen. Finally, after 2000 km, we reach the magnetosphere, containing only hydrogen, which is 25% ionized. Gradually at even greater heights there is a transition to interstellar space where the pressure is 10^{-17} atmospheres and the temperature is −270°C.

3.4   The Earth during the Pre–Cambrian era

Following this reminder of the scientific view of the Earth's physical characteristics, I will briefly summarize the dominant view of the historical development of life on Earth.[3] Not much is known about the early stages of the Earth's existence (known by geologists as the Pre–Cambrian era). The first billion years of the Pre-Cambrian era is known in geology as the Azoic era. During this period there was not yet any life. Geologists are faced with the problem that they do not have any rocks or minerals dating from that period. It is generally assumed that they were still in a liquid state at that time. The Earth's crust was being formed, and was therefore thin and much more flexible and folded than it is now. The liquid layers of rock were in constant motion. One wonders whether the seas were formed straightaway, and about the composition of the air. Some scientists imagine that the Earth's crust was exposed to violent movement and volcanic eruptions, a hot dry landscape. The composition of the atmosphere during that period was probably more similar to that of the present atmosphere of the enormous outer planets, Jupiter or Saturn, than to that of the smaller inner planets, Mercury or Venus. In the latter the light hydrogen gas, which was present at the beginning, could escape into space because of the smaller effect of gravity and the higher temperature resulting from their proximity to the Sun. During the first billion years the Earth's atmosphere probably comprised methane, ammonia, water and carbon dioxide, as well as hydrogen.[4] These gases escaped from the heated mass of the Earth and collected in the atmosphere. Estimates have shown that in addition to the violent movements and high temperatures, the Earth's crust was also exposed to strong ultraviolet radiation from the Sun, which was later reduced when the ozone layer was formed. In addition, there was much more radioactive radiation than there is now, because the radioactive materials in the Earth's crust, such as uranium, had not yet dissipated. Four billion years ago uranium is believed to have contained approximately 15% of the radioactive isotope U_{235}. In many places at that time there were also natural nuclear reactors which — as fossils in Gabon in Africa have shown — remained active until two billion years ago.[5] Following the stage of heating up and the escape of gases from the Earth's crust into the atmosphere, the Earth started to cool down. This must have led to the Earth's crust first becoming more solid, and also to the rain from the thick layer of cloud, falling on the still flat and bare surface of the Earth, as is still the case on the hotter planet of Venus. The total mass of water on the surface of the Earth has probably remained constant since that time, and is estimated to be approximately 1.2 billion cubic km.

It is not certain whether the continents already protruded above the surface of the water of the oceans that had been formed, about three and a half billion years ago. Granite boulders found in Manitoba in Canada indicate that this was the case at the end of the Azoic period, about three billion years ago. From the way they have rolled it may be concluded that there was land sticking up above the sea, on which the rain fell. The lack of erosion in feldspar crystals found in Zimbabwe in a layer of rocks 2.7 billion years old also shows that the temperature at that time was approximately the same as it is now, and that the atmosphere was not extremely acid. Thus after the first billion years of the Earth's existence, inorganic nature had probably already adopted its present form. The Earth had oceans and a volcanic mainland, a temperate climate and the atmosphere was not particularly aggressively, though it still had no oxygen.

The second period of the Pre–Cambrian era was characterized by the first signs of life. It is known as the Proterozoic era. The appearance of the first single cell bacteria–like organisms occurred about 3.3 billion years ago. From these procariots or organisms without a nucleus, developed, *inter alia,* blue–green algae, which are able to manufacture carbohydrates and oxygen from carbon dioxide and water, through the process of photosynthesis effected by sunlight.

Approximately two billion years ago this process resulted in the Earth's atmosphere losing its oxygenless character. With the increase in the oxygen content, the hydrogen and ammonia contents quickly decreased, and an ozone layer formed at a height between 15 and 35 km, which protected life on Earth from the Sun's damaging ultraviolet radiation. After the creation of the oceans and the beginning of the formation of sedimentary rocks, this is seen as the largest change in the physical existence of the Earth.

To summarize: the Earth went through the following stages in approximately four billion years of the Pre–Cambrian era. First, the contracting mass of the Earth heated up and a liquid iron and nickel core was created from the molten rocks, while the lighter matter floated up to the Earth's surface and gases such as hydrogen, ammonia, steam, methane and carbon dioxide escaped into the atmosphere. Approximately four billion years ago the rock started to harden and rain falling from the clouds filled the deeper parts of the Earth's volcanic surface to form oceans. The continental Earth masses moved on to the more solid, deeper liquid layers of rock. These continents consisted of granite or solidified magma, and gradually of sedimentary rocks formed by erosion and the process of sedimentation. In addition, other forms of rocks were formed by repeated heating and distortion. After the first single cell life forms developed about 3.3 billion years ago, the blue–green algae which produce oxygen evolved about two billion years ago. These changed the Earth's atmosphere from containing no oxygen into an atmosphere containing oxygen. The Pre–Cambrian rocks were folded and whole blocks moved over each other. In many cases they formed the centre of the present continents which underwent great movements across the globe. The Pre–Cambrian era ended about 600 million years ago; at that time a wealth of chalk skeletons of organisms was suddenly deposited in sedimentary rocks. This meant that geologists and palaeontologists now had far more concrete evidence for reconstructing the events which took place on prehistoric Earth.

3.5 *The Palaeozoic, Mesozoic and Cenozoic eras*

Although a great deal is known about the 600 million years following the Pre–Cambrian era, I will merely give a brief summary of this era in the context of this survey. After all, the purpose is merely to allow a comparison between scientific theories and the doctrine of spiritual science on the development of the Earth and of man.

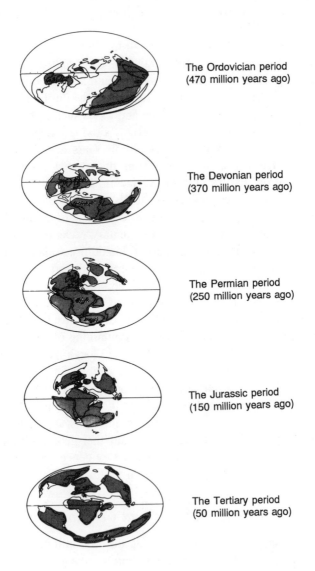

The Ordovician period
(470 million years ago)

The Devonian period
(370 million years ago)

The Permian period
(250 million years ago)

The Jurassic period
(150 million years ago)

The Tertiary period
(50 million years ago)

Table 3.3. The movements of land masses in the past 500 million years, in relation to the present continents. Shaded areas indicate the land mass then; the outlines, the supposed location of present continents.

First, there was the Palaeozoic era, which lasted from 570 to 225 million years ago. This was subdivided into the Cambrian, Ordovician, Silurian, Devonian, Carboniferous and Permian periods. This was a time of great activity with the formation of mountains alternating with quieter periods. There were also ice ages, such as the ice age during the Carboniferous era in the southern hemisphere. At the same time the climate was mild in other areas, and many different higher forms of plant and animal life evolved in the shallow lakes and swamps. The continents shifted over the Earth's surface, and in the course of time, some areas were situated first in polar and then in tropical regions, as illustrated in Table 3.3. The gradual alternation between the formation and disappearance of the seas and the succession of extreme and temperate climates had a strong influence on the evolution of particular species of plants and animals. The continents also moved in relation to each other. During the Palaeozoic era the continents of North America, Greenland, Europe and Asia drifted towards each other in the northern hemisphere. At the same time, South America, Africa, Antarctica, India and Australia were formed in the southern hemisphere, which were collectively given the name of Gondwanaland by the German meteorologist Alfred Wegener in 1915.

Wegener argued that all the continents had once been a single landmass. On the basis of similarities in the fauna it is now assumed that Gondwanaland, in the southern hemisphere, and Eurasia, the collective name for the combined continents of the northern hemisphere, did actually form a single entity during the last period of the Palaeozoic era. This land mass was called Pangaea. The creation of Pangaea was accompanied by the fertile seas receding, and the oceans becoming deeper. The end of the Palaeozoic era also had a more extreme climate, and large parts of the Earth were covered with icy wastes and deserts. As a result, many species of plants and animals became extinct.

The Mesozoic era which followed lasted from 225 to 65 million years ago. The Mesozoic era is subdivided into the Triassic, Jurassic and Cretaceous periods. During the Triassic period the shallow continental seas returned, and a hot dry climate prevailed. In the following Jurassic period the climate was

Period	Millions of years	Physical characteristics	Appearance of plants	Appearance of animals and man
PRE–CAMBRIAN				
Azoic	4600	Formation of Earth's crust		
	4000	Formation of oceans		
Proterozoic	3300	oxygen in	single–cell	
	2000	atmosphere	organisms	sponges
			algae	protozoa
		Formation of Huronian Mountains		
PALAEOZOIC				
Cambrian	570	Seas become shallower		tribolites, cepha-lopods, slugs
Ordovician	500	Northern land masses close to the equator		graptolites, fish, corals
Silurian	430	Land fuses to form two continents	leafless land plants horsetails	scorpions
		Formation of Caledonian Mountains		
Devonian	395	Lakes and marshes Gondwanaland	ferns	bony fish, insects
Carboniferous	345	covered with ice	bog plants	amphibians, reptiles
		Formation of Hercynian Mountains		
Permian	280	Formation of Pangaea, more extreme climate	extinction of many plants and animals	
MESOZOIC				
Triassic	225	Shallow seas, warm, dry climate	conifers, taxus palms	mammalian reptiles, dinosaurs
Jurassic	190	Separation of Pangaea, temperate climate		large saurians, birds
Cretaceous	136	Marked seasons, formation of deserts, catastrophe, colder	flowering plants	giant saurians stand up
			extinction of many species	
CENOZOIC				
Tertiary	65	Cooler climate		horses, whales, monkeys
		Formation of the Alps		
Quaternary	1	Ice ages		humans

Table 3.4. Stages in the development of the Earth and the biosphere.

66

more temperate, there were many marshes and swamps, and Pangaea separated further and further. First North America and Eurasia drifted away, and later Africa, South America and Antarctica. During the Cretaceous period the gap of the Atlantic Ocean became larger, and a division arose between Antarctica and Australia. The end of the Mesozoic period was characterized by the fairly sudden mass extinction of many organisms. It is presumed that an exploding star may have caused a worldwide catastrophe consisting of increased ultraviolet radiation and a huge drop in temperatures.

Finally, the Cenozoic era is our present geologic era, which is estimated to have started 65 million years ago. The first period of the Cenozoic era is the Tertiary period and covers the years up to one million years ago. The continents gradually assumed their present positions, though Western Europe and Greenland were initially joined together. In the southern hemisphere the ice receded to Antarctica. The "recent" Quaternary period was characterized in the beginning by a large ice–cap which covered the areas surrounding the North Pole.

A survey of the whole of the physical development of the Earth seen through scientific eyes soon reveals that a stable situation was achieved when the oceans were formed. For billions of years the Earth had a temperate climate which made it possible for life to survive over large parts of the surface, despite volcanic eruptions and ice ages. Nevertheless, great changes took place in the hardness of the Earth's crust, the composition of the atmosphere, the creation of seas and marshes, the climate, the interrelationship and location of the continents on the globe, and large areas of mainland were raised above sea level, or submerged by the oceans. Table 3.4 summarizes these developments.

4. The creation according to spiritual science

And He, who bears the cosmic order, went on:
*   "Only God will help you. Only He knows what was, is*
and will be. Only he knows all thoughts. The thoughts
which have already sprung up and which will still spring
up. Only he knows all the causes: also those of our
suffering."

Zarathustra, Yasna 29:4

4.1 Eras and large cycles

According to esoteric doctrine, the development of the Earth and the development of man are closely linked. I have therefore decided to outline the development of the human body alongside the description of the creation of the physical Earth. In a later chapter I will discuss the origins of the animal and plant kingdoms.

As the previous chapter showed, the classification of geological and palaeontological periods is largely determined by traces of life on Earth found by scientists in rocks and sedimentary layers. In the esoteric works this classification into periods is determined by rhythmic laws which are expressed in large and small cycles. What has been written in occult writings about the creation of the Earth initially seems very improbable because it does not directly correspond with current scientific views of evolution. Nevertheless, I would like to deal with this matter thoroughly before comparing the two views. My discussion is based mainly on the biblical story of the Creation, on elements in Greek and Germanic mythology, and on some of Steiner's works.[1] As the theories about the developmental stages of Earth and of man can be found in many different places in Steiner's books, I will arrange them more systematically.

Just as spiritual science is based on the immortality of spiritual

Earth metamorphosis	Physical character- istics				Condition of consciousness (corresponding condition of consciousness of present beings)	Parts of man					
	solid	liquid	gas/light	heat		spiritual man	life spirit	spiritual self Self	astral body	ethereal body	physical body
Old Saturn	X				trance (minerals)	X					
Old Sun	X	X			sleep (plants)	X	X				
Old Moon	X	X	X		dream (animals)	X	X	X			
Earth	X	X	X	X	object (man)	X	X	X	X		
Jupiter	X	X	X		imaginative (Angels)		X	X	X	X	
Venus	X	X			inspirational (Archangels)			X	X	X	X
Vulcan	X				intuitive (Primeval Forces)				X	X	X	X

Table 4.1. Characteristics of the seven metamorphoses of the Earth.

beings which, in the case of human souls are periodically incarnated, esoteric doctrine also postulates the reincarnation of the
Earth, and with the Earth, the solar system. The present Earth
was preceded by three incarnations or metamorphoses described
in esoteric literature, and will be followed by another three.
There are supposedly even more incarnations further back in the
past, and in the future, but little has been written about these.
During the three preceding metamorphoses and the three following ones which are more or less a reflection of these, the
Earth has a completely different appearance from the one we
know now. The present Earth is the most solid of the seven
incarnations described, as illustrated in Tables 4.1 and 4.2. The
present solid incarnation was preceded by a liquid one, and that
one by two incarnations in which air and heat respectively
formed the most condensed condition. In this it is possible to
recognize the order of phenomena which, according to the Big
Bang theory, consist of heat, light/gas, liquid and solid matter.
The three preceding incarnations of the Earth are known by the

at first sight seemingly confusing names: "Old Moon," "Old Sun," and "Old Saturn," in which the most condensed condition consists, respectively, of liquid, gas and heat, as stated above. I will return later to the origin and significance of these names.

The seven metamorphoses of the Earth are also described as the seven open or large cycles. Every cycle concludes with a period of rest, comparable to the night between two days, or the

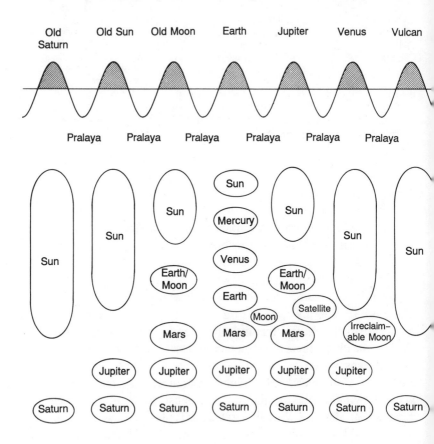

Table 4.2. Schematic structure of the solar system during the seven metamorphoses of the Earth at the time of maximum expansion in the middle of every metamorphosis.

period in which the seed of a plant rests in the soil in winter after the plants have flowered, before germinating again in the spring. These periods of rest are known as enclosed cycles or *pralayas* (see Table 4.2). The names of these conditions of metamorphosis are derived from the present components of the solar system. I will begin by briefly outlining the general characteristics of these metamorphoses.

The first metamorphosis of the Earth is the "Old Saturn" metamorphosis. I imagine this to comprise the entire present solar system. Everything which was later individualized in the Sun and the individual planets was still dissolved. At a material level, Old Saturn consisted exclusively of heat. It can be viewed as a large fireball with the present solar system at its centre. This gigantic body of heat is in a sense comparable to the primeval nebula of Kant–Laplace, although it consisted of heat rather than gases.[2] The present Sun was the centre of this ball of fire, which extended as far as the orbit of the present planet Saturn. The seed of man was planted and time was created during this Old Saturn incarnation. At this point in history, physical man should be imagined as a sort of point of heat. Before that time there was only eternity, time without movement. During the existence of Old Saturn, a large rotating ball of heat broke away from the main sphere. This was the precursor of the planet Saturn. Man's body of heat incorporated the seeds of the senses, and was like an automaton because it did not yet have its own life force (see Table 4.3).

These seeds of man are also sometimes described as "mineral man." Their movements were controlled by higher spiritual beings. They possessed a profound trance–like consciousness, that is, consciousness at an even deeper level than the consciousness of dreamless sleep. After the Old Saturn incarnation of the Earth, everything disappeared which had taken place during the period of rest, and the second Earth metamorphosis followed, known as the "Old Sun." The Old Sun was characterized by the condensing of the element of air and light from the heat, and the creation of unidimensional space in addition to time. It was a large ball of light and air. In a sense, the size of the Old Sun was comparable to a ball which had the present Sun at its centre and

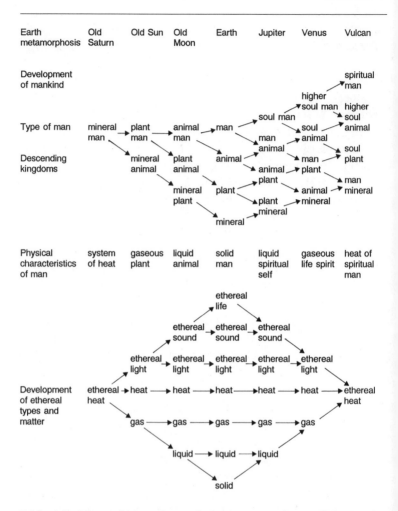

Table 4.3. The evolution of man during metamorphoses of the Earth.

the orbit of Jupiter as a boundary. Two compact currents circled the Old Sun like vital spheres: the planets Saturn and Jupiter.[3] The inside of the Old Sun consisted of wind, air and flowing gas, while the "ball" radiated light outwards. Mineral man now developed to a higher plane and now had an ethereal body, or form force body, in addition to a material body. This meant that it was alive in the sense that plants are alive. In addition to the creation of the nervous and sensory functions, their light–air body also developed as well as the seeds of the heart and lung functions. However, the development of mineral man to "plant man" was at the cost of some of man's seeds which remained behind as mineral animals with no ethereal body and no chance of acquiring a Self. The consciousness of plant man was a step higher than that of mineral man: a sleeping consciousness, reaching out to the light radiating from the inside of the Old Sun, just as plants nowadays grow towards external sunlight.

After a second long period of sleep *(pralaya),* the third incarnation of the Earth took place, known as the "Old Moon."[4] This name reveals that the Earth was separated from the Sun, which remained united with the two inner planets, Mercury and Venus. The Earth continued to form a single unity with the Moon. In addition to time, there was two–dimensional space during the Old Moon. The separation of the Sun and the Old Moon is described as the "battle in the heavens," and the asteroids between Jupiter and Mars are vestiges of this battle.[5] During its orbit around the Sun, the Old Moon only rotated on its axis once. The size of the Old Sun was now reduced to the circle which is formed approximately by the orbit of the present planet Mars. At a later point Mars broke away from the mass of the Old Moon. Part of the fiery light was condensed into watery liquid on the Old Moon. In the middle of this watery mass of the Old Moon the precursors of the later mineral kingdom developed, such as rocks in the form of scaly land masses. The scaly land masses were the bodies of the mineral animals of the Old Sun, which had continued to degenerate on the Old Moon to mineral plants with only a physical body. Steiner also described the substance of these mineral plants as a plant soup, while the atmosphere consisted of "fiery mist/air," described in Hebrew by the word *ruach.*

On the Old Moon man had developed as a creature with an astral body as well as a physical and ethereal body, so that he was able to experience feelings of joy and sorrow, love and hate. Thus plant man evolved into "animal man," who floated over the surface of the Old Moon in the watery misty element, like a sort of liquid animal creature. In addition to the head and chest, the liquid body man during the Old Moon first had a stomach with the capacity for the present digestive system and limbs. At the same time that plant man evolved into animal man, part of the seeds of man were again rejected. They formed the plant animals of the Old Moon, which did not have an astral body, but did have a physical and ethereal body. The consciousness of animal man in the Old Moon was a dream consciousness with clair-voyant experiences of his environment in symbolic images, similar in certain aspects to that later found in Atlantean man. Depending on whether the nervous/sensory system, the respira-tory/circulatory system or the digestive system/limbs were dominant, man on the Old Moon could be divided into Eagle man, Lion man and Bull man. This distinction is comparable in a way to the present classification of mammals on Earth into rodents, predators and ungulates.[6]

When this incarnation of the Earth was also completely dis-solved in the spiritual seed during the third long *pralaya,* the present incarnation of the Earth was achieved. In this the Earth separated from the Sun and the Moon. Gravity condensed the plant material of the Old Moon into a solid mineral substance, forming the land which rose up out of the oceans, and which can also be recognized in the hard mineral skeleton of man. On Earth, three dimensional space was created, as well as time. Man acquired his fourth and highest body, his Self, with which he developed self-consciousness. With the help of his senses he was able consciously to perceive the objects in his environment. His body acquired limbs, so that he could move in a vertical position, and also developed the capacity for sexual reproduction.

On the basis of the teachings of Masters of the Far East, Spalding describes a dynamic picture of the creation and dissolu-tion of the planets of our present solar system, in which the youngest planet is created from the Sun, and on the edge of the solar system the oldest planet explodes and is assimilated once more by the Sun.[7] Elsewhere in esoteric writings, reference is made to twelve planets, of which some remain to be discovered, and of which the Earth is the least developed but one.[8] The ela-boration of Rudolf Steiner's teachings provided by this descrip-tion reveals that our solar system is a dynamic entity in itself.

The present incarnation of the Earth will also pass when current developments have progressed sufficiently. Following a fourth long period of rest in which everything will coalesce, the fifth incarnation, known as the Jupiter metamorphosis, will take place. In many ways this is a reflection of the Old Moon. The development foreseen for the Jupiter metamorphosis is referred to in the Revelation to St John as "New Jerusalem." Just as the Earth is accompanied by the Moon, the planet Jupiter will be accompanied by a "satellite," which will carry that part of mankind which has remained behind in its development. During the Jupiter metamorphosis the Earth and the Moon will form a single unity once again. The hard mineral realm will no longer exist on the Jupiter metamorphosis, and the three dimensional space of the Earth metamorphosis will once again be reduced here to two dimensions. The mineral kingdom will develop as plant minerals with a watery liquid form. On Jupiter, man will develop as soul man; in other words, at the end of this metamorphosis he will have transformed his astral body with his Self. In this way the soul man will develop his spiritual Self, the lowest level of his higher spiritual essence, his higher Self. On Jupiter, man will have imaginative consciousness like Angels have now.

The Jupiter metamorphosis will be followed by the so–called Venus metamorphosis in which the Earth will be reunited with the Sun and matter will be condensed only into air. Another celestial body will break away from the Venus metamorphosis with that part of mankind which has remained behind, which Steiner termed "irreclaimable Moon."[9] The lowest realm will consist of airy minerals or regressed man, which have achieved a sort of animal–like stage, and the present plant and mineral kingdoms will no longer exist. Man will rise up to a level which could be described as a higher soul man. This higher soul man has also transformed the ethereal body with the Self, to form what is known as the life spirit, the second level of his higher Self. With this, he acquires inspirational as well as imaginative consciousness, like the Archangels. He will be able to act creatively in the animal world, as he does now in the physical world.

Finally, the Venus metamorphosis will make way for the last

incarnation of the Earth, identified with Vulcan. Like the Old Saturn, Vulcan is a planet of heat which comprises the whole solar system, and where space does not exist; there is only time. On Vulcan, man achieves his development as "spiritual man," and is able to control the physical heat of his body with his Self. During this metamorphosis, man will unite with his divine origins, with which he will achieve a state of godliness. All the present lower kingdoms will have disappeared and will have achieved a stage that mankind passed through at an earlier point. Earth's matter is then transformed into a spiritual form, and this concludes the seven incarnations of the Earth.

4.2   Small Earth cycles

The seven incarnations or large cycles of the Earth, briefly described in a rather one-sided way for the purposes of this explanation, form a rhythm which is repeated in the form of several small cycles during every individual large cycle, as illustrated in Table 4.4. In addition, every small cycle is divided in esoteric literature into seven form conditions or globes. The total development of the Earth and of man which is described therefore consists of $7 \times 7 \times 7 = 343$ form conditions.

Currently we are in the fourth large cycle (the Earth metamorphosis), and as will be described later, we are in the fourth small cycle within this and in the fourth form condition, that is, the 172nd form condition, which shows that mankind has only recently passed through the midpoint of its development. This moment is also the deepest point in the descent into his material existence. Just as large cycles alternate with periods of rest or *pralayas,* the seven small cycles are also separated by periods of rest, sometimes known as small *pralayas.* The most characteristic feature of a particular large cycle is repeated in the corresponding small cycle. In this way man's acquisition of an astral body, which took place during the third incarnation of the Earth, the Old Moon, was repeated during the third small cycle of the Earth metamorphosis. During the present incarnation of the Earth the fourth small cycle is the most essential, and the previous three small cycles are in a sense repetitions of the preceding large

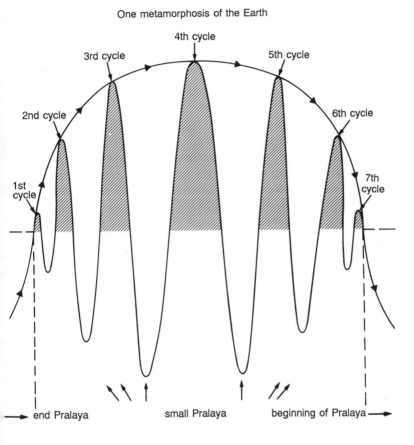

One metamorphosis of the Earth

4th cycle

3rd cycle

5th cycle

2nd cycle

6th cycle

1st cycle

7th cycle

end Pralaya

small Pralaya

beginning of Pralaya

Table 4.4. The relation between large and small cycles of the Earth.

cycles in which first a planet of heat, then a planet of light and air, and lastly a planet of water were formed. Below I will examine in more detail the events of the present fourth small cycle of the Earth in which the scientific reconstruction of the creation of the Earth can be wholly incorporated.

4.3   The fourth small Earth cycle

At the start of the fourth small Earth cycle everything was first transformed into an unrecognizable state. From this, in the spiritual world the seed condition formed earlier began to separate away from the seeds of man.

Both man and the Earth first passed through a 169th form condition in the spiritual world, which consisted of pure will and intention, and which was known as the formless Arupa condition. During the next 170th form condition, man and the Earth descended to the formed Rupa condition, which is comparable to an intention of the will, or body of thought, translated into a plan. This was followed by a further descent to the 171st form condition, the astral condition, in which an astral body was assumed, and after this man and the Earth developed an ethereal body at the beginning of the 172nd form condition, with which they achieved a condition bordering on the physically perceptible (see Table 4.5). The further development of the human body continued to take place for a while in a fine ethereal condition. At that time the ether was active in the physical elements. These elements were the end products of the ether activity concerned. The life ether was a new ether form which occurred for the first time during the Earth metamorphosis. On Old Saturn physical reality consisted of heat, permeated with ethereal heat. The beings which were permeated with ethereal heat radiated physical heat. On the Old Sun, ethereal light was added to the ethereal heat, and air was formed from the condensing of the heat. The seeds of man permeated with ethereal light radiated light, just as the Sun emits light. On the Old Moon, ethereal sound was added to ethereal light. In addition, the air was condensed to create liquid. Only creatures permeated with ethereal sound could produce sounds from within themselves. Animal man on the Old Moon was first able to do this after undergoing inner experiences. At the same time a sort of respiratory and circulatory system developed, blood flowed into animal man from the cosmos, just as air now flows on to Earth. It was the group or national identity which guided this flow of blood down for the bodies of man. Steiner describes the Old Moon as a plant mineral soup.[10] On

	7227 BC	5067 BC	2907 BC	747 BC	1413	3573	5733	7893
16807 cultural periods	Ancient Indian (8408)	Ancient Persian (8409)	Egyptian Chaldean (8410)	Graeco-Roman (8411)	Present (8412)	Russian-Slavonic (8413)	American (8414)	
2401 eras	Polar (1198)	Hyper-borean (1199)	Lemurian (1200)	Atlantean (1201)	Present (1202)	Seal (1203)	Trumpet (1204)	
343 form conditions (globes)	Arupa (intentions) (169)	Rupa (plans) (170)	Astral (feelings) (171)	Physical (forms) (172)	Higher astral (173)	Higher rupa (174)	Higher arupa (175)	
49 small cycles (circles)	Repeat of Old Saturn (22)	Repeat of Old Sun (23)	Repeat of Old Moon (24)	Present (25)	Fifth (26)	Sixth (27)	Seventh (28)	
7 Earth metamorphoses	Old Saturn (1)	Old Sun (2)	Old Moon (3)	Earth (4)	Jupiter (5)	Venus (6)	Vulcan (7)	

Table 4.5. Inter–relationship between the Earth–metamorphoses, small cycles, form conditions, eras and cultural periods.

Earth ethereal life developed, as well as ethereal heat, ethereal light and ethereal sound, and for the first time, solid matter was condensed from the liquid element. All these ethereal forms and conditions of matter were formed on Earth from ethereal life (see Table 4.3). The stage in which the Earth had a spherical body of ethereal life during the fourth small cycle is viewed as the beginning of the physical form condition, the 172nd after the beginning of the Old Saturn metamorphosis (see Table 4.5). The seeds of man were found on the large sphere of ethereal life that was the Earth, as small spheres of ethereal life. None of this could yet be perceived with the physical senses.

In our description, we have now come to the first era of the physical form condition of the fourth small Earth cycle within the fourth large cycle, or Earth metamorphosis. This first era is called the Polar era.

4.4 The Polar era

In a sense the Polar era can be seen as a miniature repetition of Old Saturn. The Sun, Moon and Earth were still one during the Polar era. The Earth organism expanded like a ball of heat to the present orbit of Saturn. Uranus and Saturn broke away.[11] In the Bible (Gen.1:1–2) this stage was described as follows: "In the beginning God created the heaven and Earth, and the Earth was without form and void, and darkness was on the face of the deep, and the spirit of God moved upon the face of the waters." (See Table 4.6.).

4.5 The Hyperborean era

On a small scale the Hyperborean era was a repetition of the Old Sun, but at a higher level of development. Neptune, Jupiter and Mars broke away. Ethereal sound or the chemical ether formed from part of the ethereal life, and this carried the chemical elements. The name ethereal sound or chemical ether indicates in itself that in esoteric terms the chemical elements are a vibration. The Earth globe receded to the sphere of the present Jupiter. Chemical ether produced the attraction and repulsion of airy substances. This was the precursor of man's subsequent rhythmic respiratory system. At the same time, the process could be seen as anticipating the real process of feeling with the digestive organs which were formed later. Man sucked up the fine ethereal substance from the environment like a sponge, and from it formed ethereal bodies which had an elongated elliptical shape. These contained the shadowy outline of the limbs and other

The story of Creation Genesis 1 (& verse)	Era	Characteristics	
		Earth	Man
2. And the Earth was without form, and void	Polar	ball of ethereal life as far as sphere of Saturn	small spheres of ethereal life
3. *The first day:* And God said: Let there be light	Hyper–borean	luminous ball of ethereal mist; gigantic oyster being	luminous, calyx–shaped ether clouds
6. *The second day:* ... a firmament in the midst of the waters, ... divide the waters		Sun breaks away	receives ethereal light from outside
11. *The third day:* Let the Earth bring forth grass	Lemurian	primeval waters of the fiery sea, sur–rounded by fiery mists; creation of plants group souls	fiery misty man; cyclops; swimming movement; centaur
16. *The fourth day:* And God made two great lights		Moon breaks away; mineral kingdom appears	division of man/woman; Adam and Eve rep–resent human being remaining on Earth
20. *The fifth day:* ... the waters bring forth ... moving creature that hath life and fowl that may fly		creation of group souls of water and air creatures; lower animals are physically present	upright man; Self; eyes; watery man; lungs/heart
24. *The sixth day:* ... cattle and creeping thing, and beast of the earth		creation of group souls of higher creatures; minerals rain down; Earth's crust solidifies	sphinx
27. *The seventh day:* So God created man in his own image		solid core; thick liquid mass with islands; amphibians; air with dense mists	gelatinous air body; return of human souls to the Earth; creation of different races
	Atlantis		

Table 4.6. The biblical story of Creation in relation to the 172nd form condition of the Earth.

organs yet to be developed. As the substances which were sucked up came from the newly formed kingdom of man, these ancestors of man should be viewed as a sort of "man–eating" creature.[12]

The remaining ethereal life was responsible for reproduction which still took place asexually in ethereal hermaphrodite man. When the ethereal mass had achieved a certain size, it divided into two parts by means of cell division, as in an amoeba, and the same physical chemical processes took place in each half. The new forms had the same soul as the mother creature. In this way "trees" were formed of the same souls. These ethereal human creatures experienced external material events in so far as the events led to movements within the ethereal body. They perceived the vibration of the surrounding ether as the effect of ethereal sound, in the form of sound. In fact, these creatures were no more than organs or shells of hearing. The ethereal Earth consisted of millions of large airy creatures inside one another, with an appearance like that of present polyps, corals, oysters and so on. The whole thing formed a gigantic ethereal slimy creature which reached as far as the sphere of Jupiter. Then the process of condensing continued and ethereal light was created from part of ethereal life. The Bible (Gen.1:3) describes this: "And God said, Let there be light, and there was light." It was the start of the first day of creation. During this part of the Hyperborean era, man had a body consisting of ethereal life, chemical ether and ethereal light, which radiated light perceptible to a clairvoyant observer. During this stage the Earth could best be described as a luminous, ethereal sphere of liquid and mist, rather like an enormous sun. Man was present on this sphere, though still invisible. Man's Self, and his astral body, were still dissolved in the spiritual essence embodied in the entire ethereal mist that was Earth. However, the physical body and ethereal body of man were starting to form as an ethereal condensing of mist from the surrounding astral body and the Self. Steiner also described man at this point as a plantlike entity with a body shaped like a regular cloud which became wider higher up, and ended in a sort of calyx–like opening irradiated with inner light.[13] Like sea-weed, this man was connected to the illuminated lap of the Earth by an umbilical cord. The umbilical cord was rather like a large root with which the seed of a plant feeds on the layer of humus on the Earth.[14]

As the ethereal substance of Earth became increasingly condensed to a more liquid element, the ethereal seed of man gradually lost the capacity to give it a direct form. Only the above-mentioned bodies could still reproduce descendants from themselves. This led to a new method of reproduction by means of the formation of buds. When the daughter creature appeared, it was considerably smaller than the mother creature, and only later grew to the same size. As the soul was no longer able to effectuate a direct form of reproduction in the dense, specialized, ethereal matter, a special part of the body was devoted to the general life principle. In this way the physical precursor of man was divided into two. On the one hand, there was the completed external body, over which the spiritual seed of man no longer had any power, and on the other, there was an inner part which was transformed into special organs, and in which external vibrations were experienced as perceptions in the form of a sort of sense of touch. As soon as the spiritual seed no longer had any power over the outer body, it decayed, and this resulted in death. The soul only remained active in the continuing asexual reproduction and in the developed inner perceptions with the help of the senses of hearing and touch.

An important event took place during the course of the Hyperborean era when the Sun withdrew, so that ethereal light and other sorts of ether disappeared from the creatures remaining on Earth. Mercury and Venus broke away from the Sun, and Mars passed through the sphere of the Earth, leaving behind the iron which later collected in the centre of the Earth.[15] The spirits of the form *(Exousiai)* withdrew to the Sun, as otherwise they would remain too far behind in their development. Man fell from a higher spiritual form of existence to a lower, more material form. The movement of the Earth around the Sun began, and the Earth began to turn on its axis.[16] In Genesis 1:6, this was described as the second day of Creation: "And God said, Let there be a firmament in the midst of the waters, and let it divide the waters from the waters." Then the creatures of the Earth received ethereal light from outside the Earth, instead of from inside it. The ethereal misty substance condensed to an ethereal watery substance. The centre of the Earth contained the ethereal primeval waters, which were not yet surrounded by ethereal light. The precursors of the present plant kingdom were already present as ether–permeated structures in the ethereal watery element.

4.6   The Lemurian era

The Lemurian era is a repetition of the Old Moon at a higher level.[17] The Lemurian continent encompassed the area that presently lies between Africa, Asia and Australia. The down-ward flow of ethereal life made everything appear on the astral-ethereal level, which is described in Genesis 1:9–13 as the bringing forth during the third day of Creation. The ethereal Earth began to condense slightly and the group souls of plant species descended into the astral ethereal sphere.

As the ethereal light withdrew to the separated Sun, ethereal heat formed from part of the ethereal light that had stayed be-hind, and this made it possible for the living creatures on Earth to develop their own heat.[18]

Man developed the faculty of vision. At this time, when the Moon was still united with the Earth, the eye still consisted of a single organ which developed a vague sensitivity to light and dark, and to the influence of the souls of surrounding creatures. Agreeable influences of souls were translated into light colours; unpleasant ones into dark images. The saga of one–eyed cyclopes and the eye of Polyphemus are reminders of this. A vestige of this organ can be found in modern man in the epiphysis or pineal gland.[19] In the body of man the fine ethereal watery and misty forms separated so that, in a sense, water and air became distinct. The body of man condensed partly into an ethereal body of air and partly into an ethereal body of water.

With the creation of ethereal heat man's ethereal body of air incorporated the element of heat or fire *(ruach)*. This so–called man of mist and fire was surrounded on the outside by its own astral body and Self, though these were still completely incor-porated in higher spiritual beings. Man did not yet feel himself as a separate Self. The fire of the man of mist and fire can be found in modern man in his hot blood. I imagine the ethereal figure of air from the beginning of the Lemurian era when I remember how the air breathed in through the lungs in our own body is taken all round the body by the blood, and in this way assumes the shape of the body.[20]

The man of mist and fire can be imagined partly as a luminous cloud floating in ethereal air. Floating rather than walking, he moved forwards, sideways, backwards and in all directions with the help of organs rather like limbs. These movements were not unstructured, but obeyed strict laws. The body of man with the dreamy consciousness of the imagery of the environment still had hardly any intelligence. It was mainly directed by higher beings which preceded the creation of man and were described earlier in Table 2.7. The spirits of the form (Powers or *Exousiai*) attempted to introduce the intellect in man and prepare his body for this purpose.

When man broke away from the parent creature,[21] he was still imperfect. The continued development of the organs, which was completed later inside the mother figure, still took place outside the parent in a protected environment. The whole event was reminiscent of the hatching process of an egg, and disposing of the shell. However, in this case there is no solid eggshell. Man's organs of movement were now considerably developed, and with these man performed the movement described above, alternately in the watery and airy parts of the ethereal Earth. Man himself also had a luminous upper part and a lower part, which was also an ethereal liquid, often submerged in the watery substance. At that time this lower part had reached the stage that is found in modern times in a different form in fish.[22]

For this floating, swimming movement, ethereal man had a sort of swim–bladder, which modern fish still have. Man did not yet have any lungs, but breathed the surrounding fiery mist through gills. In addition, there was a system comparable to the circulation of the blood in the form of a sort of umbilical cord through which substances from the fiery, misty atmosphere of the Earth passed in and out of the body.[23] The ethereal, luminous part of man was constantly pulled down by the evil forces which had remained behind in the water–Earth. Former plant man had changed into a creature which eventually achieved an amphibian stage. In myths and sagas this creature with its dual character is often embodied in a fiery dragon, or in the Old Testament it takes the form of the serpent which tempted Eve. As a degenerated form of the developmental stage reached by man at this time, the serpent indicates the depth to which man descended in his evolution.[24]

Emil Bock[25] pinpointed the place where the most important events occurred on the north edge of the Lemurian continent, where the ethereal world of the Sun still has a real effect on the ethereal world of the Earth. This is the place which is described in the Bible (Gen.2) as "the Garden of Eden," where there is a bridge of light between the Sun and the increasingly rigid Earth. This paradise island was like a mountainous area in the ethereal world, a dynamic zenith of cosmic ethereal forces which was a kind of divine island in the middle of increasingly dark chaos. Four luminous ethereal streams sprang up here, named in Genesis 2 as Pison, Gihon, Hiddekel and Prath. The Pison is difficult to find on a modern map, and seems to refer to Arabia and India. The three others are the Nile, the Tigris and the Euphrates. God placed man on Earth on this luminous paradise island: "And the Lord God planted a garden eastward in Eden; and there he put the man whom he had formed" (Gen.2:8).

When the astral body was added to the physical and ethereal bodies of man during this part of the Lemurian era, which, as stated above, can be considered as a repetition of the Old Moon, this resulted to some extent in a hellish period. The astral body planted in man was the bearer of the wildest desires, and man's group souls enjoyed their bodies in an exceptionally indulgent way.[26] In addition, the Earth threatened to rigidify as a dead Moon. In order to put a stop to this development, another important cosmic event took place; the Moon was cast off from the Earth, along with the worst downward drawing and consolidating forces which stood in the way of man's development on Earth.

The successive stages which took place in the lower part of the human body can be recognized in a number of the signs of the Zodiac: Pisces, Aquarius, Capricorn and Sagittarius. These correspond respectively to the feet, the shins, the knees and the thighs. During the Sagittarius stage man was comparable to the centaur — the lower half, a horse, representing the animal kingdom; the upper half, human.[27]

The paradise island above the Earth did not suddenly disappear as the Earth continued to develop. A trace of this miracle could be found for some time in places in Galilee, Syria, and Babylonia. Even in our own history the oasis of Damascus was an example of this.[28]

With the cosmic catastrophe of the Moon's expulsion we have arrived in the middle of the Lemurian era, and the time described in the Bible as the fourth day of Creation (Gen.1:16): "And God made two great lights; the greater light to rule the day, and the lesser light to rule the night: He made the stars also."

The fact that light was only created at this point in the story of the Bible is understandable when we remember that up to that time light was not perceptible to the physical eye. Ethereal Earth was comparable to a gigantic egg, a viscous watery substance. The atmosphere was opaque. The formation of the hard crust of the Earth took place in an astral, ethereal form. The above-mentioned giant oysters, which consisted of a slimy mass, had discarded their shell on one side, so that the whole thing looked like a thick soup containing hard lumps. It was only at the end of the third day of Creation that the iron and nickel core of the Earth had condensed to a boiling fiery mass in the astral, ethereal state. Even after the expulsion of the Moon, the Earth remained a boiling fiery mass for a long time. While the Moon was within the Earth it had lain on one side of the Earth like the yolk in an egg. For a long time it separated away from the Earth at the point where the Earth always has a tendency to be heavy. According to Rudolf Steiner, this was the area of the Atlantic Ocean. Others, like Bock and Wachsmuth, locate the place where the Moon was expelled in the Pacific Ocean.[29] All this was still invisible to the physical eye.

We now come to the period in which the unique aspect of the 172nd form condition of the Earth started to become apparent. After the Moon was expelled, the plant mineral seeds which had originated from the Old Moon and had fallen behind, condensed from the ethereal liquid to form the beginnings of solid matter.

For the first time things became physically perceptible. This was the beginning of the mineral kingdom we know and of death in the modern sense. For a long time the mineral kingdom retained a very plastic character.

As the process of solidification continued because of the remaining effect of the Moon, manifest in gravity, the human soul, which was both male and female, could no longer prescribe its own laws on matter. It had to bend to the laws of external nature on Earth. There was a separation of male and female, although this first became visible in animals, and only much later in man. Every male creature was given a female ethereal body, and every female a male one. The Bible (Gen.2:18) refers to this stage with the image of the creation of Eve. The centaur was still asexual, but after the expulsion of the Moon, man's figure acquired a form which corresponded to the animal level of development which can be found in the sexual Scorpio of the signs of the zodiac.[30] The density of matter obstructed part of the reproductive force which no longer functioned fully in a single-sex body. The unused reproductive force was inwardly transformed into the capacity for thought.

We have now reached the period described in Genesis 1:20 as the fifth day of Creation: "And God said, Let the waters bring forth abundantly the moving creature that hath life, and fowl that may fly above the Earth in the open firmament of heaven." The group souls of these creatures of water and air were created in the surroundings of the Earth. They could only develop in the ethereal atmosphere of the Earth after the expulsion of the Moon. The precursors of the plant kingdom had already formed in the astral ethereal sphere. Man continued to condense.[31] For the first time, the beginnings of incarnation became possible as man had acquired a Self. Meanwhile the spine had grown and the brain was formed. Up to then man's spine had been horizontal; now it started to draw itself up. The sign of the zodiac which refers to this stage of development is Libra, in which the forces of the Sun and Moon acquired an equilibrium, and the hips and vertical spinal column developed. The single organ of perception for qualities of the soul disappeared to make way for two eyes. As a result the ability to perceive the quality of the souls of spiritual creatures was lost, and the human soul increasingly became a reflection of the outside world.[32]

At this point the Earth, with its boiling mass, was increasingly filled with a watery and airy substance. Some shapes like islands separated away from this fiery liquid state. The first lower molluscs developed.

As the heat largely started to dissipate, the fiery mist gradually dropped, although the air remained suffused with clouds of water vapour. Man of mist and fire became water man. The vertical human form transformed itself, and the lower half with the two organs for movement metamorphosed to become predominantly a vehicle for digestion and reproduction. The upper half turned upwards, and the hands were created from the organs of movement.[33] Breathing in the fiery mist through the gills changed as the swim-bladder was transformed into lungs. In this way man was able to assimilate in the air he breathed in, higher spiritual creatures which he had initially felt radiating down on him in the form of light in his luminous ethereal state. In this way he started to make a seed of the first level of his higher Self, the spiritual self or *manas*.[34] Steiner pointed out that this change is described in the Bible in Genesis 2:7: "And the Lord God formed man of the dust of the ground, and breathed into his nostrils the breath of life; and man became a living soul." However, breathing in the air also entailed a consciousness of life and death. The Egyptians expressed this in the murder of the sun god Osiris by Typhon, the symbol of the hurricane, breath and air.[35] The stage in which the lower half of the human abdomen was formed is indicated with the sign of the zodiac, Virgo.

With the expulsion of the Moon, another important cosmic event took place before the beginning of the fourth day of Creation, which is described as the planet Mars going through the Earth for the second time.[36] The red planet Mars again left iron behind on Earth, which was then incorporated in man's blood, which had been colourless up to that time. From this moment man became a warm blooded creature. The heart entered the body at the same time as the Self, and the circulation supported the new respiratory process which had developed. In this way man had separated himself even further from his environment. At that time man's ethereal form began to move over the surface of the Earth, and he moved alternately with hopping movements, walking, and floating up into the air. The early dinosaurs revealed tendencies which correspond with this to some extent. The body was still very supple and flexible, and was transformed as soon as the inner life changed. Geographical regions and the climate formed a strong external influence.[37] However, no vestige of this man has remained in the Earth's crust in a form that can be discovered by geological means. This is because the physical body of man had not yet condensed beyond the stage of a body of heat. Since the time that man reached the Libra stage, the ethereal body, the astral body — and later, the Self — had increasingly become more active in helping to form the higher human organs, such as the lungs, the heart, and the larynx. Because of the dominance of one of these four bodies, there were four types of people, some with grotesque figures. When the physical body was strongly dominant and corresponded with the development of the lower parts, this resulted in the apocalyptic image of the bull, Taurus. This type can be found in a degenerate form in related creatures such as cows and steers. The group of people in whom the ethereal body was dominant, and in whom the parts of the trunk connected to the heart were strongly developed, can be recognized in Leo, the lion. The type of man in whom the astral body was dominant has been preserved in a degenerate form in the kingdom of birds and is shown in the Apocalypse as an eagle. Where the Self developed strongly, a creature evolved which could be considered as a combination of the other three characters because the Self combined all three parts in a harmonious way. The image of this group from which man developed is preserved in the Sphinx, which has the characteristic body of a lion, the wings of an eagle, the trunk rather like that of a bull, and a human face at the front.[38]

During the sixth day of creation (Gen.1:24), the group souls of the later land animals were created: "And God said, Let the Earth bring forth the living creature after his kind, cattle and everything that creepeth upon the Earth after his kind: and God saw that it was good." In retrospect it could be said that with the creation of the mineral kingdom, man was liberated from a tendency to become condensed too quickly. With the creation of the plant kingdom, man was liberated from a surfeit of vitality, and by leaving behind the animal kingdom, man was able to cast off an excess of desire. This history of the development of mankind repeats itself to some extent with the creation of the above-mentioned group souls of the land animals.

The essential aspect of the Earth, the hardening process into solid mineral substance, became increasingly prominent. The rocks of the primeval mountains, quartz and silicic acid, dripped down from the ethereal albuminous atmosphere surrounding the Earth like drops of wax. Everything still had a transparent character.

These rocks originated from the mineral plants which went back to the Old Moon metamorphosis, which formed por-phyry.[39] Granite and gneiss were created from the leaf–shaped mica which was deposited in horizontal layers that slid over each other. In the vertical direction a quartz framework formed across this. Both these minerals became solid as the space in between was filled up with feldspar. Coral creatures with the density of gelatine floated about in the ethereal liquid albumen atmosphere like albuminous shoals. The remnants of the Earth in the form of a living plant animal dripped down on to Earth from the surroun-ding atmosphere as a chalky rain of coral deposits.[40] These layers of chalk partially covered the above–mentioned layers of primeval rock. Gradually the silicon/magnesium (sima) layer of the Earth's crust became more dense. The layers of rock, which were soon to acquire a physically perceptible form, in this way still gave an impression of their previous development. The upper layers of the Earth lost their heavier coarser substance to the lower parts, and gradually a substance evolved higher up which was still mixed with water, but which was eventually to assume the form of our modern atmosphere.[41]

The gaseous Self was not created until the seventh day of the Creation, at the moment that the *Exousiai,* or spirits of the form, rose to a higher plane.[42] As yet no physical plants had sprung up on Earth, which was surrounded by dense clouds of mist. The atmosphere was as warm as an oven, so it was impossible for anything we know to have grown there. Some plant life did develop in the vicinity of the Earth, which caused the above-mentioned granite to rain down like black leaves.

In the centre of the Earth a solid nucleus formed, surrounded by a syrupy simmering mass.[43] During this last stage of the Lemurian era the physical senses could have perceived islands on some parts of the Earth protruding above the syrupy surface. These islands still had a rather soft consistency and fiery forces had free rein between them, so that the islands were constantly raised up by volcanic eruptions, only to be submerged again. Although some strange figures were already walking around on the most solid areas, man was still invisible in the dense misty mass.[44]

During the time of increasing solidification before the expulsion of the Moon, fewer and fewer human souls were able to assume a bodily form, and in the end only a very few couples remained, described in the Bible as the main couple, Adam and Eve. Other souls departed for other planets: Mercury, Venus, Mars, Jupiter and Saturn. Only the few remaining souls still had the strength to assume this recalcitrant human substance for their bodily form. When the Moon had been expelled, the departed souls gradually returned to the bodies of the descendants of this main pair. In doing so, Steiner relates how they formed the five different races of mankind, depending on the planet they came from.[45] In the revelations of the psychic couple referred to by the name Ramala, only four races are mentioned: the black, white, yellow and red races, which are related to the four rivers which arose in the Garden of Eden, as mentioned above.[46] In this, each race made its specific and equal contribution to the development of mankind. The red race in the west represented the element of fire, which is cleansing. The yellow race in the east represented the element of water and wisdom. The white race in the north was related to the element of air and the perfection of thinking, while the black race in the south was to bring harmony throughout the Earth. Steiner also distinguished the brown or Malaysian race.

At the end of the Lemurian era, man's body consisted of thick air rather like a cloud and of a gelatinous substance. Man had a culture in which signs were made in the air which immediately disappeared.[47] About this time when man returned to Earth, Genesis 1:27 says, "And God created man in his own image, in the image of God created he him; male and female created he them." The male Lemurian described in Genesis 4 as Cain, was the perfect master of his will and a born magician.[48] Thus he was able to lift up enormous loads simply by an effort of the will. Because of the enormous clairvoyant imagination of Lemurian women, they understood the life force of animals and the physical and chemical forces of so-called lifeless things. As mentioned above, Lemuria was a place where the turbulent movement of the Earth had come to rest. The Lemurian colony was one of the most advanced species of man. It was led from the temples by higher spiritual creatures in whose service the initiated entered. A fairly detailed description of religious and social life in Lemuria is given by the English psychic, Chavarinis. Man had a great influence on the changes in his body and on the bodies of animals and plants. Methods of cultivation were passed on to him by spiritual leaders belonging to higher hierarchies, and with these they exercised an immeasurably large influence on the surrounding nature. Although man's conduct was unconscious, it bore witness to great wisdom. Almost everywhere there were mighty volcanoes which constantly spread their destruction, producing a very hot climate.[49]

Because of the magical relationship between man's will and the fiery forces, the soft balanced character of man had a peaceful effect on the natural element, and land was formed. In contrast, the magic will of emotional fiery man caused the fiery masses to be brought to life, tearing open the thin crust of the Earth. The savage world of desires of the Old Moon period once again presented itself at the end of the Lemurian era in man's newly-created individual souls. As a result, the land inhabited by the Lemurians went under in a stormy volcanic sea of fire. Only a small part of mankind survived this catastrophe, and continued to develop in northern areas. A complete survey can be found in the above-mentioned Table 4.6.

In summary, the seven biblical days of creation can be seen as a reflection of the seven metamorphoses of the Earth and of the great steps forward in the development of mankind. Following the creation on the first day, of the luminous, ethereal, cup–shaped seed of man, the bodies of the first ancestors of sexual man, Adam and Eve, adapted for the later physical Earth, were created on the fourth day of Creation. After the catastrophe of solidification had been prevented on about the fourth day by the expulsion of the Moon, the body of man was able to develop further to a stage in which the departed human souls could be reincarnated on Earth on the seventh day of Creation. At the end of the Lemurian era man was ready to enter the essential stage of the Earth's 172nd form condition. This is the Atlantean era, in which man and his Self descended from the spiritual world into his physically solid body to find the way back in a state of freedom.

The above reveals that the struggle of the soul of "man on his way" is constantly reflected in nature and the state of the Earth. I will deal with this in more detail at a later stage.

4.7   The Atlantean era

Some of those who survived after the downfall of Lemuria settled in Atlantis, the mainland that used to exist between America and Europe, which now forms the bed of the Atlantic Ocean.[50] According to Hagemann, at the end of the Lemurian era the raining of rocks was concentrated in the area from which the Moon had been expelled, the continental block of the later Atlantic continent. This was followed by a cooling process which took place on and above the surface of the Earth, where no seas or men had yet appeared.[51] The last vestiges of smoke soon vanished from the fiery mist in the atmosphere and the sky merely held a huge mass of mist, which constantly blocked out the Sun. The Germanic sagas about Niflheim or Nebelheim are reminders of this time. At the beginning of the Atlantean era, man was still not visible to anyone looking with senses as we know them. However, after some time the physical body of man had become so condensed that it was visible.[52] Man was assimilated in the water of the misty sea, and his body condensed from the water was still completely transparent. At this early stage of Atlantis, man still had a rather vague awareness of the spiritual astral world at night. When he inhabited his liquid physical body in the day, it was night for him and there was a certain lack of consciousness. Gradually the physical organs formed, and with these he learned to see the misty, indistinct contours of Atlantis. His daytime consciousness became clearer and clearer and in this way man separated himself spiritually from an association with higher spiritual beings.

The water from the misty atmosphere which fell as rain had almost finished, and had filled up the seas and oceans. At the same time the Earth continued to shrivel up and became more condensed. In the middle of the Atlantean era man's physical body had become so dense that he had flesh and increasingly hard bones. A complete human figure had formed from the figure of the Sphinx. At first it was asexual, unlike the body of animals, but later the characteristic features of men and women started to appear. Gradually sexual reproduction took place in a physical sense.[53] This took place sooner in some peoples than in others.

Now that the Earth had become more solid, man descended from the misty atmosphere to the bed of the Earth. As his bones hardened, he started to walk for the first time. It was not until this period that man had limbs.[54] During the Atlantean era, the magical influence which Lemurian man had on the fiery misty sea, and on events on Earth, gradually disappeared.[55] In the early stages man still had a magical influence on the growth of plants. When he held his hand above a plant, he was able to make it grow faster with his will. To an important extent the will of the Atlanteans was directed by higher beings in the form of Archangels and Angels. These higher beings lived on in Greek mythology as Zeus and Apollo, or as the Germanic gods, Wotan and Thor. The whole life of the Atlanteans was closely connected to nature. They developed a powerful memory, and language also evolved during this period.[56] The word of the Atlanteans not only had meaning but also had a magical power over things and people; for example, cures could be found and animals tamed with a word. In later times this power declined, and made way for ambition and self-interest, which were curbed by the increasing strength of logical thinking and powers of judgment.

The climate in Atlantis was different from today's climate. In particular the northern areas to the west of Scandinavia and Ireland were completely shrouded in mist. In these regions man never experienced the alternation between sunshine and rain, as we do now.

The Atlanteans possessed a power which was described earlier as a life force or ethereal force.[57] This is the power which makes a physical plant grow from a seed. Modern man is unable to call on this power spontaneously, but must leave it to nature.

The Atlanteans not only grew plants for food, but also to use the life force dormant in the plant for methods of transportation and industry. With this form of energy, floating carriages could be moved forwards just above the ground, and with steering systems, these carriages could be raised far above the Atlantean mountains. The present Pico Alto on the Azores was the highest mountain at that time (5000 metres) and was known as Atlas. In our own time the carriages would be useless because the air in the Atlantean era was still much denser than it is now, while the water was much thinner.

The Atlantean was also able to increase his physical powers if he needed to do so for his activities. The human settlements of the Atlanteans at first looked like a garden in which the organic houses were made of trees which were cleverly interconnected with interwoven branches. Man fashioned the stones and used them with the growing trees.[58] What was built from nature by the Atlanteans was considered to be communal property. Thus social life in Atlantis was very different from life nowadays, although states started to form and rules were laid down. Man still had the real power to transfer his talents to his descendants.[59]

With the increase in thinking to control the mineral world, the dominance of the life force was gradually lost. Man learned to make greater use of tools and implements made from mineral substances, and he called on fire to help with this. In this he was led by human initiates, holy teachers, though these only rarely used their higher powers, and then only to stimulate man to think independently.

At the end of the Atlantean era the body of man started to assume its present form. Intelligent men were small, while the unintelligent were giants.[60] The ethereal body, which had up to that time protruded far above the head, was completely withdrawn into the physical body. Thus the head assumed a shape more like the present human head, and man's intelligence increased. Because of the complete assimilation of the ethereal body into the physical body, man learned to say "I," and became conscious of himself. The group in which this took place left Atlantis when the land was increasingly engulfed by large masses of water and air, a result of the growing egotism of the majority of Atlanteans. They went to Europe and Asia. In Tibet the most developed group founded the first centre of the post–Atlantean cultures, referred to above as the Ancient Indian culture. The downfall of Atlantis was caused because a large number of Atlanteans, including initiates, were starting to misuse the growth and reproductive forces of animals and man. Because these forces were interrelated to the effects of air and water, this led to an air and water catastrophe. The wondrous natural phenomenon of the rainbow, which did not exist in ancient Atlantis, is a reminder of the great flood of Atlantis, which is known as the Flood in myths and sagas. It was only after the Atlantean continent had been flooded that the dense mist started to clear from the air, and the Sun began to penetrate through the layer of clouds. This made it possible to see the rainbow, as described in the biblical story of Noah, the first man to see the "bow in the cloud" (Gen.9:13). At first, the Sun and the Moon were still surrounded by an enormous rainbow circle, but later they became visible to human eyes, together with the stars. With the end of the age of Atlantis and the floods and ice ages of this time, began the time of which more is known from the history of mankind. A brief summary of the post–Atlantean cultural period, which started almost ten thousand years ago, was given in Chapter 2.[61]

This summary was based on the plan outlined by Rudolf Steiner. Another historical account of the creation of our solar system and the Earth is given in the Urantia book.[62] Because of the sheer number of names and concepts already covered here, I will not include the contents of that book here.

As stated above, man's main purpose in the post–Atlantean era was to learn to follow his own thoughts and to find the way back to the spiritual world as a free and independent Self, so that this would bring harmony, not only in himself but also to the Earth.

4.8   History of man and Earth in human embryology

The historical development of man and the Earth in spiritual scientific terms can also be followed in an abbreviated form in human embryology. This has been described by Karl König and Hermann Poppelbaum.[63] An outline is given in Table 4.7.

The first weeks of the development of the human seed are reminiscent of the earlier three metamorphoses of the Earth, during which the egg membrane and appendices were formed. Old Saturn, where mineral man was created, and where the solar system was still united in a ball of heat, is reflected in the unity of the fertilized egg. This was followed by the Old Sun, the ball of light and air, on which mineral man developed as plant man, and where the outer planets, Mars, Jupiter and Saturn, first broke away. This separation is expressed in the formation of the trophoblast and the embryoblast. The trophoblast is the part of the egg that is responsible for feeding and protecting the embryo which develops from the embryoblast. The trophoblast later developed as the outer egg membrane or chorion. In the continued division into three at the time of the liquid ball of the Old Moon, animal man developed. In the cosmic division into three of the outer planets, the Sun and the Earth, still united with the Moon, this embryonic division was reflected in the form of the trophoblast, reticular magma, and embryonic seed.

The fourfold division of the outer planets, the Sun, the Moon and the Earth, which took place during the fourth metamorphosis of the Earth, happened before the embryo started to develop — because the amnion and yolk sac developed, reflecting the expulsion of the Moon. The amnion is the inner of the two egg membranes. It encloses the yolk sac, which contains the amniotic fluid and the embryo. In this way the embryo is contained in the outer membrane, the chorion, which developed from the trophoblast, the placenta, which is on the wall of the uterus, and the inner egg membrane or amnion (see also Table 9.3). These

Cosmic situation	Development of man	Development of biosphere in the physical world	Embryonic/foetal development
Old Saturn	mineral man	mineral Earth	Fertilized ovum (morula)
Old Sun	plant man	plant Earth	Trophoblast and embryoblast
Old Moon	animal man	animal Earth	Trophoblast, reticular magma, embryo nucleus
Earth	man	present Earth	Placenta, chorion, amnion, embryo nucleus
Polar era	ethereal ball	single cell organisms	undifferentiated seed (physical body)
Hyperborean era	two–part ball	eucaryots	sandal stage with primeval verte- bra; descent of ethereal body
Sun breaks away			(after 3 weeks)
Lemurian era	shell form, swim bladder, gills, umbilical cord, man of mist/fire	crustaceans, fish, amphibians,	curved hemi- sphere; extrem- ities; primitive heart; descent of astral body (after five weeks)
Moon breaks away		dinosaurs	
	sexuality; upright position; lungs and heart	birds mammals	enlargement of head; neck ex- tends; limbs develop; Self descends (after twelve weeks)
Atlantean era	solidification of bones and flesh; externalization in the world	apes man	development of bones; birth (after 38 weeks)
Post–Atlantean era	self–conscious- ness with dev- elopment of thinking	(Sun breaks through the clouds)	use of "I" for the Self in the third year of life

Table 4.7. Parallels between individual human development and the history of the cosmos, Earth's biosphere and man.

membranes represent the cosmic record of the creation of man and the Earth.

The development of the embryo itself takes place in a way which can be viewed as a biological account what happened during the 172nd form condition of the fourth small cycle of the Earth. Once again, history repeats itself. During the first days the physical seed of the embryo is still undifferentiated, like the human ethereal spheres of life during the Polar era. This corresponds to the period when the Earth was still an ethereal ball of life, and was still united with the Sun and the planets.

In the Hyperborean era the Earth condensed into a luminous ball of mist and man developed a two-part ethereal body. At the start of the third week the ethereal body of man joins the physical embryo. The embryo develops by means of cell division to the so-called "sandal" stage, in which the basic vertebrae of the backbone develop in a plantlike way; the segments are reminiscent of the stem of a plant.

In the Earth's development, this was followed by the start of the Lemurian age when the Sun withdrew, as a repetition of the Old Moon. Man of mist and fire moved in the misty smoke above the sea of fire on Earth with an ethereal body formed from a spherical ear with gills as the organ to feel the vibrations of sound in the surrounding form-giving cosmos, with a swim bladder as the organ to help with movement. It was connected by a cosmic umbilical cord to the atmosphere which fed him. In the corresponding period the astral body descends into the embryo in the fifth week as it grows at the end of the umbilical cord, following the development of the swelling hemisphere in which the first sensory organs are becoming visible: the mysterious gill openings in the neck, and the mighty heart starting to operate in the chest.

During the third month of the foetus's life the head starts to increase in size considerably, and the trunk becomes stronger. This is reminiscent of the events in the middle of the Lemurian era when the Moon was expelled and man stood up. The foetus is endowed with the Self. It is a repetition of what happens in later Lemurian man, who was present in the ethereal watery mists above the slowly developing soft land masses. The following months constitute the period which corresponds to the Age of Atlantis. The hard bones of the human skeleton are formed, just as mineral rocks, formed from the plant seeds of the Old Moon, solidify. The exit of man into the visible physical world, and the Sun breaking through the thick layers of mist at the end of the Age of Atlantis after the flood of Atlantis, are reflected in the breaking of the waters and in birth, when direct sunlight streams in. The development of thinking and the arrival of the Self and self–awareness in the present post–Atlantean era is mirrored in the child when it first starts to use the word "I" of itself at the age of three.

The history of man and the Earth reflect each other. Every step in the evolution of man as a spiritual being can be recognized in the evolution of the Earth. When man is cut off from his spiritual destiny, this results in catastrophic events on the Earth. Knowing this gives us an awareness of our enormous responsibility even today.

5.   The creation of the Earth's biosphere

Therefore let us call upon the Lord. And let us stretch out our hands to him. Let us do so together: you and I, to seek help for the suffering Earth.

Zarathustra, Yasna 29:5

5.1   Overview

Thus far I have given a general survey of the scientific theories on the creation of the physical Earth and of the evolution of Earth and man in terms of what is called "spiritual science" by Rudolf Steiner. I shall now try to synthesize the whole picture of these two preceding chapters from a detached position on the wall between the physical and spiritual worlds. Then I shall also attempt to draw up a picture of the development of the plant and animal kingdoms on Earth based on scientific insights and the principles of spiritual science. In this way I hope to arrive at an overview in which physical and spiritual viewpoints are united.

In contrast with the description of the previous chapters, I will try to use time as a yardstick in displaying the information that has been collected together. In order to do this in a fruitful way, it is first necessary to answer two questions. On what are scientific calculations of time based? And how should time be understood in spiritual scientific literature? These questions are important, as there seem to be large differences in the dates used.

5.2   Time as a yardstick

As explained in Chapter 3, which described the scientific view of the creation of the physical Earth, the age of the Earth is estimated to be about four and a half billion years. This age is usually calculated on the basis of the decay of radioactive isotopes of elements. In this decay there is spontaneous nuclear fission when atomic particles and gamma radiation are emitted. This decay is not influenced by temperature or pressure. Assuming that the speed of decay of an isotope, its so-called "half-life," is constant, the time of creation can be calculated from the ratio of the isotope to the decayed product. This assumes that the decayed product was present at the creation of the Earth. To date minerals that are billions of years old, scientists use the decay of radioactive uranium to lead; and for shorter periods, up to 40000 years, the radioactive carbon (C_{14}) absorbed by plants. It was only after radioactive carbon dating was used that the age of the Earth was estimated to be 4.5 billion years. Before this, Lord Kelvin (1824–1907) calculated the Earth to be 100 million years old, on the basis of the estimated internal temperatures. In 1654, the Irish archbishop James Usher calculated that the Earth was created in the year 4004 BC on the basis of all the generations in the Bible.[1] Although we nowadays speak in terms of absolute methods of dating, modern calculations are still based on assumptions which cannot really be verified. Therefore it is not surprising that new methods of measurement can unexpectedly result in different estimates of the Earth's age. For example, in July 1987 the Dutch astronomer Harvey Butcher reported his conclusion that the universe was not twenty but ten billion years old, on the basis of his radioactive dating of the stars.[2]

On the basis of the radioactive dating methods described above, there are geological indications that continents already surfaced above the oceans three and a half billion years ago, during the Pre-Cambrian era. The first signs of single-cell organisms date from about the same time. According to geologists, at the end of the Pre-Cambrian era, about six hundred million years ago, a wealth of remnants of organisms with calcium skeletons suddenly appeared. This was followed by a period from which the remains of higher forms of life have been found, as we will discuss in greater detail below, finishing with the remains of the first real humans, *Homo sapiens,* who replaced Neanderthal man living in northwest Europe, about 70000 to 40000 years ago. According to geologists, this brings us to the time of the last ice ages, which ended about 10000 years ago.

103

Spiritual science includes this period in the final stage of the Age of Atlantis, which ended in approximately 10000 BC with the disappearance of the last remnants of Atlantis. Plato referred to the end of Atlantis in his description of the myth,[3] and it was similarly described in the pronouncements made by the American medium Edgar Cayce.

Going back to about 10000 BC, the clocks on either side of the wall may have been showing roughly the same time but, before that, the question of time presents increasing confusion and differences. For example, Steiner describes a period at the end of the Lemurian era in which visible semiliquid volcanic islands protruded above the surface of the Earth.[4] The strange precursors of modern amphibians and reptiles walked round on these islands. These creatures were only partly visible, although their bodies consisted of air and liquid. This period is similar to the time at which science pinpoints the solidification of the continents protruding above the oceans, which took place more than three billion years ago. However, according to Steiner, the end of the Lemurian era was considerably nearer in time. Discussing the Akasha Chronicle in his book, *Cosmic Memory,* he stated that the Atlantean culture which followed the Lemurian era, existed for about one million years.[5] In his lectures on the *Theosophy of the Rosicrucians,*[6] he related that the separation of the Earth and the Moon, which occurred during the Lemurian era, took place many thousands of years ago. In his writings on Atlantis, Cayce said that the world has existed for 10.5 million years. Looking back at the time when the Earth became solid, there is therefore a difference in the dates of the two disciplines by a factor of 100 to 1000.

Even when an explanation for this great difference in time is sought by including the previous metamorphosis of the Earth in the whole process, this does not help much. Thus with regard to the length of the Old Sun metamorphosis of the Earth, Steiner refers to a period of millions of years in which we see the Old Sun changing and moving away, and after many more millions of years it lights up again from a twilight condition. This is the beginning of the Old Moon cycle. From Steiner's remarks I get the impression that he does not attach a great deal of significance to the length of the period mentioned. While he says "many thousands of years ago" for the time of the Moon's expulsion in the middle of the Lemurian era,[7] he refers elsewhere to the duration of the subsequent Age of Atlantis alone being about a million years. Perhaps his reference to millions of years should be to billions of years. Nevertheless, Steiner rejects this possibility in his lectures, saying: "If someone in our time only takes into account the forces which are operating on the Earth, he would come to the conclusion that the Earth looked different millions of years ago. In doing this he takes the cosmos into consideration. As we have already seen, when you take into account what comes out of the cosmos, the periods involved are not really that long. If you go back six, seven, or eight thousand years, the Earth and its rocks were very different from what they are now, if not externally, then internally. Going further and further back, you arrive at a time when the Earth was soft."[8]

In the same series of lectures, Steiner mentions even more directly the applicability of modern scientific insights about the time for which he described the extrapolation method of geology in the same series of lectures: "Anyone who studies geology in great depth nowadays will tell you: twenty-five million years ago the Earth was like this or like that. For example, they study what happens at the Niagara Falls. They take a stone which the water flows over constantly, and work out how much of it has been eroded in a year, and then go on making calculations. In this way they arrive at twenty-five million years. This is like studying someone's heart now and a month later to find out what the heart was like three hundred years ago. But the heart didn't exist then. The sums are right, but the things themselves didn't yet exist. The same is true for the question of what the Earth looked like twenty-five million years ago. The sum is exactly right, but the Earth did not yet exist. In the same way, geologists work out what the Earth will look like in twenty-five million years time. However, the Earth will no longer exist. If you come back in 25 815 years time, the Earth will have dissolved. The Earth will no longer exist; you will have been liberated from it. You will have risen up to your higher life."[9]

Elsewhere in the same series of lectures, he describes some

other characteristics of the condition of the Earth in the future and in the past, detailing these strange ideas which seem quite unbelievable to scientists: "We are familiar with our high mountains and the dead granite masses. The Sun rises over an Earth on which everything is dried up and destroyed. This was also the case 25 920 years ago (the Sun was in the same place in the signs of the Zodiac). It has not been there in between these two times. We do not have to go back more than at most 15 000 years to find the time when the Earth appeared in the guise of a plant as a result of the completely different position of the Sun, and it was even later that it appeared as an animal. Therefore when you go back in time you must imagine that the rocks were liquid, about as liquid as iron in a foundry. When the Sun is once again in Libra in about 8000 years time, the Alps will have dissolved, the Earth will become plantlike, men and animals will return to their earlier condition. One could actually say that in relation to the cosmos the Earth is merely sleeping."[10]

Thus spiritual science suggests that the scientific calculation of time and the imagery of the creation of the Earth are a long way from the truth, and are actually much more dynamic, based on the cyclical progression of the signs of the Zodiac, rather than on the static principles of the present natural laws. This means that the scientific timepiece of the radioactive decay of isotopes is not quite as reliable as we imagine. Alice Bailey describes that in the middle of the Lemurian era the natural kingdoms were greatly stimulated by the spiritual world: "In the mineral kingdom, for instance, certain of the minerals or elements received an added stimulation and became radioactive, and a mysterious chemical change took place in the vegetable kingdom. This facilitated the bridging process between the vegetable and animal kingdoms just as the radioactivity of minerals is the method of bridging the gulf between the mineral and vegetable kingdoms."[11]

This description suggests that with the appearance of radioactive elements, the production of oxygen started and the change from the anaerobic to the aerobic atmosphere took place, in the middle of the Lemurian era. This was after the expulsion of the Moon. In addition, this description indicates that extrapolating into the past on the basis of the radioactivity theory does not always lead to reliable results. According to spiritual science, changes take place much more rapidly than indicated by scientific calculations, and Steiner even goes so far as to say that time itself is subject to variations. This may be illustrated by a few examples. In *Occult Science,* he wrote: "The laws which at the present time underlie the moulding and shaping of forms in the kingdoms of Nature can certainly not be extended to the more remote ages of the past."[12]

And in *Manifestations of Karma,* he said: "...the answer to this question: What is matter? What is the soul? must also vary. It must at once be emphasized that the answers which will be given are only those which the earth–man can make, and are of significance only to the earth–man."[13]

Finally, on this subject he wrote in his lectures on *Man's Being, his Destiny and World Evolution:* "There is one thing that is not known: that the applicability of natural laws decreases with distance (like the strength of light and gravity), that our Earthly natural laws no longer apply when we are in cosmic (spiritual) space."[14]

Steiner is even more explicit about the value of the concept of time as a unit of measurement in science or in terms of spiritual science, when he says: "Time in the heavens is different from time on Earth. We try to make time on Earth go as evenly as possible. This cannot be done with heavenly time which sometimes goes faster and sometimes goes slower because it carries life within itself. Man kills Earthly time, and that is why it is so regular. Heavenly time is alive, and therefore it is not regular."[15]

He explains this statement in greater detail in his book, *Cosmic Memory,* where he indicates that, in fact, the speed of development is not the same on all the planets [Earth metamorphoses]. "Life proceeds with the greatest speed on [Old] Saturn, the rapidity then decreases on the [Old] Sun, becomes still less on the [Old] Moon and reaches its slowest phase on the earth. On the latter, it becomes slower and slower, to the point at which self–consciousness develops. Then the speed increases again...On Jupiter the speed of the [Old] Moon, on Venus, that of the [Old] Sun will again be attained."[16]

The idea expressed above is a good argument for not using time as a unit of measurement to compare the two types of scientific doctrine. In any case, Steiner's indications initially appear to have a qualitative rather than a precise quantitative sense. This explains how, on one and the same page, the Age of Atlantis supposedly existed for about a million years, and at the same time, for many thousands of years. The apparent discrepancy is also explained by the fact that the spiritual world, beginning with the astral level, can only be understood when one steps outside time. According to Blavatsky, there is no time outside the physical body. Steiner states that in the spiritual world, time becomes space.[17]

Nevertheless, this attempt to compare time scales shows that spiritual science considers the scope of application of natural laws to be restricted to the spatial surroundings of the Earth, and the temporal surroundings of the present period, which lasts from approximately 10000 BC to AD 10000. In the more distant future and the more distant past, our current measurement of time loses its real significance to a large extent.

Thus Cayce wrote that in the Age of Atlantis, reaching the age of six or seven hundred years was equivalent to no more than an age of sixty or seventy years now. In contrast with Steiner's indications of time, Cayce's writings contain precise dates for particular events which took place during the Age of Atlantis. However, in relation to this sort of teaching, the question arises whether existing scientific insights were taken into account to fit in with this teaching, or whether they have an absolute meaning.

Another point of correspondence with Steiner is that before the development of human sexuality, under the sign of the Scorpion, could progress to the physical shape of the hips, under the sign of Libra, the Sun first had to move through all the signs of the Zodiac, which took 25920 years.[18] In earlier times there had to be even more orbits before this could happen. Therefore the familiar method of calculating time of the post–Atlantean period cannot be applied to earlier periods. The Sun first had to move through all the signs of the Zodiac — in the past, even several times — before there could be any progress in evolution. Thus the formation of the parts of the body which required a more powerful build also took much more time.

All this suggests that every developmental stage in man's evolution during the Lemurian and Atlantean eras lasted several hundred thousand years. If it is maintained that the Age of Atlantis ended about 10000 BC, this means that according to modern calculations of time, the Lemurian era must have ended millions of years ago. In fact, Bailey states that the middle of the Lemurian era was 18 million years ago. This brings us to the outer limit of what can be deduced from the mainly theosophical and anthroposophical literature on calculating the age of the physical world. It seems as though we have come to a dead end along the trail of time as a comparative unit of measurement. In this context Bailey warned that anyone who tries to map out these matters and draw them up in a detailed table, will find themselves in areas where mistakes are inevitable, and will totter through a mist which will eventually engulf him.[19] I am beginning to feel like this myself.

Finally, Wachsmuth and Hagemann shed some light on this question by pointing out that Steiner often referred to a million years to indicate unimaginably long periods.[20] Years as we know them are only meaningful as a unit of measurement from the middle of the Age of Atlantis, when the movement of the Earth around the Sun became established at its present orbital speed. Several of Steiner's followers placed the middle of the Age of Atlantis between 15000 and 20000 BC.[21]

Elisabeth Vreede, who divides the Age of Atlantis into periods of 7 × 2160 years, indicates that this classification goes back to times when chronology in the modern sense of the word did not really apply.[22] These years are calculated merely to provide a basis for comparison with our own time. Her calculation for the end of the Lemurian era in 24000 BC should therefore be seen in this light, though it is clear that there is absolutely no connection with the hundreds of millions of years used in the scientific world. One possible solution for the huge difference in dates is that the calculation of time in spiritual science only relates to developments in the ethereal world. This is a world which has time but no space, though the time is different and more variable than time in the physical world, as Steiner indicated. As soon as a being turns to the physical world from the ethereal world, the more rapid course of time is reduced to the long periods recognized in geology for the different stages of evolution.

These considerations have shown that this calculation of time is not a good unit of measurement for comparing developments in the spiritual and physical worlds. The developmental stages of man and of plant and animal forms of life provide a better basis for comparison.

5.3   Early metamorphoses of the Earth

In order to arrive at an understanding of the relationship between man and nature, it is necessary first to find out how the seeds of the lower kingdoms originated. Steiner described the physical relationship between man and the animal and plant kingdoms, *inter alia,* in his lectures on *Man as Symphony of the Creative Word.* In order to grasp these images, we shall need to immerse ourselves again in these ideas. Table 5.1 contains a summary. It should be noted that all the seeds first originate in the ethereal world. It is paradoxical that the seeds which were formed last in evolution, namely, single cells, appeared first in the physical world, as shown in Table 4.7.

During the Old Saturn metamorphosis, at the same time that the foundations were laid of man's senses, the seeds developed for butterflies and other insects in the ethereal heat. Steiner referred to the butterflies, dragonflies and other insects as the gifts of Saturn, Jupiter, Mars and the Sun, at a time when they were still united. The effect of the Sun can be recognized in the butterfly egg, the effect of Mars in the growth and movement of the caterpillar, the effect of Jupiter in the chrysalis, and the effect of Saturn in the butterfly itself. The butterfly is the cosmic embodiment of the sensory system, and more particularly of the memory.[23]

The seed of the bird originated in the first half of the Old Sun metamorphosis. It is a creature of heat and air, and the body is virtually all head. The seed of the bird, for example, the eagle, originated at the same time as the formation of the human head.

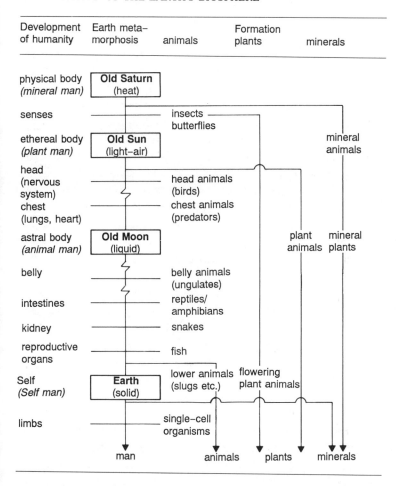

Table 5.1. Parallels in the original formation of the body of man and the animals, plants and minerals in the ethereal world.

The bird can be viewed as a sophisticated head, like the nervous system of a mammal. The feathers, which developed later, can be viewed as a materialized form of its thoughts.

During the second stage of the Old Sun, when the outer planets broke away from the Earth, which was still united with the Sun and the inner planets, plant man developed the beginnings of a chest and spine like a stem, and twelve pairs of ribs

111

like twelve leaf stalks. In this chest cavity the rhythmic systems of respiration and the circulation of the blood also developed. At the same time the seed was sown of animals which are all chest, such as lions. The lion's maw is the repercussion of the inter-action between the heartbeat and respiration.[24]

For the development of mineral man from Old Saturn to plant man of the Old Sun, it was necessary for some of the seeds of man to return to the level of mineral animals. On the Old Moon these seeds degenerated into mineral plants from which the first mineral rocks were formed on Earth, as explained above. These primeval rocks therefore had a plantlike character on the Old Moon. During the Old Moon metamorphosis man's first digestive organ, the belly, developed before the separation of the Sun. The cow and the bull are representatives of the digestive animals or ungulates which were first formed during this period. Following the separation of the Sun, lower forms of purely digestive ani-mals originated during the Old Moon metamorphosis at the same time as the continued development of the seed of man. The intestines corresponded with amphibians and reptiles, which are no more than walking intestines. It was only during the Earth metamorphosis that they acquired a head. The kidneys corres-ponded with the snakes. The development of man's reproductive organs during the last stage of the Old Moon corresponds with the development of fishes and the even later water animals. The development of animal man on the Old Moon was at the expense of the second group of seeds of man to be cast back and remain behind as plant animals. The non–flowering trees developed from these on Earth, as indicated in Table 4.3. The seeds of flowering plants formed in a different and special way. They developed from some of the insect seeds formed on Old Saturn, which were influenced on the Old Moon by forces pulling downwards, and as a result, were pulled down to the physical world from the ethereal world. This meant they lost their capacity to move, and became immobilized images of the creatures fluttering around in the insect world. Parallel with the development of the butterfly from the egg, roots developed on Earth from the seed of the plant under the influence of the forces of the Moon. Under the influ-ence of Venus, leaves spiralled upwards. It is like observing the effect of gravity on a caterpillar. The calyx is the chrysalis developing on Earth with the help of the forces of Mercury. Just as the butterfly develops from the chrysalis, the flower develops from the calyx. The seed then returns to Earth. This plant cycle had its beginnings on the Old Moon. To summarize, a flowering plant can be seen as a butterfly imprisoned in earth.[25] The internal organs which develop in a butterfly become visible in the flower as leaves and blossom.[26]

Finally, seeds of man were cast back on Earth by man for the third time, so that he could rise higher. At the eleventh hour the lowest animal seeds developed from these, some of which degenerated into single-cell organisms. During this period man's limbs developed. This developmental process reveals how man builds up his body in the spiritual world, descending from the head to the chest, belly and limbs. This is very different in the belly animals, which develop the chest and head from the belly upwards. Chest animals develop from the middle, both upwards (to the head) and downwards (to the belly). As mentioned above, in the subsequent Earth metamorphosis, when the process of solidification started to take place, we see that the most degenerative forms are materialized first in the husks left behind by man as he develops. From that time their capacity for further spiritual development was interrupted for a long time. However, they were still able to specialize in the function which they assume in the physical world.[27]

I will return at a later stage to the conclusions which can be drawn for Darwin's theory of evolution from this developmental history.

5.4   Ethereal development and geological parallels

Polar and Hyperborean eras

I will now try to give an overall outline of the development of the Earth's biosphere, interrelating the insights of science and spiritual science as much as possible. I should like to take the classification of spiritual science[28] as a starting point, although this sometimes contains conflicting information. I will begin by using the classification of Wachsmuth and Poppelbaum as much as possible. This seems to be particularly directed at developments in the ethereal world. For every period and its characteristic stages of development, I will seek a parallel in geological eras.

During the 172nd form condition of the Earth metamorphosis (see Table 4.5) ethereal life was the highest ethereal condition, and at the same time, the origin of life on Earth. Ethereal life originated during the 172nd form condition. The lowest form of man in the Polar era did not condense any further than this ethereal life. Table 5.2 shows how the natural kingdoms descended in the form of spiritual seeds before this time, during the 169th to the 171st form condition. After the formation of the ethereal seeds of man and Earth in the 169th form condition, animal seeds originated in the 170th and plant seeds in the 171st form condition. The seeds of minerals formed only during the 172nd form condition during the Polar era. In the subsequent Hyperborean era, ethereal air and chemical ether, or ethereal sound, developed from ethereal life (see Table 5.3).

On the first day of creation, according to Genesis, the Earth had not condensed beyond an ethereal ball of air comprising our whole solar system. The ethereal ball of air originated from the group souls of the minerals, which were created by the spirits of the form.[29] As described above (see Chapter 4), the ethereal body of man consisted of a single–cell egg which sprouted and was no more than an organ of hearing. The chemical ether allowed for rudimentary feeding, and had a strong influence on forming the body. When these bodies were formed, some of the seeds were cast down. These later formed the first animal kingdom on physical Earth. They have an ethereal air body, slightly reminiscent of a snail's shell. The later species related to these include snails, worms, coelenterates, sponges and so on. In addition, some of the seeds degenerated. They consisted solely of ethereal life and decayed to form the subsequent single–cell organisms such as bacteria.[30] The creation of these single–cell organisms corresponds most closely to the second half of the geological Pre–Cambrian era, although it should be noted that according to spiritual science, there had not yet been any physical

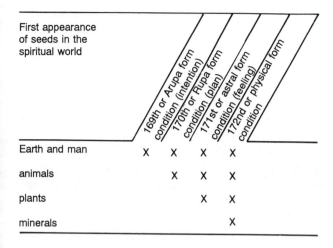

First appearance of seeds in the spiritual world	169th or Arupa form condition (intention)	170th or Rupa form condition (plan)	171st or astral form condition (feeling)	172nd or physical form condition
Earth and man	X	X	X	X
animals		X	X	X
plants			X	X
minerals				X

Table 5.2. Creation and descent of individual seeds to the lower spiritual levels during the 169th–172nd form condition.

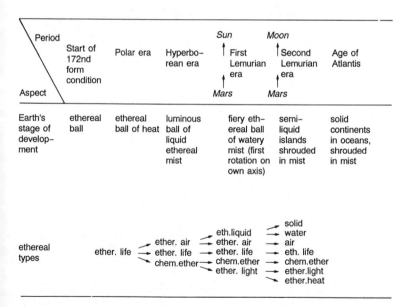

Table 5.3. Survey of developmental stages of the Earth and the development of ethereal types during the 172nd form condition (see also Table 4.3).

solidification, and there were still no oceans. All these developments took place in an ethereal, albuminous atmosphere.

During a later stage of the Hyperborean era, described above
as the second day of Creation, the ethereal body of man contained a cell with a seed, and had the form of an ethereal cloud
with a calyx–like opening. The body radiated inner light, and
reproduced by creating smaller descendants. Following the sense
of hearing, the sense of touch was also acquired. At the same
time as the higher development of the human ethereal body, a
group of coarser astral beings was again cast down and animals
with an ethereal water–air body developed from these. Presumably these were the corals, cephalopods, graptolites, tribolites,
and so on, which eventually appeared. Tribolites were very common from the Cambrian to the Silurian period. Their numbers
then dwindled, and at the end of the Palaeozoic era, they became
extinct. Large coral reefs formed from the coral creatures,
particularly during the Silurian period, and these still cover a
larger surface area of the Earth inland.

In addition to the two groups of lower animals and single–cell
organisms which developed, plantlike beings also appeared when
the Sun separated away. However, these did not yet have the
same form as plants now. The group souls of these plants were
created by the Angels,[31] and have a body of ethereal air and
ethereal light.[32] Then they appeared as shining plant forms,
swirling through the ether. Later their bodies consisted of ethereal
light and air, combined with ethereal water. The first traces of
rooting psilophytes were found during the Silurian period. According to Poppelbaum, the end of the Hyperborean era probably
coincided with the transition of the Silurian to the Devonian
period. At that time the gigantic oyster–like creatures described
above formed the nebulous, albuminous atmosphere in which the
ethereal single–cell organisms and lower animals lived. However,
these ethereal bodies could not yet leave behind fossilized im-
prints. Thus, according to geologists, the fossils dating from this
period, and coral reefs built up then, must have been imprinted
in physical substance from the ethereal remains of these organisms at a later stage when the layers of rock rained down. I will
return later to another possible explanation. Table 5.4 gives a

general survey summarizing all the information discussed above as systematically as possible. Once again the table shows the six days of creation from the first book of the Bible, Genesis. Steiner provided some valuable insights into this matter during a series of lectures in Munich in August 1910.[33]

The Lemurian era up to the expulsion of the Moon

After the separation of the Sun, and the beginning of the Lemurian era, ethereal light largely disappeared from the Earth which was left behind, and the creatures alive on it. Ethereal heat developed from part of the remaining ethereal light, giving rise to the fiery element which enables the body to generate heat. According to Genesis, the group souls of plants and higher animals needed the input of ethereal light from outside on the third day of creation, and they turned to the Sun, which was now present externally. The Earth slowly started to turn on its axis, resulting in the differentiation of day and night. The first stage of the formation of the continents took place as they separated away in the fiery ethereal liquid shrouded in mist. Thus the Polar, Hyperborean and Lemurian eras, up to the expulsion of the Moon, were a repetition of the Old Saturn, Old Sun, and Old Moon metamorphoses.

Early ethereal Lemurian man moved around like a floating cloud on the borders of the ethereal layers of air and water. His body of fire and mist was rather like a cyclops, with organs of movement. The lower, most condensed part of the body, moved about in a liquid element, and was fish-shaped. The upper part of the body reached up into the astral world. It had gills, and under the influence of sunlight, the eye started to develop. During this time man was increasingly drawn down to the lower regions. Higher man transformed the fishlike body to a body which is quite similar to that of modern snakes, and later that of reptiles and amphibians.[34] The above-mentioned animal seeds, which initially originated on the Old Moon, used these husks of bodies, so that increasingly highly developed animal species were formed from the developing seed of man. In this way the developing husks of man provide a body for the seeds which do not wish to wait any longer for the completion of the husk. In this process

117

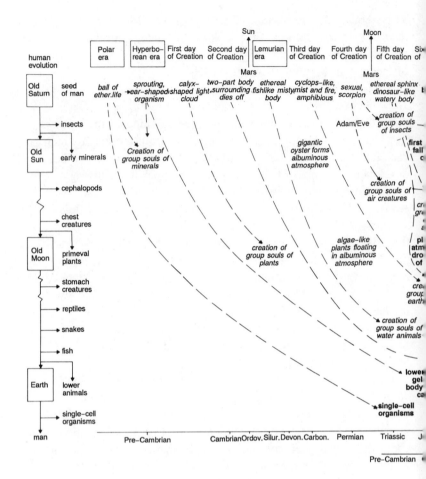

Table 5.4. Evolution of man and creation of the biosphere in the 172nd form condition.

the seeds which originated last were first to descend down to the physical Earth. The successful evolution of reptiles throughout the land which took place during this period is also related to their propensity to lay eggs with a shell, which eventually became a hard shell. Higher plant seeds joined the creatures descending to the Earth, such as horse's tails and ferns, whose liquid forms were metres tall, and spread over the Earth in spraw–

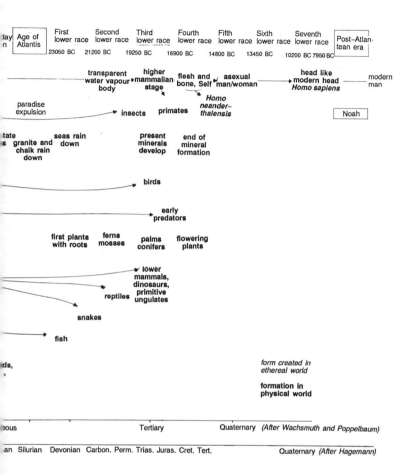

day n	Age of Atlantis	First lower race 23050 BC	Second lower race 21200 BC	Third lower race 19250 BC	Fourth lower race 16900 BC	Fifth lower race 14800 BC	Sixth lower race 13450 BC	Seventh lower race 10200 BC 7950 BC	Post–Atlantean era

transparent water vapour body • mammalian stage higher • mammalian stage • flesh and bone, Self • asexual man/woman → modern head head like Homo sapiens — modern man

paradise expulsion → insects primates Homo neanderthalensis Noah

tate s granite and chalk rain down seas rain down present minerals develop end of mineral formation

birds

early predators

first plants with roots ferns mosses palms conifers flowering plants

lower mammals, dinosaurs, primitive ungulates

reptiles

snakes

fish

ds,

form created in ethereal world

formation in physical world

eous | Tertiary | Quaternary *(After Wachsmuth and Poppelbaum)*

an Silurian Devonian Carbon. Perm. Trias. Juras. Cret. Tert. | Quaternary *(After Hagemann)*

ling forests. According to Wachsmuth and Poppelbaum, these developments took place from the Devonian to approximately the Permian period, that is, the beginning of the Mesozoic era. At the end of the Permian period the plants and animals which had developed had a gelatinous body[35] which could not yet have been fossilized as in the preceding stages. However, the ethereal remains of plants were responsible for the subsequent organic

119

carbon deposits which have been found in the carboniferous layers of the Earth's crust. Hagemann's explanation is more probable, in which the Carboniferous period coincides with the Age of Atlantis, as explained below.

The end of the Palaeozoic era is a time at which developments took a new direction in various respects. As long as the Moon was still united with the Earth, and the Earth lacked the former direct contact with the Sun, there was a dominating, unbalancing, rigidifying tendency. With the expulsion of the Moon on the fourth day of creation, there was a possibility for developments to take an upward turn.

The period following the expulsion of the Moon
The expulsion of the Moon probably took place at the beginning of the Mesozoic era, according to Poppelbaum, during the transition from the Triassic to the Jurassic period. The expulsion resulted in chaos on Earth. Earth still looked little like it does at present. When the Moon was expelled with the most condensed parts of the Earth, it was once again able to open up to the influence of the Sun. After the catastrophe the mineral kingdom recovered first, followed by plants, then animals, and finally, man. During this time Mars also passed through the still very plastic Earth sphere, leaving a lot of iron behind. The role of the iron in the blood is a reminder of this event. The air and water creatures which were created after this on the fifth day of creation are the hot-blooded species. For the first time mineral seeds solidified to become physically perceptible, and on the sixth day of creation they dropped down from the atmosphere in the form of wax as the first rock. The heavy particles containing iron collected in the centre of the Earth and the continents started to form as semi-liquid areas.

The atmosphere was still full of black mist and smoke. The soft bed of the Earth was watery and covered with many springs.[36] The climate was very warm.[37]

As explained above, man stood upright after the expulsion of the Moon. This image is embodied in the Sphinx, which is composed of the three types of animals — the bull, the lion and the eagle — with a human face at the front. The group souls of the land animals which appeared in the Jurassic period were created on the sixth day of creation. Before the higher mammals separated away as degenerated seeds of man, snakes, reptiles and amphibians, lower mammals and the dinosaurs one by one assumed physical form, following the expulsion of the Moon. The highest mammalian species from this time were probably the marsupials, such as kangaroos. The dinosaurs were a type of a monster form which had not yet acquired the passions of man governed by the Self. Poppelbaum describes them as tremendous predatory animals, half–fish, half–crocodile, walking mountains of land creatures, half–elephant, half–kangaroo; ghostly giants of the air, half–lizard, half–bat, they all bore witness to he irresistible arrival of a demonic age. At the end of the Cretaceous period they all became extinct following a catastrophe.

After the seventh day of creation and the creation of the physical sky, the oldest animal seeds, those of insects started to appear in a physical form at the beginning of the Age of Atlantis. Their first appearance to a great extent corresponded with appearance of the seeds of flowering plants (angiosperm plants), which were formed from the insect seeds on the Old Moon. The insects, with their higher consciousness, which is revealed in the strict laws governing a swarm of bees or an anthill, appeared on Earth[38] at the same time that the Self descended into man. According to spiritual science, this is a sign of the deep relationship between man, as a spiritual creature, and animals and plants. Nature shows that the most important moment in the development of the Earth, man becoming conscious, was happening then. The parallel arrival of flowering plants during the Cretaceous period was preceded during the Jurassic period by a tremendous growth of gymnosperm plants, such as conifers and palmate cycads.

According to Wachsmuth and Poppelbaum, the end of the Lemurian era was characterized by the presence of a volcanic island which constantly rose up and sank in the middle of a hot, semi–liquid mass of rock, surrounded by oceans and air heavy with thick mists. The water was thinner and the air thicker than in our own time. On the volcanic island there were forests of palm trees and physical creatures moved about which reproduced sexually and were precursors of the reptiles and amphibians of our own time.

The Age of Atlantis

During the Age of Atlantis the element of fire disappeared from the surface of the Earth, just as the smoke disappeared from the atmosphere which was still heavy with mist. The Earth continued to solidify under the influence of gravity, and the seas and oceans formed as the mists rained down. As geological surveys have shown, there was a mainland where the Atlantic Ocean is now during the Tertiary period, stretching from western Europe almost to North America. This geological reconstruction corresponds closely with Steiner's descriptionof the old continent of Atlantis: "This continent was encircled by a warm stream which, strange as it may seem, was seen clairvoyantly to flow from the south through Baffin Bay towards the north of Greenland, encircling it. Then, turning eastward, it gradually cooled down. Long before the continents of Russia and Siberia had emerged, it flowed past the Ural mountains, changed course, skirted the eastern Carpathians, debouched into the region now occupied by the Sahara and finally reached the Atlantic Ocean in the neighbourhood of the Bay of Biscay. Thus it followed a strictly delimited course. Only the last remaining traces of this stream are still extant. This stream is the Gulf Stream which at that time encircled the Atlantean continent. Now ... the Greeks experienced a memory of the spiritual worlds. The picture of Oceanus which is a memory of that Atlantean epoch arose within them."[39]

As matter became harder, the higher mammals were the last to enter the physical world. At the same time, birds and insects developed extremely quickly, especially mammals with a placenta. In the middle of the Tertiary period the first horses, rhinoceroses, predators and *Proboscidea* developed from the primitive predators and ungulates. In all these animals the original upright position assumed by some dinosaurs, and which is still visible in kangaroos, was lost again. An explosive development also took place in flowering plants. In the middle of the Age of Atlantis, one group was left behind once again, which was halted in its development at the last moment. These were the primates, from

human foetus at birth

young gorilla

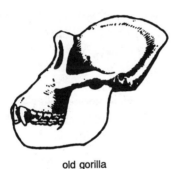

old gorilla

Table 5.5. The development of the skull of man and gorilla.

which in particular the apes developed. Basing himself on research by Louis Bolk, Poppelbaum showed how the skull of a
young gorilla, which is almost identical to that of a human
foetus, tragically develops so that the jaw moves forwards and
the eye sockets become heavier in a way that is characteristic of
the primitive gorilla (see Table 5.5).[40] In this way the physical

123

development shut itself off from the influence of the Self by the uninhibited effect of the astral body.

It was not until the middle of the Age of Atlantis that man assumed a visible form in which his bones became hard and he walked around the Earth in an upright position. Sexual reproduction started to take place at this point. Man learned to use the pronoun "I" to refer to the Self, and became self–conscious. By the end of the Age of Atlantis the human form had assumed its present shape.

Man first made an appearance during the Quaternary era, which started with the Pleistocene period, as well as higher animals, such as the sabre–tooth tiger, the mammoth, and the cave lion. When palaeontologists discovered the first remains of man, he already had all the essential physical and cultural characteristics. In fact, these representatives, such as sinanthropus and neanderthal man, do not even represent the mainstream of man's development. They are not the direct ancestors of mankind, but degenerated offshoots which were again the first to be halted in their development, and give an excessively negative picture of the advanced human culture of the Age of Atlantis. Following the Atlantean catastrophe caused by ice ages and the Great Flood, when all the vestiges disappeared under the surface of the Atlantic Ocean, the present geological period began about ten thousand years ago, known as the Holocene period of the Quaternary era, and modern post–Atlantean man developed.

5.5   Two schools of thought about geological eras

With a little juggling of the facts, I have outlined the classification of geological eras drawn up by Poppelbaum and Wachsmuth in relation to the eras used in spiritual science. In doing this I was rather confused by the totally different classification used by Hagemann. For the first two authors the Pre–Cambrian era starts in the Polar era, while Hagemann believes that the Pre–Cambrian era began after the expulsion of the Moon, in the Lemurian era. It is worth noting that this gives rise to the survey also shown in Table 5.4. In general terms the classification given above by Poppelbaum and Wachsmuth is directly derived from the steps in the development of mankind itself at an astral–ethereal level. For example, fish are presumed to have developed at the time that the husk of the seed of man had the shape of the nebulous body of a fish, while amphibians are thought to have evolved in the stage of amphibious fire and mist, so that this period is presumed to fall into the Carboniferous period. Hagemann bases his classification on a much later creation of the group souls of animals, which then make use of the astral–ethereal husks left behind by man, and inhabit them. Physical embodiment only took place after the Earth had physically solidified, which happened in stages after the expulsion of the Moon. In this light, both interpretations can be shown to contain an element of truth. Wachsmuth and Poppelbaum describe the development of man at an astral–ethereal level, while Hagemann relates the geological eras only to the rapid solidification of the physical Earth after the expulsion of the Moon. I consider Hagemann's explanation to be the more appropriate on a physical level, and it was used as the starting point for Table 5.4. However, some questions do remain. The extinction of many species of animals at the end of the Cretaceous period can be explained in Poppelbaum and Wachsmuth's theory by the downfall of Lemuria. In Hagemann's theory the catastrophe which caused many species, such as the dinosaurs, to become extinct, took place in the middle of the Age of Atlantis. This is the time from which we calculate our present period. It is also the time at which man left the watery atmosphere and stepped on to solid ground. Possibly it was the general solidification which caused many species to become extinct. Furthermore, according to Hagemann's reconstruction, the disintegration of Pangaea coincided with the zenith of the Age of Atlantis. This means that the vast mainland of Pangaea would have been identical to Atlantis. According to Hagemann's classification, this suggests that Lemuria must have coincided with the Ordovician period. As Table 3.3 shows, there was certainly a large land mass at that time, stretching from the South Pole to the northeast, beyond the Equator. The submergence of part of this continent and the large south-western movement during the Silurian period would then coincide with the downfall of Lemuria.

The attraction of Hagemann's briefly outlined schema is that it coincides more closely with the solidification of the mineral kingdom. His classification also corresponds with Steiner's views,[41] for example: "In the Lemurian era the Earth was populated by man and the lower animals; at first there were only a few higher species on Earth." This must have referred to man when he was still transparent, and the lower animals, while the seeds of the higher animals were still being formed. Here is another example: "After the expulsion of the Moon the Earth looked more or less like the Old Moon. In that time some lower species of animals developed through condensing too prematurely."

This confusion arises very easily because Steiner does not always state explicitly whether the condition of the bodies which have formed takes place on an astral ethereal level or on the level which can be perceived with the senses. In both cases he sometimes refers to bodies of air or water. The survey in Table 5.3 provides the most reliable summary which I can reconstruct at the moment. Undoubtedly it will be necessary to elaborate and verify this in more detail, particularly because Hagemann's classification gives rise to an even greater gap between the calculation of time in the physical world used in geology, and the calculation of time used in spiritual science for the initially ethereal world. According to Hagemann, the period which corresponds with the Cretaceous period was approximately 17 000 years ago. The speed at which the ethereal biosphere developed must have been unimaginably great in terms of current scientific standards. The hard data of science are completely different in relation to events in a few thousand years' time. I find it difficult to comprehend the significance of these starting points.

5.6   Evolution or degeneration

Both from the point of view of natural science and spiritual science, the development of the Earth's biosphere reveals connections which can provide new insights into matters which have been difficult to explain up to now. The fossilized remains of organisms reveal the perfected, solidified bodies of animals, giving rise to the question how one species developed from another. The connecting links between the developmental stages of organisms in an ascending line are often missing. The missing links in series of intermediary forms of families and species of organisms become even more noticeable as the collections are more complete, and the gaps increase when higher levels of the hierarchy of families, orders, classes, and species are examined. Thus there is no connecting link between reptiles and amphibians or between reptiles and birds. The intermediary species which might have been considered developed much too late, which means that they were degenerated forms of descendants rather than precursors. It is also very difficult to be persuaded that a specialized solidified organism, which has survived for a long time, can be sufficiently flexible to explain the wealth of subsequent higher species with the help of Darwin's law of natural selection. A very different light is shed on evolution when each of the fossilized species is viewed as being a descendant of creatures which have fallen behind in the development of ethereal man, and which then adapted to conditions on Earth as well as possible. In this case the plasticity required is not sought in the fossilized organism, but in the ethereal forms of primitive man preceding them.

The plasticity of the many forms of life is also easier to understand if we proceed on the assumption that the mineral kingdom only acquired its present solid form in the late Lemurian and early Atlantean era. Poppelbaum's views necessarily imply that family trees increasingly consist of single bare branches, and that the animal form is most easily derived from the preceding form of primitive man. The original characteristics of animals are retained most clearly in the body of man. Man's physical development has been held back; presumably the human hand developed into the mole's digging claws, the fishes' fins and the bird's wing, not the other way round. According to Poppelbaum, the human head evolved to specialize in the tools of the beak and the bill. I must admit that his ideas suggest a breathtaking unity in the animal and human kingdom, and it is difficult to understand why science has not pursued this line of thought in more detail. With his theory of evolution, Darwin did provide an approximation of man's evolution, but he turned his attention to degenerated "snails," and imagined that these left–behind species could evolve from one another. His theory that higher species evolved from lower ones only works for the evolution of the ethereal human body; it does not work for the countless physical creatures which fall by the wayside. Small, refined adaptations took place in these organisms as they became paralysed in their evolution, but these were dead–end developments in a spiritual sense. In the future they will once again have the chance to enjoy spiritual development. All the lower species fell under the influence of Earth forces which drew them down at an early stage: animals with their horizontal stance rather than the human figure striving upwards, plants with their roots rooted into the Earth, and minerals in their petrified state. The oldest mineral kingdom developed from the plant minerals on the Old Moon, and the more recent chalk and silica developed from deposits of the lower animal species. Again lower forms developed from higher forms. In this way, everything around man is connected with his own developmental history. The Earth's biosphere is a mirror of man's essence, and the lower species enable man to exist in the physical world.

In his work, *Study of Man,* Steiner explains this connection even more clearly.[42] In his thinking, man's head assumes all the animal forms. Every thought arising in a human head has become independent and visibly present in the form of an animal, just as a flowering plant is the visible expression of the inner essence of a butterfly. Mees considered this in great detail.[43] The fact that the human head does not assume the shape of a wolf, a lion, a snake, and so on, is because his trunk and limbs prevent this. Man metamorphoses these animal desires into thoughts which only appear in an extra–sensory world.

Thus the trunk is related to the plant world. This is clear from the structure of the backbone, the twelve pairs of ribs, which are reminiscent of a stem with twelve pairs of leaves. If man did not breathe out carbon dioxide, but removed the oxygen from it, a new plant world would develop in man's chest. If the head and limbs allowed it, the human trunk would constantly assume forms from the plant world. By breathing out carbon dioxide, man creates the plant kingdom outside himself, so that he does not become a plant. Steiner refers to human respiration as a sort of anti–plant kingdom.

Finally, the human limbs, bones and muscles must develop a constant tendency to oppose the crystallization of minerals by earthly forces, to dissolve minerals. This requires the same force which dissolves the nutrients stored in the seed of a plant in spring, so that it can grow a root.[44]

In this way man appears as a creature in whom external processes are reflected. He must dissolve the solid mineral kingdom within him, turn about the expanding kingdom of plants, and transform or spiritualize the animal kingdom, which is full of desires.

In the evolution of man, in which man turns away his lower kingdoms so that he can rise higher himself, it is understandable that these processes must still be actively pursued by man if he is to exist as a healthy organism. One day man will have to pay the debt that he owes the lower kingdoms which have offered themselves to him, by helping them to raise themselves.

5.7   The myth of the creation of the animal world

In Greek mythology there is a story of the creation of the animal world which reflects the insights of spiritual science on many points. Steiner's account of the head animals left behind in the first part of the Old Sun, the chest animals during the second part of the Old Sun, and the development of belly animals on the Old Moon, bears remarkable similarities to the description in Plato's *Timaeus:*

"Birds were produced by a process of transformation, growing feathers instead of hair, from harmless, empty–headed men, who were interested in the heavens but were silly enough to think that visible evidence is all the foundation astronomy needs. Land animals came from men who had no use for philosophy and never considered the nature of the heavens because they had ceased to use the circles in the head and followed the leadership of the parts of the soul in the breast. Because of these practices their forelimbs and heads were drawn by natural affinity to the earth, and their forelimbs supported on it, while their skulls were elongated into various shapes as a result of the crushing of their circles through lack of use. And the reason why some have four feet and others many was that the stupider they were the more supports god gave them, to tie them more closely to earth. And the stupidest of the land animals, whose whole bodies lay stretched on the earth, the gods turned into reptiles, giving them no feet, because they had no further need for them. But the most unintelligent and ignorant of all turned into the fourth kind of creature that lives in water. Their souls were hopelessly steeped in every kind of error, and so their makers thought them unfit to breathe pure clean air, and made them inhale water, into whose turbid depths they plunged them. That is the origin of fish, shellfish and everything else that lives in water; they live in the depths as a punishment for the depth of their stupidity. These are the principles on which living creatures change and have always changed into each other, the transformation depending on the loss or gain of understanding or folly."[45]

This Greek myth gives a striking picture of the way in which animals fell behind in man's development, and at the same time it reminds us of the events of the earlier metamorphoses of the Earth.

6. The nature of the Earth's biosphere

Then the voice of God resounded, Who knows all causes;
for Whom nothing is concealed:
"Before I created the world there was only I. Every-
thing has its ultimate cause in me; both your reason for
existence and your thoughts. I created you to serve as food
for the people. That is the only reason for your existence.
Therefore: do not complain and do not grieve. I know
your suffering and your pain, even before you have spoken
them."

Zarathustra, Yasna 29:6

6.1   The wall and I

Step by step I have changed position. I began by following the
path of the great scientific thinkers. Scholars such as Francis
Bacon, René Descartes and Isaac Newton still carried on the
tradition of medieval religious thinking. As a result of their
thinking, the connection between visible reality and the spiritual
world was gradually lost. In the end the spirit was denied, or
explained as a product of a self–organizing nature. In the foot-
steps of the founders of modern science, I saw how mechanistic
thinkers built an increasingly high wall between the two worlds.
Many have even forgotten that the wall exists at all, or that there
might be anything behind it.

I have tried to find the wall and stand astride it. From this
position I have been able to examine the reports of those who
claimed that their journeys to the other side had provided a
breathtaking panorama of the origins of the biosphere. According
to spiritual science, true evolution took place in the ethereal
world, while natural scientists have identified the side shoots
which have come to a dead end as essential links in a process
taking place in the physical world. Spiritual science provides a

true unity between the fragments which I found in religion and in science. This unity is more profound than the holistic thinking of the new age movement. I have to admit that it has deeply affected me, and that I no longer want to return to a science which denies that it is inspired by a spiritual world. It is as though the wall which I climbed has shrunk. I find myself back at ground level, though the panorama has not disappeared. The wall seems to have become lower. However, there is a price to pay for continuing along the road I have taken. The certainties of scientific assumptions start to become blurred; the inviolable boundaries of space and time fall away; the rock-solid certainty of the static mountains becomes relative; laws have only a limited applicability, and periods of billions of years are reduced to thousands of years. How can I share these panoramic views with others, and convince others, if I cannot base these relativities on my own spiritual observations, as is possible for anyone who follows a modern training? For these insights have merely come about as an intuitive acceptance of the truth of other people's views. However, even if I had observed these things directly with an enlightened consciousness, would I be able to convince others? My own observations could not simply be repeated by any other researcher, and thus they would lose their credibility in the eyes of such a researcher. Only the idea itself has the power to convince others, by its simplicity and elegance; to put aside the familiar assumptions for the moment, so that when the panorama is spread out before the spiritual eye, others are inwardly convinced.

Thus the aim of my work is not to convince others directly. It is an attempt to describe one aspect of the idea behind the creation of Earth and man in such a way that the idea itself becomes radiant for others. Thus it is rather like bearing witness. Anyone is free to be open to this or to dismiss it as nonsense.

I would like to start from this point of the link between spirit and matter, religion and science, and then examine what consequences the insight obtained about the creation of the Earth and its biosphere has for the way in which the essence of the Earth functions. A clearer insight into this must lead to a more clearly defined feeling for the way in which man can live in harmony with this great essence. On the basis of the interconnection of natural science and spiritual science, I want to find a direction for my deeds. It is necessary to appeal to the will through thoughts and feelings for human technology to be incorporated harmoniously in the essence of the Earth.

6.2   Earth and the solar system

My aim was to study the functioning of the Earth and its biosphere in their totality, from the points of view of natural science and spiritual science. In doing this, I discovered that spiritual science gave rise to a comprehensive plan for the development of mankind. This plan cannot be confirmed by scientific findings, but nor can it be disproved. Modern science does not extend beyond those things that can be perceived with the senses, and this limits its scope. Spiritual science outlines a plan for mankind. What is the role of the Earth which supports mankind and everything related to it? Is the Earth a spiritual being? Is the Earth alive as an organism is alive? In spiritual science the Earth is viewed as a living being, as will be shown below. However, seeing the Earth as a living organism implies that the solar system and the larger systems beyond also function as living entities. Therefore, by way of introduction to the study of the Earth being, I would like first to examine the solar system in order to understand better how spiritual science views the context of the Earth's existence.

In Steiner's account, a sun which is created at the beginning of the development of a solar system must first place its planets outside itself before it can develop itself. When this development has progressed sufficiently, and until the sun can be reunited with its planets, it becomes a zodiac, an environment. According to Steiner, in our solar system the moons form the Sun's corpse, the planets her physical body.[1] Everything directed by the fixed stars forms its ethereal body, and all the beings of the higher hierarchies which inhabit the husks of the physical and ethereal corpse, form the astral body. Finally, the comets gather all the astral substances which have a negative effect within the solar system, and cast them out into space. In this way we see that in

133

the organism of a solar system, physical bodies and higher spiritual bodies are found together at the same time. The sun of a solar system is a carrier of the spiritual essence. Bailey describes how the spiritual essence that bears our solar system, the Sun Logos, is built up from a body with seven centres. The Sun Logos itself forms the heart of an even greater cosmic being.[2]

In our solar system, the Sun Logos, the basic principle full of worldly wisdom, the inner Word, is formed by the sum of the seven biblical Elohim, or spirits of the form. The Egyptians identified these seven creative forces as the architects, the *Khnumus,* while the Zoroastrians called them the seven *Amshaspends.* The Hindus had seven *Prajapatis,* the Assyrians the seven *Lumazi,* and the Brahmans the seven *Kumaras.* According to Blavatsky, the seven Elohim were not "God," they were created by the One God, the unrevealed Logos, the Demiurge, the true creator. Their creation contains the end of the formless, the void, the dark. The seven Elohim are: Ildabaoth, Jehovah, Sabaoth, Adonai, Eloeus, Oreus, and Astanphaeus. The Jews see Jehovah as the leading god among the seven Elohim. According to Steiner, this is in connection with the ancient Hebrews, who saw Jehovah as the spiritual group soul of their people. Blavatsky indicated that the identity of the seven divine figures known from antiquity corresponds to the seven spirits for the Thrones of the Roman Catholic Church. In ancient mysteries these seven "Builders" were called the *Kabiri,* the "greatest gods," the "mighty" and the "planetary" spirits. In the Christian Cabbala the names of the Archangels were given to the seven centres of our solar system as the leading planetary spirits: Michael to the Sun, Gabriel to the Moon, Samael to Mars, Anael to Venus, Raphael to Mercury, Zachariel to Jupiter, and Orifiel to Saturn. In other disciplines the places of these "directing forces" are different. These inspiring godheads of the seven "planets" also correspond with the lower *Sephiroth* of the Jewish Cabbala, or the sons of Brahma born of wisdom, called the *Kumaras,* who have the following names: Sana, Sanat–Sujata, Kapila, Sanat–Kumara, Samanda, Sanaka and Sanatana. As an example of the correspondence between the Christian Archangels and the Brahman Kumaras, Blavatsky describes how Sanat–Sujata has the same characteris-

Planetary characteristics	Spiritual beings which have an influence	Comparable aspect of man
Physical form	Spirits of the form	physical body
Internal movements	Spirits of movement	ethereal body
Lowest form of consciousness	Spirits of wisdom	astral body
Movement in space	Spirits of the will	sentient soul
Order in solar system	Spirits of harmony	intellectual soul
Order in Milky Way galaxy	Spirits of love	consciousness soul
Order in universe	Trinity of divine life	higher Self

Table 6.1. Present influence of higher spiritual beings on the planets, and the comparable aspects in man (see also Table 2.5).

tics as the "invincible virginal warrior, the Archangel Michael." According to theosophy, Sanat–Kumara is the leading spirit of the Earth.[3]

According to Steiner, the Sun Logos is not the sum of these seven Elohim, but of six Elohim. The seventh, Jehovah, joined with the Moon after the Sun separated away, and continued to prepare man to develop the Self from there.[4] Within the solar system the seven Elohim or Kumaras have a position comparable to the seven power centres in the head of man, which are connected with the other centres (*chakras* or lotus flowers) in the body, distributing the power of the Self.[5] As Table 6.1 shows, the physical form of the centres of the solar system is determined by the spirits of the form (Elohim). Internal movements within the planets are the result of the influence of the spirits of movement (*Dynameis*), while the spirits of wisdom grant the planets the lowest form of consciousness. The spirits of the will bring about the movement of the planets in space. The Cherubim determine the order of the planets in the solar system, while the Seraphim control the order of the solar systems in the Milky Way galaxy. Finally, the trinity of divine life, Father, Son and Holy Ghost, governs the order of the universe.

In an occult sense, the planets are not only celestial bodies, but also the fine ethereal substance which directs life processes and is located between the Earth and the orbits of the planets. This space has a lens–shaped flattened form. The boundaries of the ethereal planetary form are also determined by the spirits of the form which inhabit the Sun. Every planet is actually a hole in the ethereal celestial body, where a break has occurred in the form, creating visible matter.[6] The world view of the Italian, Dante Alighieri (1265–1321) was also based on this occult wisdom. Following the Greek astronomer, Ptolemy, he did not see the solar system simply as a physical system, but regarded it as an ethereal system of processes at a spiritual level. In this system the physical planets mark the boundary of the ethereal sphere of influence of the higher spiritual beings. This is based on the development of mankind, with the Earth as the focal point. The starting point used is the situation in which the spring equinox of the Sun is in the sign of the Zodiac, Gemini. This was the case in 3000 BC at the time of Zarathustra. At that time Mars, Jupiter and Saturn were on one side of the Sun, while Mercury, Venus and the Earth, with its Moon, were on the other side. In this con–

Sphere of influence from the Earth to	Spiritual beings
Moon	Sons of life (Angels)
Mercury (Venus)*	Spirits of the fire (Archangels)
Venus (Mercury)*	Spirits of the personality (Archai)
Sun	Spirits of the form (Exousiai or Elohim)
Mars	Spirits of movement (Dynameis)
Jupiter	Spirits of wisdom (Kyriotetes)
Saturn	Spirits of the will (Thrones)
Comets	Spirits of harmony (Cherubim)
Zodiac	Spirits of love (Seraphim)

* In ancient literature, these were reversed.

Table 6.2. Present sphere of influence of higher spiritual beings on the solar system and the Zodiac (see also Tables 2.6 and 2.7).

stellation the sphere of influence of higher spiritual beings was very apparent, as described in Table 6.2.

The sphere of influence of the Angels is on the Earth and as far as the Moon, that of the spirits of the form is on everything within the ethereal sphere of the Sun, while the Thrones' influence extends to the edge of our solar system, the sphere of Saturn. The Cherubim and Seraphim are physically expressed in the comets and the stars of the zodiac. In ethereal terms the Earth should be seen as being completely surrounded by the sphere of the Moon. The Moon is a large ethereal body, with the Earth as a solid kernel. The Earth and the Moon are within the ethereal body of Mercury. Finally, the outer planet Saturn comprises all the other ethereal spheres. Beyond all this are the heavens, with the encompassing fixed stars of the Zodiac.

Steiner pointed out that Dante described the ethereal world correctly, and this description still applies in correspondence with the physical description initiated by Nicholas Copernicus (1473–1543).

Steiner also pointed out that every planet has its own spirit of the form (Elohim) and spirits of movement. The individual planets were created because the different spiritual beings created places to live which corresponded with their developmental stage. Thus Venus and Mercury were formed because the spirits of the form, whose development had fallen behind when the Sun broke away, were looking for a dwelling place with a finer substance than the Earth and a coarser one than the Sun. Mars is related to Earth, but is at an earlier developmental stage than Earth. Mars is a repetition of the Old Moon metamorphosis. In the beings that inhabit Mars the Self has not yet descended into the astral body.[7] The other planets are a dwelling place for higher ethereal life forms than those we know on Earth.[8] Jupiter is a repetition of the Old Sun, and Saturn of Old Saturn. The modern Moon is a vestige of the Old Moon's metamorphosis. Steiner wrote that originally the planets Neptune and Uranus did not belong to our solar system, and were only later incorporated into it.[9] This is why they are not considered in the esoteric writings on our solar system. Just as Jehovah is the ruler of the Moon, Steiner names Christ as the highest planetary spirit of the modern Earth.[10]

Whenever Christ is referred to, it should be remembered that according to the esoteric doctrine, this is a reference to the connection of the Sun spirit with the individual, Jesus of Nazareth; this is how the Christ–impetus was achieved on Earth. Like Man, the solar system is shown to be a cosmic being, composed of seven centres. Within the solar system the Earth has an ethereal position, as though the concern of the higher hierarchies must be directed to it. This is where the development takes place of man and Angels to higher spiritual beings, led by the spirits of the form, or Elohim, which inhabit the Sun. Thus in a spiritual sense the Earth is by no means the most developed planet in our solar system.[11] The solar system is an ethereal world, full of life, in which the Sun and the Earth are central poles for the development of man. At some point the Sun and the Earth will be re-united, and according to Steiner, this is possible because the leading spirit of the Sun, Christ, has united himself with the Earth since Golgotha.

For a comparison with the composition of man's physical body, it is important to understand the functions of the planets in the solar system. Steiner wrote about these functions, which are summarized in Table 6.2. The higher hierarchies have a scope of operation which penetrates space at ever greater depths and, in this process, the Earth is the ethereal basis. Each one of these ethereal spheres is specifically related to the function of one of the human organs. At the same time, these ethereal spheres function as the organs of the solar system. In this the Sun is the heart in the centre of the series of spheres of influence which reaches from the Earth to the comets orbiting through our solar system, and pointing to the Zodiac. Saturn and Jupiter form the solar system's ethereal nervous and sensory system, Mars and the Sun form the ethereal respiratory and circulatory system, while Mercury, Venus and the Earth represent the digestive system and the limbs.[12] As the planet of love, the Earth is a characteristic product of this solar system and of the being inspired by the spirits of love, the Seraphim reaching as far as the Zodiac.

6.3   The spirit and the Earth's Self

The preceding paragraph showed how the Earth is incorporated in the scope of operation of the higher spiritual hierarchies. The Earth is the planet on which man can freely develop love. After the ideas expressed above, it comes as no surprise to learn that spiritual science considers that the Earth has a soul.[13] The Earth's soul comes from the Sun. The six Elohim radiate light and love to the Earth from the Sun, and Jehovah reflects these rays from the Moon on to the Earth. The light of the Sun is the purest manifestation of the physical body of the Sun Logos.

The planet Logos of our Earth, related in theosophy to Sanat–Kumara, the Lord of the World, and by Steiner to Christ, adopted an ethereal incarnation halfway through the Lemurian age, and descended to Earth. Up to the middle of the Lemurian era, when the Moon was still united with the Earth, Jehovah or Yahweh was the leading spirit of the Earth, and his physical presence was experienced by man in the ethereal air and wind.[14] The planet Logos transmits the will of the Logos of the solar system to man and the angels. Sanat–Kumara leads the planetary hierarchy, which comprises the three Kumaras or Buddhas of labour, according to Bailey. The three reflections of the will, love and the intellect, aspects of the Sun hierarchy, are revealed in these. The aspect of the will is represented in the leader, Manu; the aspect of love/wisdom in the Bhodisattva, which is identified with Christ in theosophy, and the aspect of the intellect in the Mahachohan. Below them there are the Masters which still have a coarse material body, and below them, various levels of initiates and disciples.[15]

According to theosophy, the central house of the planetary hierarchy is Shambala, a centre in the ethereal world near the Gobi desert, also known as the White Island. Several Masters live in the Himalayas nearby. Spalding[16] was one of many authors to write about this. In his lectures on *The Gospel According to St John,* Steiner wrote that the aura of the Earth was changed by the mystery of Golgotha because the Sun Logos started to unite with the Earth at that moment. Since the mystery of Golgotha, the Sun Logos of the Elohim has been striving to be reunited with the planetary Logos of the Earth. Since that time, Christ has been the spirit of the Earth and the Earth has literally become the body of Christ. According to Steiner, this is also the meaning of the Last Supper. In this context Steiner cites John 13:8, which he translates as: "Who eats my bread, walks on me." From this moment Christ became the spirit of the Earth.[17]

As spiritual beings are not named as individuals, but by their function, it is not surprising that their names change as their development progresses, although this does create considerable confusion.

In addition to its planetary spirit, the Earth also has a Self, just as man has a Self. In *Universe, Earth and Man,*[18] Steiner wrote that the Earth organism's Self consists of the total of the plant Selves. The Self of the plants is in the centre of the Earth.

The Earth's Self sucks into itself the soul of the Sun through the astral bodies of its plants. This is another expression of the link between the power of Christ and the Earth. In this way the spiritual content of the Sun's rays is led to the centre of the Earth.

The Self of man forms part of the Self of Christ. It is through Christ that man exists on Earth as a spiritual being.

6.4   The Earth's astral body

The astral body or soul of the Earth surrounds its ethereal and physical body, and its centre is also in the centre of the physical globe of the Earth. According to Steiner, the astral body of the Earth consists of a multitude of spiritual beings, which arrange everything related to rhythmical processes and the changes of the seasons. The spirits of the cycles play an important role in this, and I will return to this point in Chapter 8. The astral body of the Earth is the area inhabited by man when he is asleep. The Earth is able to accommodate animals by means of its astral body. The cycle of water is an example of a process which reveals the astral quality of the Earth. The physical body of the Archangels is expressed in currents of air. Reptiles and amphibians are animals with a strong sense of these astral qualities, the climate and meteorology. For example, a frog reflects the feelings which the

Earth experiences during a period of rain or drought.[19] As long ago as the sixteenth century, the German astronomer Johannes Kepler (1571–1630) wrote: "The earth must have a soul. The earth is an animal. The fact that the earth truly has a soul is revealed most clearly by observing the weather and the aspects by which this is constantly influenced. The whole earth is animated and this leads to great harmony, both on earth and between it and the celestial bodies. The soul affects the whole body of the earth, but is located in a particular area, just as the human soul has its seat in the heart; and thence it influences the oceans and the earth's atmosphere, as from a source or focal point."[20]

It is not only man who breathes his psyche in and out throughout the year. According to Steiner, when winter is coming in December, the Earth's soul is completely drawn into the Earth.[21] It is then that the Earth has its most intense psychological life. At the end of June the northern hemisphere has breathed out completely, and its soul is given over to the super-terrestrial cosmic world, for the Earth's soul reaches out to the stars, wanting to know the life of the stars. While the Earth's soul draws within itself on the south, it reaches out in the north to the cosmos, which can be seen as a comet's tail by the clairvoyant. The festivals of Christmas and Easter, and the summer mysteries which survive in the north, originate in this breathing process. Recently Cloos studied the meaning of the seasons for the life of the Earth's soul. He shows how the Earth's soul is fertilized by the cosmos in summer, and that in winter this power brings about the fertilization of the planetary seeds at about Christmas, at the moment that the Earth is breathing in most deeply.[22] When man became conscious that the Earth was round, he became less dependent on the seasons. As a result, man's deep feeling for recurring festivities and for the breathing of the Earth's soul has disappeared.

Apart from this breathing of the Earth's soul, the Earth also has a pattern of sleeping and waking. Just as man breathes in and out on average 25 920 times per 24 hour day, the Earth's soul breathes in and out 25 920 times in one Sun–day. A Sun–day lasts 25 920 years, the time it takes for the spring equinox of the Sun to pass once through the signs of the zodiac. Steiner pointed out that the Earth is sleeping now, just as it was 25920 years ago.[23] The Earth is now dried up and cut off from the cosmos. No more than 15000 years ago everything on the Earth was soft, the Earth was a sort of plant, and later a sort of animal. At that time the Earth was awake and linked to the whole cosmos. In the future, when the Sun is once again in Libra, the Alps will be dissolved, and man and the animals will return to their original liquid condition. In this way the Earth's biosphere has a cycle of 25920 years, waking and sleeping, in which the life of the Earth returns each time to a higher level of development.

6.5 The Earth's ethereal body

As is the case for the astral body and the Self, the centre of the Earth's ethereal body coincides with the Earth's physical centre. The ethereal body of physical nature is not a unity like the human ethereal body. It consists of many differentiated beings, including the natural spirits, which will be discussed in Chapter 8. Plants can exist on Earth when their seeds have germinated with the help of its ethereal body.[24] Wachsmuth distinguishes four areas on the Earth's surface which have different ethereal climates, expressed in the shape of the leaves of plants.[25] These are categorized in a triangular shape of a leaf resulting from the influence of ethereal light, the semicircular shape with chemical ether, and the square or diamond–shaped leaf with ethereal life. When ethereal heat is dominant, this is expressed in abundant pollination, as in conifers, and birch tree catkins (see also Table 9.7). In addition, Steiner states that the ethereal aura towers above every part of the Earth's surface[26] with a basic tone which suddenly changes when a nation leaves its home territory. This ethereal aura does not depend only on what rises up from the ground, but also on the nation living there. The way in which man treats the land is also important: for example, cutting down forests, agricultural activity, or water projects. The spirits of the people influence these ethereal auras, and therefore influence everything affected by a living, organizing principle. The spirit of the people can affect physical relationships through this ethereal aura, though not directly. Water is the bearer of the Earth's ethereal element. Running water and clouds form the physical body of the Angels. Fish feel strongly in tune with the flowing of ethereal forces in summer and their withdrawal in winter. Fish experience the ether as the Earth breathing. The Earth's ethereal body is revealed to man when he allows the physical world to have a moral effect on him.[27]

6.6   The physical Earth

The present physical body of the Earth experiences physical change, just like that described in relation to the astral body.

The form of the surface of the physical Earth is determined by the spirits of the form. These bring to rest the powers of the Thrones, Cherubim and Seraphim, radiating from the centre of the Earth, and the powers of the spirits of the second hierarchy, radiating from the cosmos to the Earth.[28] If they did not do so, the surface of the Earth would have a constant, undulating movement. When the hard mineral surface is broken up or dissolved by erosion, the Earth's soul feels joy. When the mineral solidifies from a soft state by a process of crystallization, the Earth's soul feels pain.[29] Therefore the Earth's soul suffered when the Earth

Earth layers	Effect
Mineral Earth	functions as an "eggshell"
Liquid Earth	destroys life
Air Earth	destroys feeling
Form Earth	changes form into its opposite
Fruit Earth	full of pent-up growth energy
Fire Earth	consists of passions
Earth's surface	reflects qualities by opposites
Fragmenter	basic cause of all disharmony
Earth's Core	seat of power of spiritual evil

Table 6.3. Layers of the Earth and their effect.

solidified following the expulsion of the Moon, as soon as it could carry man.

According to Steiner, the solidified Earth consists, in esoteric terms, of nine layers which gradually merge with each other (see Table 6.3).[30] The upper three layers are described as mineral Earth, liquid Earth, and air Earth; the middle three layers as form Earth, fruit Earth and fire Earth. Finally, nearest the centre, there are three more layers: the Earth's reflecting layer, the Fragmenter, and the Earth core. Every layer has a separate effect on man and as the layers are closer to the core of the Earth, and therefore further away from the Sun, their effect is more malevolent. The evolution of man will transform the centre of the Earth and spiritualize it. In the next chapter I will deal with this more fully. We must link the dark forces below our feet with the shining forces above.

In the same way, man must learn to know the animals, plants and minerals, so that our debt to them can be paid and they can be delivered from their retarded situation.

In this way, in addition to the solid physical Earth which is familiar to us, there is the fluid process of learning as a bearer of the ethereal body of the world, and the gaseous process as a bearer of the astral body. Light and heat represent the Self of the Earth, which is borne by the plant Selves feeding on the sunlight which is drawn into the centre of the Earth. At the same time we are confronted with the astonishing fact that the worlds which can be distinguished above the solid Earth surface spiritually reflect each other below the Earth's surface. The effect of this mysterious phenomenon will be discussed in a later chapter.

7. The Earth as organism

Once again God raised his voice; and his Spirit came over the Earth, and trembled through it to its lowest depths. Then the Earth trembled and spoke:
"My soul is converted. But who can serve as a voice for me to tell the people that my soul is no longer en-snared in itself, but exists only to serve others."
                                        Zarathustra, Yasna 29:7

7.1   Morality and health

In writing the previous chapter I had the feeling that I had col-lected a lot of useful facts from an esoteric source, but that the essence of the Earth as a living organism had still eluded me. What are the characteristics of the Earth that should determine the direction of man's activities nowadays? In what light should we view human intervention in the ecosystems on Earth? Can anything be said about this on the basis of the role played by higher spiritual beings in the development of the Earth and its inhabitants? Are not the cosmic periods of time much too large to provide meaningful guidelines for man's actions in the next ten to one hundred years? When I think of the catastrophes which are before us in the long term, I am assailed by a feeling of despair. What is the point of behaving more responsibly with regard to ecology when overwhelming catastrophes are rooted in Earth's destiny, for example, if the mountains are to melt in ten thousand years time? I will have to find an answer to these questions before there is any point in continuing.

In Steiner's description, the Earth as an organism has already passed the zenith of its flowering.[1] As indicated in Table 4.5, we have already passed the middle of the Earth metamorphosis. However, according to Steiner, if man did not pass his forces on to the Earth, the development of the Earth would have come to

145

an end a long time ago. The evolutionary process of the Earth is kept going by man. Man ensures that the minerals continue to develop their capacity for crystallization, that plants continue to flower, and that the lower animal species can live on Earth. However, man does not grant the Earth these forces directly in his acts, but by the life forces released from the material remains of the dead. The materials and forces left behind after death are different from those received at birth. They are metamorphosed during man's life. These changes are the result of the development of man's individuality, his Self, and from this these changes affect the astral body, the ethereal body and the physical body. Man is the medium through which extrasensory forces are constantly seeping into the physical world.

From this I conclude that life on Earth is possible to the extent that man transmits the influence of higher spiritual beings. The more man acts in accordance with the moral laws of the spiritual world, the more the higher hierarchies can affect the Earth like a yeast, creating life, through people of "goodwill." The consequence of this is that when man does not act in accordance with the standards of higher hierarchies — and man is now quite free not to do so — the development of the Earth will be broken off, the Earth will age much more rapidly, will solidify even more, and provide fewer opportunities for the spiritual beings linked to the Earth to develop. The time in which man can develop into a particular higher stage will then be shortened, and a larger number of human souls will only achieve this development at a later stage. If the Earth did not function properly, this could even disrupt the development of our solar system.[2] Moreover, Steiner points out that in the future a "dead Earth" will lead to a "dead Jupiter." Man's heritage will have far-reaching consequences.[3]

Chapter 6 indicated that man has a direct influence on the localized ethereal body of the Earth. Steiner's writings on spiritual science suggest that man's uninhibited, amoral conduct will result in violent reactions in the atmosphere, the circulation of water and the Earth's crust. Hurricanes, floods and earthquakes could result. In this context, Steiner revealed in *Manifestations of Karma* that there is a higher wisdom which unleashes counter-forces such as hailstorms and volcanic eruptions when man is tempted to pursue comfort and luxury, in order to ensure that man's spiritual development does not stagnate.[4] The Earth and man are closely related. Man must make it possible for the Earth as an organism to pursue its development. In doing so man also lays down the conditions for his own development and that of his companions: the natural kingdoms and the hierarchies.

The question remains in what light human activities — and technology in particular — should be viewed in more concrete terms. This is undoubtedly the extent to which the connection with the spiritual origins of the physical world can play a part in our affairs. Is man choosing for morality, or for an increasingly large–scale exploitation of the Earth's resources? Is man capable of moral technology?

I revealed above how the development of man and the natural kingdoms have a common background. Stones, plants, and animals can all be viewed as beings which were brought forth by us. The Earth's biosphere is a being that is closely related to man: both were formed from cosmic forces. Man now has the freedom to help to determine Earth's destiny by acting on the basis of good or evil. This is quite a responsibility, and an enormous challenge in wielding the gigantic forces of technology. The Earth is already ailing as a result of man's intervention. How can it be cured?

When the Earth organism is compared with the human organism, which we know better, in order to answer this question, it can be reformulated: what is moral healing? This is the most practical way of asking the question, though it is still not easy to answer. It is not for nothing that nowadays medicine is confronted with deep moral dilemmas, such as the acceptability of organ transplants, the conception of test–tube babies, the manipulation of the genetic code of DNA in bacteria, plants, animals and eventually man, and finally the problems of abortion and euthanasia. Man's capacity for intervention in the life processes of the human organism runs parallel to his capacity to intervene in the Earth organism. In both cases man is obstructing the spiritual world rather than helping it. We are rather like clumsy infants who want to help with the washing up in keeping house

147

for the Earth. There is a similarity between test–tube babies and the increasingly large areas of cultivated land which disappear behind glass in greenhouses, and are regularly doused with dis–infectant gases. Artificial limbs are comparable with the high–rise flats, bridges and tunnels which are built into the body of the Earth. When civil engineers re–route large rivers this is the same process as the heart bypass operations performed by heart sur–geons. The fast–food diet of increasing numbers of people is not very different from the use of artificial fertilizer and excessive pig manure on the land. Euthanasia results from the same line of thought as that which leads to the threat of world disaster posed by a hole in the ozone layer or a nuclear winter following a nuclear war.

By the foregoing comparisons, I simply mean that the choices made in health care are the same choices as those which should be made in caring for the biosphere of the Earth. Because of the possibilities of technology, man is forced to consider the morality of his acts. In doing so, the realization that man, the Earth and the natural kingdoms have a common spiritual origin can be a spur to ensure that one's actions are aimed at healing rather than exploitation and destruction.

When individual life is seen only from a materialistic point of view, an attempt will be made to keep the organs of the body in good condition as long as possible by means of courses of vac–cinations, special diets, exotic holidays, drugs and psychotherapy. When these no longer work, there is a great deal to be said for a painless death by injection. However, when man's health is viewed from an awareness of the existence of a spiritual world, reincarnation and karma, this results in a different attitude. Illness and suffering are viewed as challenging forms of resistance on the developmental path, which serve to awaken man's moral and spiritual essence, and allow it to flourish. These obstacles are ways of smoothing out former imperfections, of creating a new spiritual harmony in the individual's life, and of getting closer to the image of man as a bringer of salvation to the natural king–doms in their time of need. Health care without the spiritual element of the human soul is then seen as inadequate care. Only doctors with spiritual sympathy and understanding will be able to heal future man. In many aspects we are each other's doctor and our own physician. We ourselves can find the inner harmony to cure illness and help others to do so. However, no one else can cure us if we do not follow the path ourselves. This does not mean that medical expertise is not essential to reinforce the healing processes and gain time.

In the context of the Earth's biosphere the above clearly shows that it is man who disturbs the Earth's balance and who would be able to heal the Earth by increasing the moral content of his acts. The morality of our conduct is of paramount importance. In order to find a specific touchstone for this conduct it will be necessary to go one step further. How can I enable the Earth to develop through my own day–to–day behaviour?

In health care we have seen an increase in the popularity of homeopathy and of medicine which is based on man as a spiritual being. The health of a person as a whole can be determined from nearly every organ. The eye, and the techniques of iriscopy based on the eye, are an example of this in medicine. Every organ is a miniature person. A thorough knowledge of the role of parts of human organs and the cosmic significance of medicinal properties of plants and minerals are used to treat diseases in alternative medicine. Promoting the spiritual learning process linked to the disease is an important basic principle of anthroposophical medicine, and should not be obstructed.

Thus some of the basic principles which can be borrowed from health care are that disease should be seen as a moral learning process, that room must be created for this learning process, which is ultimately even more important than combatting the symptoms of the disease as quickly as possible, that the spiritual causes of disease should be understood, and that the spiritual effects of medicines and therapies should be examined.

Quite simply, illness in man can be caused by external wounds or by internal causes. Steiner states that the origin of internal diseases should always be sought in the digestive processes.[5] In contrast, the circulation of the blood is a constant healing process which is held in check by respiration. The circulation of the blood is an internal process, while respiration provides an interaction with the outside world. Both these circulatory processes contribute to healing. In this way, man breaks down the influences in food which cause disease. This leads to a process of development. I will study these processes in more detail in a later chapter. According to Steiner, spiritual development follows in the nervous and sensory systems from these healing forces.

This can also be described in a different way. Man was born as a spirit on Old Saturn. He acquired the power to cure himself in the circulatory process on the Old Sun and encountered substances causing disease in food on the Old Moon (see Table 5.1). The translation of these spiritual insights into human health to the Earth as a living organism means that we must learn to see the Earth as a living spiritual being, a being whose normal development can be disrupted by man. Man can harm the external Earth. Moreover, man also constantly intervenes increasingly in the Earth's digestive processes, which can make the Earth organism ill, just like a human organism. When the Earth's biosphere is diseased by its digestion, mankind as a whole must learn to develop more in harmony with the essence of the Earth. Man can work at making the Earth healthy through the circulation of the blood and respiration. In this way the spiritual development of man is linked to the ecological crisis which increasingly threatens the Earth. Moreover, the solar system needs a healthy Earth so that its destiny can be fulfilled.[6]

For a more detailed account of the urgent appeal made to man's behaviour nowadays, I shall try to draw a clearer picture of the organs of the Earth organism and of the processes which influence the Earth's health.

7.2   Organs and processes in the Earth organism

At this critical point in our study, we need to arrive at a description of the Earth's anatomy and physiology. Without such a description, man would have to care for an organism of which he did not even know the organs or how they worked. Furthermore, learning to understand the Earth organism as a parallel with the human organism could help man to become conscious of his responsibility for curing this member of the cosmic family and for

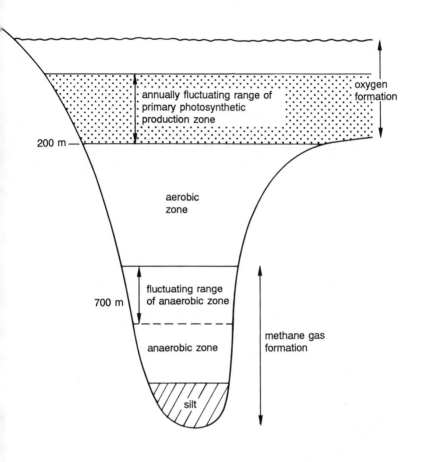

Table 7.1. Oxygen–regulating mechanisms off the coast of Venezuela.

securing his own future. Science has identified certain global cyclical processes which are indicative of organic functions. However, there is a lack of insight into the interrelationship of these processes and their relation to man's cosmic organization which is presumed to exist behind these organs and processes.

Having decided to describe the Earth organism, it took me a while to figure out how to do this. It is difficult enough to

151

describe the functions of the human organism correctly. This is even more true of an organism of which only few people are aware, and which is also much larger and more difficult to understand in its entirety.

For months I read everything I could find about the Earth organism. The books are often difficult to find, and in addition they are difficult to read. As this is the essence of my quest, I will briefly describe the various means of access I eventually found. The Gaia hypothesis described by the English chemist, James Lovelock, is the most accessible of these. This theory argues that the Earth is a self–regulating living being. Lovelock's book, *Gaia, A New Look at Life on Earth,* sums up a large number of scientific arguments which form a rational support for the ancient Greek myth about Gaia, the Earth goddess.[7] Another means of access is through mythology itself. For as a bearer of ancient wisdom, it sometimes contains important ideas about the essence of the Earth organism.

Finally, the work of Rudolf Steiner and its elaboration by some of his followers, are a wealth of information. I will return to this in the next chapter. After examining the Earth through these four different sets of spectacles, I will try and synthesize the common elements. On this basis, I hope to establish some characteristics which will indicate a direction for man's relationship with the Earth which he inhabits.

7.3   Lovelock's Gaia hypothesis

At the beginning of the 1970s, Lovelock — later with Margulis — put forward the theory that the Earth is a self–regulating mechanism with the capacity for keeping our planet healthy by controlling the chemical and physical environment.[8] In the 1960s Lovelock had already started thinking about the characteristic qualities of a "living" planet in order to be able to test other planets in our solar system for any physically perceptible forms of life. This research was part of the NASA Space Programme. Lovelock discovered that others, such as Alfred Redfield,[9] had already published a hypothesis that the chemical composition of the atmosphere and the oceans are biologically controlled. Like

Erwin Schrödinger,[10] Lovelock defined life as an open and continuous system that is able to lower its internal entropy, a measurement of chaos in a system, at the cost of free energy which is taken from the environment. According to the second law of thermodynamics, entropy always increases in a closed system. Life can only exist as an open system which receives the energy required for life from outside — in our case, from the Sun. Viewed from space, the evidence for life on Earth is the constant chemical imbalance in the composition of gases in the atmosphere. If there were a chemical balance, the Earth's atmosphere would be very similar to that of Venus and Mars, where the atmosphere consists mainly of carbon dioxide. On Earth, nitrogen (78%) and oxygen (21%) are predominant. Every year at least 2000 million tonnes of oxygen are produced on Earth to maintain the oxygen content. In this way the Earth's atmosphere is an extension of the biosphere. Lovelock states that all living things on Earth, from whales to viruses, from oaks to algae, can be considered as a single living being composed of different parts, which is capable of manipulating the Earth's atmosphere under changing external circumstances in order to satisfy all its requirements. The atmosphere is a biological construction like a bird's feathers or a wasps' nest. The planet and its nature is not a primitive force which must be contained, nor a demented spaceship which eternally describes pointless circles in the solar system.

Then Lovelock gives some examples of processes which comprise the physiology and toxicology of the Earth. The Earth has mechanisms for regulating the oxygen content of the atmosphere, for controlling the climate, for processing toxic waste, for regulating the acidity of ground and surface water, and for monitoring the salt content of the oceans.

According to scientific calculations, the Earth's climate has been virtually constant for the last three billion years, between 45 degrees latitude North and 45 degrees latitude South, which accounts for 70% of the Earth's surface. Although the heat radiated by the Sun has increased by approximately 30% during the last few billion years, the average temperature has only varied between 10 and 20°C. Possible explanations for this include the high carbon dioxide and ammonia content of the atmosphere in the early stages, and possibly the reduced reflection of light on the Earth's surface. Then, when life started to develop, the atmosphere's composition started to change because the carbon, nitrogen and hydrogen were taken from it. Possibly this is why the atmosphere's ammonia content declined at the same time as the radiation of heat from the Sun increased. Apart from the reduction in the atmosphere's ammonia content, the reflection of light by cloud formation may have been another mechanism for slowing down the increase in temperature. Maintaining the correct ammonia production is an example of a self-regulating mechanism.

Lovelock goes on to illustrate the importance of keeping the oxygen content constant in the change from an anaerobic to an aerobic atmosphere, which is calculated to have taken place approximately two billion years ago. An oxygen content higher than 21% would lead to spontaneous combustion. A lower oxygen content would result in reducing biological productivity. He describes how this content is actively regulated by microbiological methane production, on the one hand, and deposits of carbon in deep anaerobic zones of the oceans and marshes, on the other hand, as shown in Table 7.1. The deposits of carbon in the oceans provide a net gain of oxygen because oxygen is released during the photosynthetic formation of carbon compounds from carbon and water. Later this is no longer a compound when the carbon is burnt to form carbon dioxide. The Earth also has mechanisms for rendering toxic waste harmless. Some of the non-degradable substances include metals which are taken from the Earth's crust by mining and waste disposal. In the long term these can poison the sediments of lakes and oceans. This is prevented by combining them in insoluble compounds and by microorganisms which transform toxic metals such as mercury, lead and arsenic into gaseous, methylated products. These are diluted in the atmosphere and dispersed over the surface of the Earth.

The fact that the Earth has not become too acid would also be incomprehensible if it were not a living organism. The oxidation of ammonia to form nitrates, of methane to form carbon dioxide, and of sulphides to form sulphates always results in acidity. Mars and Venus have become acid. Probably this has not occurred on Earth partly as the result of the erosion of chalky rock.

The constancy of the salt content of sea water is also of vital importance for life. Every year rivers have deposited approximately 540 million tonnes of salt in the oceans, and yet their salt content has hardly changed in the past few billion years. There must be a salt separation mechanism which is controlled biologically. This makes one think of the sedimentation of chalk and silicic acid from the skeletons of diatoms. Chlorides and sulphates can crystallize out in shallow lakes and bays, of which the formation is also biologically determined. An example is the formation of lagoons by coral reefs. The methylation of sulphur by marine algae into the volatile substance, dimethylsulphide, also plays a role.

The essential element, iodine, is transformed into the volatile substance, methyl iodide, by algae in seawater, and is distributed over the land via the atmosphere. In the atmosphere methyl chloride is formed from methyl iodide and chloride ions. Methyl chloride could serve to regulate the ozone layer.

These regulating mechanisms suggest that the Sun feeds the Earth with light and heat, that the atmosphere and the cycle of water ensure the exchange and transportation of substances in the form of rhythmic processes, that functions resembling those of organs such as the liver (detoxification) and the kidneys (desalination) take place in the shallow parts of seas and oceans, while the rivers meander over the skin of the solid Earth's surface, rather like veins. Finally, the photosynthesis of the woods, forests and upper layers of the oceans provide a reflection of the respiratory process which takes place in the lungs. Lovelock and others[11] point out that man has speeded up the carbon cycle by 20%, the nitrogen cycle by 10% and the sulphur cycle by more than 100%. This is not surprising when it is remembered that in the past few thousand years it has been scientifically calculated that the world population has increased by a factor of more than 1000, and that the per capita energy consumption of the population has increased by a factor of between ten and one hundred.[12] The role of the tropical rainforests and the shallow seas off the continental coasts is particularly important. Currently they are most critical for the functioning of the self–regulating Earth mechanism. Although Lovelock considers the survival of micro-organisms to be more important for the continuity of the Earth's biosphere than the survival of man, he also suggests that mankind as a species could constitute the nervous system and brain of Gaia. The conclusion is that man must accept his role as a partner of Gaia.

I support this conclusion of Lovelock's. I would now like to compare his scientific picture of the organs and regulatory processes with the views presented by other sources. Lovelock did not think of the name "Gaia" for his hypothesis himself. He admits that it was suggested by someone else. He did not investigate the deeper meaning of Gaia in Greek mythology, as I will do now, and Lovelock does not really see Gaia as a true living being. He wrote: "Gaia theory suggests that we inhabit and are part of a quasi–living entity that has the capacity for global homeostasis."[13] According to Richard Kerr, the Gaia hypothesis is dead because it cannot be verified by means of tests.[14] In 1988, Lovelock published a sequel to his work, entitled *The Ages of Gaia,* in which he wrote a biography of our living planet and also commented on the religious significance of the Gaia hypothesis. In this work, he said: "Living itself is a religious experience ... For me, Gaia is a religious as well as a scientific concept, and in both spheres it is manageable ... It is otiose to try to prove that Gaia is alive. Instead, Gaia should be a way to view the Earth, ourselves, and our relationships with living things ... Individuals interact with Gaia in the cycling of the elements and in the control of the climate, just like a cell does in the body ... Gaia's unconscious goal is a planet fit for life ... That Gaia can be both spiritual and scientific is, for me, deeply satisfying."[15]

Lovelock's balancing act to keep a foot in both worlds has been attacked by many critics. The Gaia hypothesis is considered unsuitable for making predictions or for optimalizing the conditions of life. In the *Scientific American* of December 1989, Tim Beardsley remarked: "Gaia, the smile remains, but the lady vanishes." The wall between mechanistic and spiritual ways of seeing once again towers over us. However, I do not expect that this will reduce the attraction of the Gaia concept, as many studies have shown.[16]

7.4   Gaia in Greek mythology

The Greek goddess Gaia, Gaea or Ge, is seen as the personification of Mother Earth. According to Bartelink, the same deity is personified in a religious and historical sense in the Greek Demeter, the Roman Tellus, and the Germanic Nerthus.[17] In the Egyptian religion the Earth deity Geb was male rather than female and the goddess Isis was comparable to the Greek Gaia. For the Greeks the mother goddess Gaia represented the source of all life to which the seeds of life also returned. As mother goddess of the pre–Greek tribes of Asia Minor, Gaia appeared in many different deities, including Artemis Ephesia, who is depicted with many breasts.

According to Greek mythology, Gaia arose from Chaos, and she gave rise to heaven (Uranus), the mountains and the sea. Subsequently all things were created from the marriage between Uranus and Gaia, the gods of heaven and Earth. For example, the Titans sprang from the blood of Uranus. These were giants whose body ended in the body of a serpent. Typhon is one of the best known. In the myth of creation described by Plato in *Timaeus,* Gaia and Uranus had twelve children, the Titans. These included Oceanus and Tethys. In their turn Oceanus and Tethys were the parents of the Oceanids and river gods. According to the Greek poet Homer (*c.*800 – *c.*750 BC), Oceanus is the river which flows round the world. Chronos and Rhea were the children of Oceanus and Tethys. Chronos dethroned his father Oceanus, and married his sister Rhea. Chronos and Rhea had daughters, Hestia, Hera and Demeter, and sons, Hades Poseidon and Zeus. However, Chronos swallowed his children when they were born. Only Zeus escaped from his father because Rhea gave Chronos a stone wrapped in nappies after the birth of Zeus, which he immediately devoured without realizing what it was. Zeus grew up on Crete, and when he became an adult he vanquished Chronos, who spewed up his other children in reverse order. Chronos became a popular symbol of time, who devours the years he has engendered.

Steiner describes how, according to Pherekydes of Syros, the Ancient Greeks regarded Zeus as the leader of the Sun spirits, the spirits of the form.[18] In addition, Pherekydes of Syros, who was the esoteric teacher of Pythagoras (575 – c.500 BC), described how just as thoughts arise from the force of man's soul, Zeus evoked rainbows, lightning and thunder, and the red morning sky from his essential being. Zeus is the infinite ether, the omnipresent, alive in itself. According to Pherekydes of Syros, the abstract transient nature of time in Chronos is more like a being which gives rise to the elements of air, fire and water. He learned that this development is based on the principle of Zeus, Chronos, and in the third place, Chton. Chton is the description of the chaotic condition of the Earth at the time of the expulsion of the Moon. Chton became Gaia, the present Earth, because Zeus gave her the gift of ears of corn. It is the symbolic representation of the effect of the Sun beings on the chaotic Earth in the Lemurian era. In contrast with the ancient Greek myth, in which Gaia is depicted as the mother goddess, she is later identified with the physical Earth as revealed in this explanation of Pherekydes of Syros and in the works of Homer. Zeus became the most important god of the Greeks, the father of gods and man.

According to Greek mythology, Zeus married his sister Hera after conquering the Titans. He divided his dominion with his brothers Poseidon and Hades, who were assigned the sea and the underworld. Zeus had children by many other goddesses, as well as with Hera. For example, Persephone was born from the union between Zeus and his sister Demeter, the goddess of agriculture and the fruits of the Earth. Persephone was trapped by Hades and had to remain in the underworld. The Earth dried up when Demeter was mourning Persephone, so Hades allowed her to return to Earth, as long as she did not eat a pomegranate. As she disobeyed, she had to spend half of the year in the underworld. She is a symbol of human life, of a grain which dies in the Earth, of birth, flowering and death, and of the desire for immortality. All these ideas were expressed in the so-called Eleusinian mysteries.

Steiner recounts that Persephone was the leader of the ancient art of clairvoyance.[19] When she was carried off by Hades or Pluto, clairvoyant powers were suppressed. Now she has sunk into the depths of the soul, where she works on reinforcing our Selves. The Akasha Chronicle confirms that Persephone was the daughter of Demeter. Demeter is the greatest representative of the basic force which is now described by the term "chastity": a chastity which represents a fertile reality which is not ascetic, but implies the fundamental love of mankind. Clairvoyant powers spring from this force. Demeter was not only the source of food for early mankind, but also the lawgiver. She was the moral stimulus for external relationships. When she later withdrew, she founded a school of mysteries in Eleusis to replace the laws based on natural forces by laws based on a more abstract intellectual morality. In modern man it is still the force of Eros which makes him alive and healthy. However, the era of man meant that the forces of Eros were transformed into the forces of Demeter, representing the force of fertile chastity. After the abduction of Persephone, Demeter retained only the forces which bring about withering and fruiting.

Now that we have seen how Greek mythology is rooted in the deeper sources of spiritual science, it is time to examine a Greek myth of the Earth in closser detail. It is a spiritual reflection of the Earth, in contrast to the physical image of the Earth as presented by Lovelock, and we find it described at length by Plato in his *Phaedo*:

"... the real Earth, viewed from above, is supposed to look like one of these balls made of twelve pieces of skin, variegated and marked out in different colours, of which the colours we know are only limited samples, like the paints which artists use; but there the whole Earth is made up of such colours, and others far brighter and purer still. One section is a marvellously beautiful purple, and another is golden; all that is white of it is whiter than chalk or snow; and the rest is similarly made up of the other colours, still more and lovelier than those which we have seen. Even these very hollows in the earth, full of water and air, assume a kind of colour as they gleam amid the different hues around them, so that there appears to be one continuous surface of varied colours. The trees and flowers and fruits which grow upon this earth are proportionately beautiful. The mountains too and the stones have a proportionate smoothness and transparency, and their colours are lovelier. The pebbles which are so highly prized in our world — the jaspers and rubies and emeralds and the rest — are fragments of these stones; but there everything is as beautiful as they are, or better still. ...

"There are many kinds of animals upon it, and also human beings, some of whom live inland, others round the air, as we live round the sea, and others in islands surrounded by air but close to the mainland. In a word, as water and the sea are to us for our purposes, so is air to them; and as the air is to us, so the ether is to them. Their climate is so temperate that they are free from disease and live much longer than people do here; and in sight and hearing and understanding and all other faculties they are as far superior to us as air is to water or ether to air in clarity ...

"Such is the nature of the earth as a whole and of the things that are upon it. In the earth itself, all over its surface, there are many hollow regions, some deeper and more widely spread than that in which we live, others deeper than our region but with a smaller expanse, some both shallower than ours and broader. All these are joined together underground by many connecting channels, some narrower, some wider, through which, from one basin to another, there flows a great volume of water, monstrous unceasing subterranean rivers of waters both hot and cold; and of fire too, great rivers of fire; and many of liquid mud, some clearer, some more turbid, like the rivers in Sicily that flow mud before the lava comes, and the lava–stream itself. By these the several regions are filled in turn as the flood reaches them.

"All this movement to and fro is caused by an oscillation inside the earth, and this oscillation is brought about by natural means, as follows.

"One of the cavities in the earth is not only larger than the rest, but pierces right through from one side to the other. It is of this that Homer speaks when he says

Far, far away, where lies earth's deepest chasm;[20]
while elsewhere both he and many other poets refer to it as

Tartarus. Into this gulf all the rivers flow together, and from it they flow forth again; and each acquires the nature of that part of the earth through which it flows. The cause of the flowing in and out of all these streams is that the mass of liquid has no bottom or foundation; so it oscillates and surges to and fro, and the air or breath that belongs to it does the same; for it accompanies the liquid both as it rushes to the further side of the earth and as it returns. ...

"Among these many various mighty streams there are four in particular. The greatest of these, and the one which describes the outermost circle, is that which is called Oceanus. Directly opposite to this, and with a contrary course is Acheron, which not only flows through other desolate regions but passes underground and arrives at the Acherusian Lake; where the souls of the dead for the most part come, and after staying for certain fixed periods, longer or shorter, are sent forth again to the births of living creatures. Half way between these two a third river has its rise ... This is the river called Pyriphlegethon, whose fiery stream belches forth jets of lava here and there in all parts of the world. Directly opposite to this in its turn the fourth river breaks out, first, they say, into a wild and dreadful place, all leaden grey, which is called the Stygian region, and the lake which the river forms on its entry is called Styx ... and its name, the poets say, is Cocytus.

"Such is the conformation of the earth and its rivers. And when the newly dead reach the place to which each is conducted by his guardian spirit, first they submit to judgement ... Those who are judged to have lived a neutral life set out for Acheron, and embarking in those vessels which await them, are conveyed in them to the lake; and there they dwell, and undergoing purification are both absolved by punishment from any sins that they have committed, and rewarded for their good deeds ... Those who on account of the greatness of their sins are judged to be incurable ... these are hurled by their appropriate destiny into Tartarus, from whence they emerge no more.

"Others are judged to have been guilty of sins which, though great, are curable ... These too must be cast into Tartarus; but when this has been done and they have remained there for a year, the surge casts them out — the manslayers down Cocytus and the offenders against their parents down Pyriphlegethon. And when, as they are swept along, they come past the Acherusian Lake, there they cry aloud and call upon those whom they have killed or misused, and calling, beg and entreat for leave to pass from the stream into the lake and be received by them. If they prevail, they come out and there is an end of their distress; but if not, they are swept away once more into Tartarus ...

"But those who are judged to have lived a life of surpassing holiness — these are they who are released and set free from confinement in these regions of the earth, and passing upward to their pure abode, make their dwelling upon the earth's surface. And of these such as have purified themselves sufficiently by philosophy live thereafter altogether without bodies, and reach habitations even more beautiful, which it is not easy to portray — nor is there time to do so now."[21]

In this impressive myth, Plato describes the processes of the Earth which take place in the spiritual world, and the destiny of man after death in the spiritual world surrounding the Earth. This is referred to several times with concepts such as "when seen from above," "there," "that other world," "what is water to us is air to them," "our air is ether to them," and "the true Earth." It is important to gain a better idea of "the nature of the Earth as a whole" from this. This is the Earth as a physical and spiritual being. This whole nature is expressed particularly in the liquid element, which seems to flow freely through the dividing wall between the physical and spiritual Earth. For example, Oceanus flows around the world, but comes out in the subterranean Tartarus. Lava is also considered as the liquid element which is present in the Earth. These are all indications of the Earth's ethereal body. In the centre of the Earth there is a "swing," a sort of heartbeat which maintains the cycles of streams of lava and water and currents of air. Here we seem to have come across an important organ, one of the life processes of Gaia. This life process provides connections which take us a step further than is possible with Lovelock's Gaia hypothesis. But before following this line of thought, we shall first reflect on the image of the Earth depicted in Germanic and Nordic mythology.

7.5   The Earth organism in Germanic mythology

Germanic and Nordic mythology is set between Asgard, the house of the gods, located high above central Germany, and Midgard, the home of man. According to Rudolf Steiner, this mythology is the purest description of the creation of the Earth in terms of spiritual science.[22] Ginnunga–gap, a Germanic-Nordic chaos, reflects the moment at which the Earth re–emerges from the pralaya after the last metamorphosis of the Old Moon. Ginnunga–gap, which means "yawning chasm," is a deep abyss shrouded in mist, which lies in the middle of space. The only thing there is the tree, Yggdrasil, under whose three roots — the past, the present and the future — as yet unborn time is still concealed, the beginning of the Old Saturn metamorphosis. The northern part of the abyss is called Niflheim, the realm of mists and biting cold. To the south of the abyss there is Muspelheim. This is the world of fire and light, and is guarded by the giant Surtur. Muspelheim evokes an image which is reminiscent of the Old Sun. At the beginning of time the rain of sparks from Muspelheim melted the ice in Niflheim. When the glow of Muspelheim combined with Niflheim, this gave rise to the giant productive cow Audumla, and the first giant Ymir. The giant Ymir was fed on Audumla's milk, just as man was fed from the environment through an umbilical cord in the Old Moon. While he was asleep, a son and a daughter were born from the sweat under his arm, and the six–headed Thrudgelmir from his feet. The God Buri, the producer, sprang from the salt rime which the giant cow Audumla ate from the ice covered rocks. This heralded the Earth metamorphosis with solid matter. Buri begat the god Börr. Börr then married the giantess Bestla. Börr and Bestla were the ancestors of the Ases who lived in Asgard. Asgard is the spiritual centre of inspiration for northern and western Europe, and has strong links with the Grail mysteries.

Börr and Bestla had a one–eyed son, Odin. The one–eyed Odin is reminiscent of the cyclopes which reflected the development of man during the Lemurian era. Odin was the most important god, as Zeus was in Greek mythology. Apart from Odin, the sons Wili and We were born from the union of Börr

163

and Bestla. Odin married Frigga and gave birth to her sons Baldur and Hermond. Baldur was the god of light, beauty and peace, and was loved by god and man.

There were now twelve palaces in Asgard where the gods lived. These palaces were built of gold and precious stones, and they housed Odin (Wotan), Thor (Donar) and the others. Valhalla, the hall of the slain, was also situated in Asgard. Asgard was surrounded by mighty rivers and sharp swords. In addition to the twelve gods, the female Ases, such as Frigga and Sif, also lived there.

In a long battle of the giants against the gods, the first giant Ymir was killed by the brothers Odin, Wili and We. Then the Ases rolled Ymir into the abyss and formed the world from his body. His flesh became the earth, his blood the seas and rivers, his bones the mountains, his teeth the stones and rocks, his skull the heavens, his hair the trees, and his brain the clouds. Midgard, the garden which lies between the heaven and the centre of the Earth, was created from his eyebrows as a place for man to dwell. Finally, the Ases took the sparks which flew from Muspelheim to the Earth and placed them in the heaven as the Sun, the Moon and the Stars (planets). These are the celestial bodies which, on the Old Sun, still formed a single unit with our own Sun. In this myth the Earth organism is derived from the body of a giant, and the sea and rivers were his blood, a body which stretched from the centre of the Earth and in which his bones reach to the clouds formed from his brain.

Just as the solar system is produced from the tree Yggdrasil, man comes from the two holy trees, the Ask (Ash), and the Embla (Alder). From these two holy trees Odin created the first human couple, together with two other gods, Hönir and Loki. Odin gave man life and movement. Ancient Germanic, Nordic man, who was to some extent clairvoyant, saw Odin's domination in the elements, in the wind, in breathing and in speaking, which is related to breathing. Steiner indicated that the individuality which was represented in northern Europe as Odin is the same as that which appeared later as Buddha.[23] Buddha became a container for Odin. Hönir, one of Odin's brothers, granted man intelligence, and feeling, the force behind imagination. Loki or

Lödur gave Germanic man his own characteristics and light skin colour, his racial characteristics. The three gods Odin, Hönir and Loki always play a collective role in the myths.

In Steiner's lectures on *The Mission of the Individual Folk-souls,* he describes how the world of the gods and Ases comprises Angels and Archangels.[24] Odin, or Wotan, is the leading Archangel, who broke off his own development in order to bring speech to man. Thor, or Donar, and his wife Sif gave individual man his Self. In an occult sense, Sif means "group Soul." Even in early times consciousness was displaced from the observation of the spiritual world to observing the physical world. Steiner showed that once man had received his Self consciousness, Loki gave man his freedom and independence. However, at the same time, Loki burdened man with desires which draw downwards, for behind the Loki figure there is a Lucifer who attempts to obstruct the development of man foreseen by the gods. To the extent that man is affected by Loki's influence, he becomes blind to the spiritual world. This is expressed in a myth in which Loki engineers the murder of the clairvoyant Baldur by the blind Hödur.

Frigga is the goddess of love and marriage. She protects the flowers and the spring. In this respect she is very similar to Nerthus, the Germanic Earth goddess of fertility, and to Ostara, the goddess of spring and the regeneration of nature. The Oster festival, the German Ostern (Easter), celebrates Ostara.

In her palace Frigga receives women when they have died, just as Odin awaits men after death. In this way Frigga, Nerthus, and Ostara are symbols of death and rebirth, of Earth and man.

A comparison with the Greek myths immediately suggests a similarity between Gaia and Audumla, and between Rhea and Bestla. The battle of the gods against the Titans is also the same as that against the first giants. Zeus and Odin are the same characters, as are Demeter and Frigga. Moreover, there is a great deal of similarity between Persephone and Baldur, who must stay in the underworld in the power of Hades and Hell. Finally, in both cases, it is the great stream of the Tartarus and of the heart and veins of the giant Ymir, which flow through the body of the

Earth, and make it into a whole. Later I will try to fit these images into a more all-encompassing context.

In the next chapter, I will expand on the broad view of the Earth organism that has emerged from the sources consulted in this chapter. Anthroposophical views tend to be complementary to these rather than contradictory. The picture becomes increasingly detailed, but is not yet conclusive. In view of the broad and fragmentary nature of anthroposophical literature about the Earth, I do not claim to provide a comprehensive survey in the chapter which follows.

8.   The Earth organism in anthroposophy

> *Then the Earth was moved by pity and inner compassion.*
> *She said:*
> *"I see the weakness of man. What I felt to be his*
> *cruelty is only his weakness. I need man and he cannot*
> *survive without me. And yet I wished to abandon him. Yet*
> *who can serve as a voice that man will know I am well*
> *disposed towards him?"*
>
> Zarathustra, Yasna 29:8

8.1   Interaction with the higher hierarchies

Rudolf Steiner emphasized the function of the Earth as a living organism in many of his lectures. He expressed this most profoundly when he stated that the planetary spirit of the Earth has the task of bringing about the interaction of the Earth with the other celestial bodies surrounding it.[1] It is his task to direct the Earth and guide it in such a way that in the course of time it will achieve the right relationship with other celestial bodies. At the same time, the planetary spirit is the Earth's great sensory organ, which enables the Earth to achieve the correct relationship with its environment. It is the planetary spirit which leads the planet through space and gives the whole planet its purpose. As described in an earlier chapter, the planetary spirit was brought into contact with the Christ. Then Steiner summarizes the most important characteristics of the Earth organism, as described in Chapter 6, in a way which supplements what was written earlier. He does this by drawing broad parallels between man and the Earth.

Everything which can be observed about the Earth through the senses corresponds with our physical body. The Earth's ethereal body is formed by the world of natural spirits or elemental beings. These are mostly deviations in the form of Self–less servers of the spirits of the third hierarchy, the Archai, Archangels and Angels. These are the gnomes, elves, nymphs, and fiery spirits or salamanders which are familiar from fairy tales. These creatures guide the flow of liquids throughout nature and were described in detail by Ernst Hagemann on the basis of Steiner's work.[2] They are the architects of the natural kingdoms in miniature, but they have no responsibility. They carry out the tasks of the ethereal world. Then the world of the so-called spirits of the cycles forms the Earth's astral body. These spirits have broken away from the spirits of the first hierarchy, the Cherubim, Seraphim and Thrones. They are the organs which carry out the tasks in all processes which reveal a rhythm, such as the alternation of day and night and summer and winter. They direct the work of the above-mentioned natural spirits or elemental beings and form a spiritual sphere surrounding the Earth. They carry out the plan of the Seraphim, Cherubim and Thrones. Finally, the planetary spirit itself is comparable to man's Self.

Apart from the outline of this all-encompassing picture, Steiner seems to have written only briefly about the parallels between the organs and digestive processes in the human body and in the Earth's body. In his lectures on education, he also gave a description of the structure of man which can be translated in terms of the Earth.[3] For example, as described in a previous chapter, the head constantly produces figures which correspond to the animal kingdom around us. In the body these animals are transformed into thoughts. They only exist in the extrasensory world. The plant kingdom would develop in man's chest, which accommodates the respiratory and circulatory systems but for the fact that man breathes out the carbon dioxide which is formed, thus preventing the plants from developing. When a person is too weak to do this, he falls ill. Every contagious disease is actually related to a species of plant. Respiration is an anti-plant system. Finally, the movement of the limbs helps to counteract the tendency of minerals to crystallize, which causes gout and diabetes. Thus the animal kingdom can be found in the head, the plant kingdom in the chest, and the mineral kingdom in the digestive system and limbs. The head transforms animals into thoughts, the chest reverses the processes of the plant kingdom, and the limbs dissolve minerals. On this basis, parallels should be found with the Earth.

For example, the towering thunder clouds miles above us can be seen as gigantic structures of mist, rooted like plants on the Earth's surface and flowering high in the troposphere, the Earth's chest. By contrast, the animal passions of the Greek underworld are housed inside the Earth in the Earth's head.[4] In the outer layers of the Earth matter is dissolved and radiation is dominant.

Steiner also points out the parallels between man and the solar system. Something which constantly emerges from his writings is the close interconnection between higher spiritual hierarchies and the beings which broke away from them during the development of man and the Earth. Although I will continue my attempt to compare the organs and processes, I am starting to realize that the life rhythms of the Earth organism are so strongly directed by the cosmos and the spiritual hierarchies, that it is difficult to see man as being in autonomous control of the Earth. According to Steiner, volcanic eruptions and great changes in the climate are caused by the cosmos, and the Sun and the intensity of sunspots play an important role.[5] Man does have a responsibility as well, particularly with regard to the capacity for destruction of modern weapons and technology. This responsibility can only be fully developed when man approaches the Earth organism, which is so different and so much larger than himself, with respect and uninhibited attention.

8.2   The threefold division of planet Earth

One of Steiner's most important ideas was the principle of the threefold division.[6] The number 3 and the threefold division relate to the functions of the human soul and the social order within society. In addition, the number 4 has an esoteric connection with the Earth in the form of its four points of the compass and the four natural kingdoms. Moreover, the number 4 can be found in the four triangles which, according to Steiner, comprise the Earth.[7] These four triangles form a pyramid with points at the South Pole, the Caucasus, Japan and the west of the United States. The sides of the pyramid are areas with the most intensive volcanic activity. The number 7 has come up before with regard to the structure of the centres in the ethereal body of man and of the solar system. Steiner also distinguishes seven life processes related to the seven planets. Finally the number 12 is related to the twelve spiritual forces emanated by the signs of the zodiac, which are reflected in the human senses, of which Steiner also identifies twelve.[8]

In order to understand the anatomy of the Earth, the physical threefold division in man provides a helpful perspective. Steiner emphasizes the three aspects of man on the basis of a polarity between head and belly, taking and giving, contracting and radiating, breaking down and building up, past and future. Between these two extremes the present, the connection, is always a middle link. Thus a distinction can be made in the human figure between the head–chest–belly/limbs, and parallel with this, the three aspects of thinking–feeling–the will. In this, thinking is related to the past, feeling to the present, and the will is aimed at the future. In spiritual terms the three aspects relate to society with regard to its spiritual life, legal life and economic life, with their respective ideals: liberty, equality and fraternity.[9] The way in which these three aspects hark back to the creation of man during the previous Earth metamorphosis was discussed in Chapters 4 and 5. As man's steering mechanism, the physical head is the most immobile part of the body, while the belly and limbs, where commands are carried out, are the most mobile. The rhythmical processes of respiration and the circulation of the blood bring about the connection and harmony between the two poles. The physical threefold division in man can be identified in every living organism. For example, in cells or unicellular organisms a distinction can be made between the nucleus as the concentration and steering mechanism, and the cell wall, and possibly the pseudopod as the area for expansion, digestion and movement. The exchange of nutrients and waste products takes place through the cell wall. The pseudopod can be seen as the most primitive form of a limb. The area between the nucleus of the cell and the cell wall is the central area where respiration takes place in the so-called mitochondria. In the spherical shape of the cell, the steering mechanism is therefore in the nucleus, the connecting link in the protoplasm, while the cell wall carries out the commands.

The model of a cell can help to bridge the gap between man, who moves about in an upright position, and the globe of the Earth, which floats in space. As in the cell, the three aspects of the physical Earth can be identified in the spherical layers. The concentration and steering mechanism is contained in the Earth's core. I described earlier how the plant kingdom and seams of metal ore in the Earth can be viewed as the Earth's nervous and sensory system, passing impressions of the outside world to the centre of the planet. In this way the whole of the Earth's crust, mantle and core forms the head or steering mechanism of the Earth organism. This shows once again that the Earth and man have an opposite orientation in space. The plant kingdom has the same orientation as the Earth. In plants, the roots are the centre of concentration, sucking water and mineral salts from the Earth. The stalk is the connecting link, and the leaves and flowers constitute the digestive and reproductive systems from which substances are dispersed into the environment. The "bellies" of plants are turned to the Sun, as is Earth. The contrast between man and plants is also expressed in the fact that man and animals breathe out carbon dioxide and breathe in oxygen, while these processes are reversed in plants in the daytime.

The Earth's chest comprises the hydrosphere and the lower part of the atmosphere. It is the ring which is situated between the lithosphere, with the rocks, and the higher atmosphere. The processes of the circulation of water and air, of the heart and lungs, take place in the Earth's chest. The lung function is aimed at an exchange with the solar system outside the Earth. The heart function can be recognized in the rain which falls on the surface of the land, just as our blood brings nutrients to the tissues of our body and removes waste products. In this respect Rudolf Steiner pointed out that the cycle of water is really Earth's circulation.[10] In this sense, the Earth's chest comprises everything which belongs to the biosphere. It is interesting that the chest represents man's most essential functions; it is the heart which is concerned with life between birth and death. The head is the product of the previous incarnation, and the belly and limbs a preparation of the

171

physical body for the next incarnation. The chest is the only part which really characterizes man on Earth.[11] In this way the biosphere, where water and air are dominant, like blood and breath, is part of the real organism of the present Earth.

Finally, it is inevitable that we return to the initially strange conclusion that the higher atmosphere, consisting of the thermosphere, the exosphere and the magnetosphere, should be seen as the belly and limbs of the Earth organism. It is the least solidified part of the Earth, in which the magnetotail forms a parallel with the pseudopod of bacteria. The magnetotail is the long extended layer of the Earth's magnetic field which exists in space behind the Earth's orbit (see Table 8.1). In the Earth's digestive system the temperature rises above 1200°C, and gases occur in a partially ionized state in changing proportions. The higher atmosphere forms the boundary with interplanetary space, from which the Earth receives its nutrients in the form of solar radiation and hydrogen expelled by the Sun.

In the Earth the most solid and immobile steering mechanism is also found in the "head" and the most mobile mechanism carrying out commands is found in the "belly," while the "chest" acts as a connecting system. In order to arrive at a better understanding of the Earth and the significance of man's social activity, I would like to take a closer look at the processes which can be distinguished in each of these three systems of the Earth. At the same time, I shall try to discover a further subdivision of these three aspects within the steering system, the connecting system and the implementation system, as is the case in man.

In this respect, Steiner distinguishes the thinking, feeling and will functions of the human head in terms of the brain, the senses and the lower jaw.[12] Using the science of organizations as an analogy, we could also refer to the steering function, the measuring function and the planning function. In this the brain is the least mobile, the lower jaw and chin the most mobile. In popular belief this can be recognized in the idea that a prominent chin is the sign of a strong will.

With regard to the chest, there are parallels with the chest cavity, the lungs and the heart. The sternum forms the solid support for the chest cavity, which is the structure surrounding

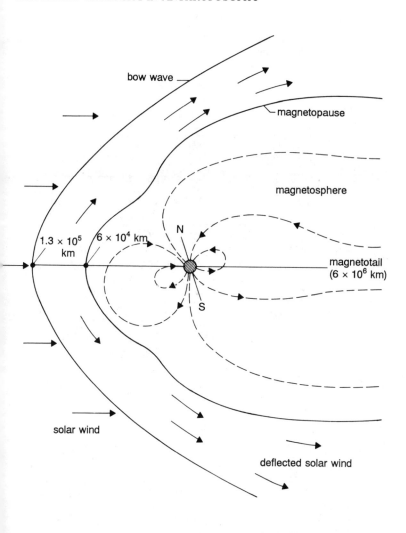

Table 8.1. Cross–section of the Earth's magnetosphere.

the lungs and heart. The lungs are responsible for the rhythmic interaction between the inside and outside world, and the cardiac and vascular system is the bearer of the will of the Self, and is responsible for the internal transportation function. The heart with

173

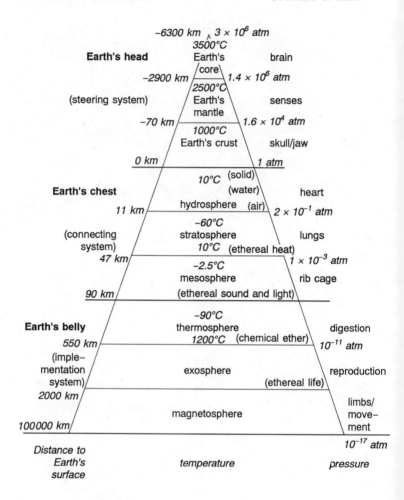

Structure of the Earth   Structure of man

Table 8.2. Comparison of the three–part structure of Earth and man.

its rapid rhythm is the most mobile component in the chest. The polarity in the chest is manifest more on the horizontal plane, as it is in the Earth to some extent, in the form of the relatively restricted height of about 200 km comprising the Earth's chest.

174

In the belly there is a reflection of the vertical order within the head. The parallels of thinking, feeling and the will, that is, of contraction, connection and radiation, can also be recognized in the limbs, the sexual organs and the digestive organs. Table 8.2 summarizes this structure. The spiritual mobility of the brain is reflected in the physical mobility of the limbs. Digestion is a characteristic transforming function, the sexual organs are responsible for the reproductive function, and the limbs take the body to its goal, and constitute a frame for presenting the body and the bones. In this way, the three aspects of the physical organization of man and the Earth can be transformed into a nine–part system.

Table 8.3 characterizes the typical functions of each part, as a frame of reference for drawing up this nine–part organization. These three systems for steering, forming connections and carrying out commands, and the nine characteristic functions embedded in these systems, are present in every organization with a capacity for life. These functions can be discerned in man, in a business, a government organization, a central heating system, and also in the Earth organism. Without these nine functions there is no organic unity. The significance of this organic ordering principle will be further elaborated below.

8.3 The Earth's steering system

The organs which correspond to man's brain, nervous and sensory system, and the skull with a mobile jaw, are contained in the Earth's "head," the steering system. Three aspects roughly corresponding to the Earth's crust, the Earth's mantle and the Earth's core, can also be distinguished in the Earth's steering system, as illustrated in Table 8.4.

From the outside inwards, Steiner first distinguishes three layers in the Earth's crust on the spiritual level:[13]

the solid mineral Earth
the liquid Earth
the air Earth.

Together these three layers form the skull of the Earth's "head";

System	Function in human body	General characteristics
steering system	brain/nerves	steering (regulating chamber)
	senses	measurement (external impressions)
	skull/jaw	planning function (bearer of plan for execution of intentions)
connecting system	circulation of the blood	internal transportation function (bearer of organization's identity)
	respiration	external transportation function (material exchange with outside world)
	chest cavity	
		enclosing function of transportation systems (accommodates the essential being)
implementation system	digestion	transformation function (carrying out characteristic transformation process)
	reproduction	
	limbs	reproductive function (maintaining conditions for the transformation process)
		product presentation function (characteristic material product of transformation process with which the organization presents itself to the outside world and moves towards its goal)

Table 8.3. General characteristics of the nine functions in an organization.

in other words, the system for carrying out the steering of the Earth. It is the most solid, but also the most mobile part. The movements consist of the shifting of the continental plates, earthquakes and volcanic eruptions. The solid mineral Earth owes its form to the spirits of the form, as described briefly in an earlier chapter. The undulating interplay of forces which are caused by the spirits of the will (Thrones) radiating outward from inside the Earth, and the spirits of movement (Forces) radiating to the Earth from the cosmos, would cause the surface of the Earth to be like waves on the sea if the spirits of the form did not freeze this movement and fix it in a permanent form.[14] The above–mentioned pyramid structure can be found in the solid continents. However, the Earth as a whole is still spherical because of the liquid rocks at deeper levels, and water.

In considering the inner layers of the Earth, we come across what is known in anthroposophy as the "subnatural," an area where technology is dominant, and which is the opposite of the "supernatural," where light dominates. Man, living in the Earth's "chest," must find a balance between these supernatural and subnatural areas, or in terms of Greek mythology: man lives on Gaia with Uranus, the heaven, above, and Tartarus, the contracting centre of the Earth, below. The origin of all disruption and destruction lies in the subnatural regions. For every heavenly force, there is a subterranean counterforce. The three above–mentioned layers of the Earth's crust were formed during the expulsion of the Moon.[15]

Electricity, magnetism, and radioactive radiation are most clearly manifest in the solid mineral Earth.

The Earth's crust, or skull, represents the physical level at which man's development takes place, and is also the solid excretory product with which the Earth's steering system presents itself to the outside world. This solid mineral Earth reaches a depth of about 70 km, where it has a temperature of approximately 1000°C, and the pressure is about 16000 atmospheres. The Earth's crust is sometimes referred to as "sial" because of the predominance of the elements of silicon and aluminium.

Steiner considers that a spiritual force is dominant in the "liquid Earth," which presumably coincides with the magma zone in which matter has a semi–liquid form. When this force is brought together with life, it expels life. It has a deadly effect, comparable to an act of observation in which we disconnect our feelings from the object. This destruction is the counterpart of the

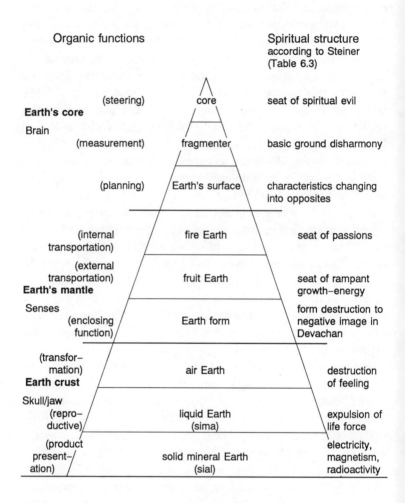

Organic functions		Spiritual structure according to Steiner (Table 6.3)
Earth's core (steering) Brain	core	seat of spiritual evil
(measurement)	fragmenter	basic ground disharmony
(planning)	Earth's surface	characteristics changing into opposites
(internal transportation)	fire Earth	seat of passions
(external transportation) **Earth's mantle** Senses (enclosing function)	fruit Earth	seat of rampant growth-energy
	Earth form	form destruction to negative image in Devachan
(transfor-mation) **Earth crust** Skull/jaw (repro-ductive)	air Earth	destruction of feeling
	liquid Earth (sima)	expulsion of life force
(product present-ation)	solid mineral Earth (sial)	electricity, magnetism, radioactivity

Table 8.4. The structure of the Earth's nervous–sensory or steering system based on physical and spiritual characteristics (see Table 6.3).

life-giving effect of the sexual organs in the lower abdomen. Without the mineral Earth, this layer would be blown away into space. The plastic magma zone is sometimes known as "sima" because silicon and magnesium predominate here (see Table 8.4).

Presumably the "air Earth," mentioned by Steiner, is located in the lower part of the Earth's crust and the upper part of the Earth's mantle to a depth of 400 km, at the border of the heterogeneous structure of rocks. Underneath this, the composition is very homogeneous, as seismic investigations have shown. In an esoteric sense, Steiner describes the characteristic aspect of this layer as destroying feeling. Every experience is transformed into its opposite, as feelings are transformed into concepts by thinking which has a deadening effect. This layer of air Earth is seeking a way out, like the steam in a boiling kettle. The essential transformation process for the steering of the Earth from observed qualities into their opposite takes place in the air Earth. These three layers of the Earth together form the implementation system of the Earth's "head organism."

In the central area of the "head organism" Steiner distinguishes:

the form Earth
the fruit Earth
the fire Earth.

These should be compared with, respectively, the enclosing function, the external transportation function, and the internal transportation function of the Earth's steering system. These three spiritual layers were formed inside the Earth when the Sun first broke away. I have not come across any description of the exact relationship between these three layers and the physical layers in the Earth's mantle. In scientific terms, the Earth's mantle is a layer with a fairly homogeneous structure which extends to a depth of 2900 kilometres, where the Earth's core begins. The main part of the Earth's mass is concentrated in the Earth's mantle. According to Steiner, the form Earth changes every form into its opposite. The form Earth consists of a substance which turns everything into what takes place spiritually in the Devachan. This is where the negative of existing matter is created. When matter is destroyed, its negative image is created in the Devachan. In this way the form is transformed into its opposite. All characteristics enter the environment. The space itself, which was taken up by the object, is empty.[16] Conversely, looking from inside outwards, the material substance of the Earth is created from the spiritual in this layer. This layer forms the first physical surround enclosing the processes taking place within it. It is interesting to note that in scientific terms, the greatest mass of the Earth is situated in a place which spiritual science considers to be empty space.

The fruit Earth is full of compressed growth energy. Every particle of the fruit Earth is constantly growing, like mould. It increases in size and can only be kept together by the upper layers. It serves the forms of the layer above it, and should be viewed as the life behind this form. A comparison with man's lung function can be found in man's constant need to breathe out carbon dioxide as a rampant plant kingdom would otherwise grow in his chest.

The fire Earth consists of passions. This is a sensitive area which constitutes the source of infinite desires and passions. This area reacts strongly to man's excesses of will and boundless passionate eruptions. This area can break through all the upper layers, and in this way cause earthquakes and volcanic eruptions.

Continuing the parallel with the human chest, the form Earth, fruit Earth and fire Earth correspond with the chest cavity, the lungs and the heart, that is, with the enclosing function, the external transportation function, and the internal transportation function. Transformations take place here which translate matter into spiritual substance, and vice versa. It is the sensory system of the Earth's "head." This is where the connection between the object and the image can be found.

Finally, Steiner names the last three members of the "head organism," which are comparable to the brain and are closest to the Earth's centre:

> the Earth's reflecting layer
> the Fragmenter
> the Earth's core.

These are comparable to the planning function, the measurement function, and the steering function. In Von Gleich's description, the origin of these three layers goes back to the earliest times, when Saturn first broke away from the remaining heat ball of the

Old Saturn metamorphosis. The temperature at the present boundary between the Earth's mantle and the core is estimated to be approximately 2000°C, and the pressure approximately 1.4 million atmospheres. The temperature in the core, which has a radius of 3450 km, and consists of nickel and iron, is believed to be between 3000° and 4000°C, and the pressure approximately 3 million atmospheres. Regardless of the pressure, some scientists believe that all substances would occur in gaseous form at this temperature. As it is not possible to recreate these extreme conditions in the laboratory, it is difficult to imagine the physical processes taking place in the Earth's core. The Earth's reflecting layer transforms all events on the Earth into their opposite. For example, light as it shines on the surface of the Earth is transformed here into electricity. Man's moral actions are turned into their opposite here. The Fragmenter is the basis of all disharmony. Under the influence of the Fragmenter all essential units are infinitely multiplied. This layer also fragments all moral substance. Dante called this layer "Caina," in the depths of the funnel of hell. Here is located the force which results in division, dissatisfaction, conflict, discord and hatred. The development of man towards love and brotherhood is a constant victory over this layer. The planetary spirit has its seat in what Steiner calls the Earth's core. The Earth's core has three organs which are reminiscent of the aspects of the will, love and intelligence, referred to in theosophy, as described in Chapter 6 in relation to the planetary spirits. According to Von Gleich, two of these organs are to some extent comparable with our brain and our heart. On the other hand, the core is the seat of the force of spiritual evil, and thus of black magic. According to Steiner, this is the centre of the struggle between Cain and Abel, related in Genesis 4. This struggle between Cain and Abel formed the core of the so-called "Volcano mysteries" which existed during the Age of Atlantis and were betrayed by practitioners of black magic, thus causing the catastrophic flood of Atlantis.[17] The name "Cain" means "own thinker," and can be found in the name of the underground god of blacksmiths, Vulcan, who was really called Vul-Cain. It is not for nothing that the last Earth metamorphosis is called Vulcanus, when evil will be conquered. With regard to the steering centre in the Earth's "head," Steiner remarked that as in every planet, the Earth contracts in the centre. He describes how, when matter is compressed from all sides towards the centre, strangely it disappears altogether in the centre. To the extent that matter disappears in the centre, it reappears in the cosmic environment.[18]

In the absolute centre of the Earth, matter is dead and becomes spiritualized, just as thinking in man is produced by the digestive processes. It is as though the Earth is speaking to the spiritual world. When this process is extended too far, and the link with the spiritual world is lost, the path is open for black magic. All the layers above serve to protect man against these evil influences which obstruct his purpose. According to Steiner, man's evolution is aimed at transforming and spiritualizing the inner parts of the Earth. Man is summoned by the processes of observation and thinking to liberate himself and the Earth. In this respect it is encouraging that the influence of the planetary spirit, the Christ, reaches to the core of the Earth.

The steering system of the Earth is characterized by the transformations which take place here of material into spiritual substance, of the destruction of life, and of feeling and form. Reasoning from inside outwards, we come across the creation of these phenomena from spiritual aspects. The seething, untamed life force, passion, and reflection, are located here. Spiritual characteristics rooted in other layers must ensure in the Earth's "head" that the destructive forces of black magic directed at the centre are kept in check. The Earth's steering system is characterized by a violent interplay of forces, a dynamic spiritual balance and apparent peace. The Earth's mantle of rock protects life on the surface against these violent forces.

The Earth's "head" remains very mysterious, because Steiner did not write a great deal about these dark processes.

8.4   The Earth's connecting system

The organs which are embedded in man's body, such as the heart and lungs, have in a sense been externalized in the Earth, and this is most clearly revealed in the Earth's "chest." In man, the

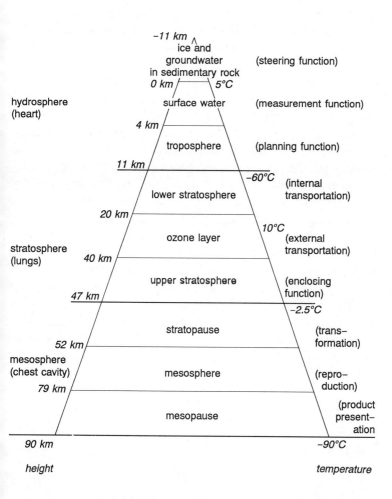

Table 8.5. The structure of the Earth's connecting system.

chest cavity protects the internal organisms from the environment, while in the Earth this is a solidified layer of rock on which the heart and lungs are placed, turned out towards the cosmos. I will now examine the vertical distribution of the three aspects of the

183

Earth's connecting system. A more horizontal division of the Earth's surface will be discussed later. This is very important for gaining a better insight into the function of the Earth's surface, for human activity is directed in the first instance at the surface.

Although it is self-evident to seek the Earth's "head" in the rocky shell, it is not so easy to locate the boundary between the Earth's "chest" and "belly." In seeking a parallel with man, the outer limit of the Earth's chest seems to be the mesosphere, where the air currents of the troposphere and stratosphere come to rest. The Earth's connecting system, the chest, containing the biosphere, is bordered by the mesosphere on the one hand, and the rocky shell, on the other. This closely corresponds to Wachsmuth's spatial description for the Earth's respiratory process.[19] The respiratory process defined by him of the daily increase and decrease in atmospheric pressure, extends to the upper stratosphere with a height of 47 km. The mesosphere, which reaches a height of approximately 90 km, together with the mesopause, acts as the diaphragm of the Earth's chest, encasing and delimiting the rhythmic respiratory process.

As in the case of the Earth's "head," three aspects can be distinguished in the Earth's "chest." As shown in Table 8.5, the functions of the heart, lungs and chest cavity can be recognized in the

hydrosphere (including troposphere)
stratosphere
mesosphere.

These three spheres in the Earth's "chest" together form an organic unity, the Earth's "chest organism," in which nine characteristic functions can again be distinguished, as shown in Table 8.5.

The hydrosphere, including the troposphere, forms the biosphere, the area on Earth where life is found. It is fascinating to see that the biosphere is located in the Earth organism's heart. The heart area, the internal transportation function, comprises the whole hydrological cycle, the ground water in sedimentary rock, the fresh surface water in rivers and lakes, the salt water of the seas and oceans, and the evaporated water in the troposphere which rains on the surface of the Earth. The heart extends from the 11.5 km deep Marianas Trench and the Philippine Trench in the Pacific Ocean to the 8.8 km high Mount Everest in the Himalayas, and from there as far as the boundary of the troposphere or tropopause. At the poles it extends upwards 8–10 km high, and above the tropics 17–18 km.

In the Earth's heart, water and air are in energetic movement, so that nutrients and waste products are transported from the land to the sea and vice versa. This transportation mechanism maintains the important cycles of carbon, nitrogen, sulphur and other elements, in which solar energy is the driving force. This was outlined in a previous chapter in relation to Lovelock's Gaia hypothesis. In *Universe, Earth and Man,* Steiner described how water forms the physical body of the Angels, as is often revealed in ancient myths and sagas.[20] Water vapour forms the physical body of the Archangels, while fire, heat and lightning form the physical body of the Archai. The Elohim, or spirits of the Form, are active in the forces of the weather and the wind, and in the Earth's ethereal body. In this way the Earth's heart is animated by the beings of the higher hierarchies. As stated above, the outer boundary of water is found at the tropopause. This is the area which is comparable to the alveoli in the lungs in the human chest, where the blood takes in oxygen and releases carbon dioxide. Regarding the Earth, there is an exchange of light and heat radiation, as well as the transportation of gases such as oxygen and ozone.

Within the hydrosphere, three aspects can be distinguished: the solid sedimentary rock accessible to water and the polar ice caps, the layer of surface water, and finally, the troposphere above the Earth's surface. Of these, the sedimentary layer is the most immobile, while the troposphere is the most mobile. Sedimentary rock, polar ice and glaciers are reminders of the past, expressed in a series of layers. The steering function of the "chest organism" is formed by the geographical relief of the land, which influences the pattern of rainfall and the speed at which water flows. The surface of the seas and oceans is constantly adjusting differences in height, and acts as a global set of scales, the measurement function of the "chest organism." The surface of the sea is the thermometer of the world's climate and the surface water is also a reservoir in which the fluctuations in the concentration of atmospheric gases and temperatures are evened out.

The temperature of the troposphere decreases at higher levels to approximately −60°C at the tropopause. The atmospheric pressure also decreases from 1 atmosphere to about 0.2 atmospheres. In the troposphere the ratio of nitrogen (78% of the gaseous matter) to oxygen (21%) remains constant. Carbon dioxide accounts for 0.3%. Water vapour is found only in the troposphere. Therefore cloud formation is also restricted to the troposphere. The planning function of the "chest organism" is expressed in the troposphere in the accumulation of heat radiation known as the "greenhouse effect," and the distribution of pressure systems around the globe. The resulting cloud formation determines the reflection of light and influences radiation in the higher layers.

In the stratosphere, the conversion of oxygen to ozone and the respiration of the Earth are key phenomena, just as the transportation of water is the main activity in the hypersphere. The stratosphere stretches from approximately 11 to 47 km above the Earth. The central part of the stratosphere consists of the ozone layer which lies between 20 and 40 km above the Earth. The ozone layer is bordered at the bottom by the lower stratosphere, and at the top by the upper stratosphere. The temperature in the lower stratosphere is virtually constant at −56°C. In the ozone layer the temperature rises to approximately 10°C. Wachsmuth also calls the ozone layer the area of ethereal heat.[21] In the ozone layer a little of the oxygen (O_2) is converted into ozone (O_3) under the influence of ultraviolet (UV) radiation from the Sun. In the upper stratosphere the temperature again falls to −2.5°C.

The atmospheric pressure in the stratosphere decreases to only about 10^{-3} atmospheres at the upper limit. At this point nitrogen and oxygen are still combined in a ratio of 4:1.

In the lower stratosphere there is a more active exchange of substances with the underlying troposphere than the exchange of substances between the upper stratosphere and the ozone layer. In this way, the lower stratosphere fulfils the internal transportation system, while the ozone layer takes care of the external transportation function which consists here of the interaction with the outside world by converting oxygen to ozone with UV radiation. The upper stratosphere, where there is a sharp fall in the exchange of substances and in temperature, in a sense encloses the transportation functions of the lower stratosphere and the ozone layer.

As stated above, the central function of the ozone layer is to combine the UV radiation coming from the vicinity of the Earth with oxygen which is the bearer of the Earth's respiration. According to Wachsmuth, Rudolf Steiner considered that where there is ozone, the life principle can be incarnated. Then the UV radiation converted to ozone is transported to the troposphere, though this only happens to 1% of the ozone that is formed. In addition, the ozone layer protects the biosphere against UV radiation, which is damaging to life.

Van Romunde also considers that the function of the ozone layer is to ensure the proper interaction between the UV radiation of the Sun, the oxygen processes in the atmosphere, and life on Earth, which is dependent on these.[22] As the stratosphere forms the lungs of the Earth, it might be said that the Earth breathes "light," just as man breathes "air."

Wachsmuth also revealed a direct relationship between the Earth's breathing and the stratosphere. He described the respiratory process of the Earth in detail, the area where this process can be observed, and the far−reaching consequences on physical processes in plants and animals. He gives a detailed description of the Earth's force field or ethereal body, which consists of a sphere of which the centre is not exactly in that of the physical Earth (see Table 8.6). This force field causes the daily double wave of atmospheric pressure which has a variation of approximately 0.3 mm mercury pressure at 60° latitude. The maximum peaks occur at 0900 and 2100 hours, the minimum troughs at 0300 and 1500 hours. This is the Earth's own rhythm, independent of its rotation round the Sun. At the same time there is a turning point in daily air movements, and mountain winds or valley winds blow in mountain regions. According to Wachsmuth, the areas where this daily respiration takes place comprise the whole of the Earth's chest area, consisting of the hydrosphere, the stratosphere and part of the mesosphere. In this respect, the characteristic lung function of the stratosphere is emphasized once again. He also points out that the biological activity of organs such as the liver, intestines, kidneys, and gall bladder fluctuate in men and animals in conjunction with this respiratory rhythm.

The mesosphere stretches from a height of approximately 47 to 90 km and is subdivided into the stratopause (47–52 km), the mesosphere (52–79 km), and the mesopause (79–90 km). It is the least mobile part of the Earth's chest, where an increasingly slow movement of air from east to west at the height of the mesopause changes to an even slower movement from west to east. The temperature falls from −2.5°C in the stratopause with increasing height to −75°C to −90°C near the mesopause at 79 km. The temperature remains constant in the mesopause. The characteristic product of the connecting system, the Earth's "chest organism," is the complete standstill of air currents in the mesopause. The characteristic transformation function located in the stratopause is the warming process from −90°C to −2.5°C and the creation of light. Wachsmuth locates the mantle of ethereal light around the Earth, which carries out the reproductive function in the chest organism, in the mesosphere.[23]

The whole of the mesosphere can be viewed as a cold layer which coincides with the enclosing function, the chest cavity function, of the chest area in the Earth organism. Moreover, the mesosphere is the highest layer where the ratio of the most common gases, nitrogen and oxygen, is still the same as in the troposphere. This brings us to the border of the ocean of air above the biosphere, and thus to the diaphragm of the Earth's chest.

8.5   The Earth's implementation system

The intense metabolic activity, which normally takes place in the belly, has a special character in the Earth. In the belly area the Earth accumulates as much radiation from outside as it can, in so

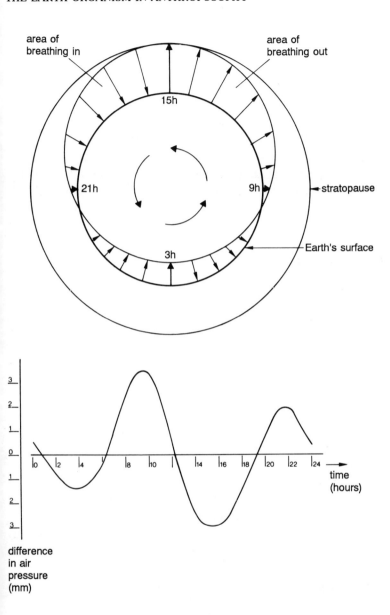

Table 8.6. Influence of the effect of the Earth's form force body on the atmospheric pressure at the equator in a 24–hour period.

far as it can be used, and the excess is radiated back. As explained in Table 8.2, the belly area comprises:

the thermosphere
the exosphere
the magnetosphere.

In the belly area, the thermosphere can be considered as carrying out the Earth organism's transformation function, converting solar radiation into a combination of vital elements for the biosphere; the exosphere as fulfilling the reproductive function; and the magnetosphere as carrying out the product presentation function, thus the limbs of the Earth. I will not attempt to subdivide further the Earth's implementation system, as I lack reliable information in this field.

In the thermosphere, which extends to a height of approximately 550 km, a number of characteristics are drastically altered.[24] Part of the gases (0.1%) start to be found in ionized form as the result of absorption of X-rays and UV radiation. The gas ions have a positive charge and negative electrons split off. The latter reflect radio waves from the Earth's surface back to the Earth. There are several of these reflecting layers which partly disappear at night in the absence of sunlight. The reflecting layers have an undulating surface, like ripples on the sea. In the thermosphere the temperature reaches very high levels as a result of the radiation absorbed (approximately 1200°C). At the very low pressure in the thermosphere of 10^{-11} atmospheres the heat content of the air is very slight. In these conditions, molecular oxygen (O_2) is dissociated more rapidly into atoms (O) than molecular nitrogen (N_2). The result is that oxygen becomes lighter than nitrogen. This leads to a different ratio between these two gases. In the mesopause the ratio of nitrogen to oxygen was 4:1, but at a height of 500 km, this ratio has changed to 1:4. According to Wachsmuth, the thermosphere is the area where chemical ether predominates, where chemical reactions take place, and as we approach Earth from space, the correct combination of atmospheric gases is forged for the lower atmospheric layers.

The exosphere is located between 550 and 2000 km above the Earth. The inert gas, helium, is predominant here, and slowly escapes into space. At 2000 km, it accounts for 90% of the total gases. In addition, there is hydrogen and free oxygen. Helium is supplied to the exosphere by being formed in the ground and escaping from the Earth's surface. According to Wachsmuth, the exosphere is the area where the ethereal life mantle is located as part of the Earth's ethereal body.[25] As discussed earlier, all ethereal and physical matter on Earth was created from this ethereal life. Thus the reproductive function of the Earth can be ascribed to this sphere. In the magnetosphere hydrogen is predominant from a height of 3500 km. The outer limit of the Earth's magnetic field is situated at the outer border of the magnetosphere at a height of approximately 100000 km. The ionization level of hydrogen has risen here to about 25%, while atmospheric pressure has fallen to approximately 10^{-17} atmospheres. This is almost the same as that in interplanetary space, where the pressure is at most 10^{-18} atmospheres, and hydrogen is also predominant. The magnetic field around the Earth is strongly compressed by the solar wind to a distance of about 60000 km, as shown in Table 8.1. This current of electrically charged hydrogen from the Sun is responsible for the extremely long "magnetotail" in the wake of the Earth, which can be measured even at a distance of approximately 10 million km. This magnetosphere and the magnetotail contain the characteristic product of the Earth with which it presents itself in space. The Earth's limbs have a magnetic nature and, as in the case of man's skeleton of calcium, they originate in the Earth's relations between solid matter and magnetism, following the expulsion of the Moon. The Moon, which rotates around the Earth at a great distance, can in a sense be seen as the most solidified form of the Earth's limbs, as its moving feet. Some of the solar wind is found in the areas of the Earth's magnetic poles, which gives rise to the polar lights. This supply of hydrogen in the atmosphere compensates for that which escapes into space.

The thermosphere, exosphere and magnetosphere are described by Wachsmuth as the "outer atmosphere" containing the inexhaustible reservoir of radiation, animation and food for the Earth.[26] It is the area where energy in the form of radiation or waves, is transformed into matter. It is the area of chemical forces, where the production function is located, and where atoms and molecules are organized and fortified into a combination which can be used in the inner atmosphere. In this inner atmosphere or chest, respiration and the heat–driven water cycle pulsate. In the region of the Earth's belly, a disordered situation still exists and the daily fluctuation in the Sun's radiation is much less apparent. In that area of the Earth energy is collected, and those things are prepared which are subsequently received by the chest area and distributed down to the biosphere below. In this way the higher atmosphere acts as a "radiation digestive organ" between the Earth and the Sun.[27] The way in which the Earth's radiation is monitored from the Sun is a scientific field that is still in its infancy. Fascinating observations have been made in these outer regions of the Earth with the help of satellites such as the Japanese MAGSAT, and the American NIMBUS. The Sun's activity has a great influence on magnetic storms in the magnetosphere, for example, years with a high intensity of sunspots correspond with periods on Earth when there were many magnetic storms.[28] Recent research has shown that electromagnetic phenomena in the magnetosphere and exosphere are strongly interrelated.[29] The electromagnetic field is influenced by the magnetosphere as far as the thermosphere. I will return in a later chapter to the possible effects of this, and the effects of fluctuating supplies of hydrogen atoms on the lower spheres of the planet's organization.

9.   The Earth as a mirror of man

Then He, who inspires a feeling of universal amity, raised his voice:
  "There is one amongst you who wishes to serve as your voice. His name? Zarathustra Spitama."

Zarathustra, Yasna 29:9

9.1   The biosphere between two poles

The preceding chapter gave an overall view of the anatomy of the Earth organism. In broad terms, this amounts to a cosmic process in which energy from the Sun is radiated to the Earth, to be changed there by the Earth and everything that lives on the Earth, and transmitted to the Earth's core by a process that cannot be detected scientifically. At the Earth's core, the energy, condensed as matter, is spiritualized. In this concept the biosphere appears as a centre between two poles: the pole of the Sun, shining and radiant, and the dark, concentrated pole of the Earth. In the biosphere, the Earth's heart, there are forces which are rich in energy but which kill life, and which are protected from the cosmos and transformed into life–supportive elements and conditions. X–rays are converted in the thermosphere, UV radiation in the ozone layer and heat and light radiation are regulated by means of the thermoregulation system. At the other pole, the Earth's core, there are also protective layers which keep in check the savage destructive forces of subnatural phenomena which draw downward. In the area between the chest and the heart, which joins heaven and Earth, man's life and nature, which is bound to man, can evolve.

Using the three aspects of the Earth organism's structure, as discussed in the previous chapter, I would now like to try to assimilate the other information which is available. In this attempt, working with the constantly found emphasis on a three-fold division is the main principle. From this broader viewpoint, what was described in terms of particular organs can now be incorporated without the potentially confusing assumption that it has an absolute meaning. For example, the Earth's kidneys, said — by some sources — to be located in the Earth's crust, can now be viewed as a relative concept for the mobile implementation system of the Earth's head, which was described by Steiner as air Earth. Many of the organ's functions thus acquire their significance within the chain of the threefold division, which in itself forms part of a larger threefold entity. The body of man is a reflection of the component parts of the Earth and of the Earth as a whole, or as is sometimes said: the body of man is made in the image of other bodies, only on a larger or smaller scale.[1]

After a closer look at the vertical structure of the Earth organism, using the threefold division as a framework, I will go on to examine these aspects further within the biosphere.

9.2   A closer look at the vertical structure

All the sources referred to in previous chapters concurred in identifying the centre of the Earth as the brain. Other sources locate the steering in the Earth's core, where energy disappears in the centre to reappear in the parallel world. For the same process, Rudolf Steiner refers to the appearance of matter in the Zodiac which surrounds the solar system. Steiner's "reflecting layer" in the Earth's core, where qualities are transformed into their opposite, is closely related to a description of the Earth in a Greek myth, as "the opposite side where the slope rises steeply." It is the border to which Tartarus extends, the area of subterranean ethereal streams extending to the centre of the Earth. Perhaps Tartarus takes up roughly the same area as that which is described as the heart, the internal connecting function of the Earth's head organism, as indicated in Table 9.1.

In this "chest" part of the head organism, it is easy to imagine the rhythmical fluctuation of ethereal, water and air currents. This motor, which is situated in the Earth's mantle, receives and sends impulses via the four large veins which flow like rivers in the subterranean regions. First, there is the Cocytus, which flows through a wild and fearful area, reminiscent of the passions of Steiner's fire Earth. Secondly, there is the fiery Pyriphlegethon, of which the streams of lava are tributaries, and which can be situated in the air Earth and liquid Earth which opens on to the area of the Earth's crust. Thirdly, there is the Acheron which flows through many desert-like regions, and is clearly connected

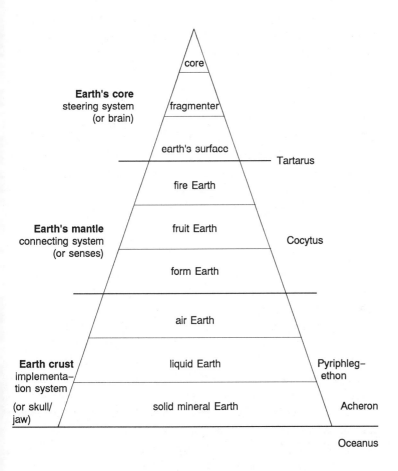

Table 9.1. The structure of the Earth's head in relation to the rivers in Greek mythology (see also Table 8.4).

to the dry solid stony shell of the Earth, while the fourth and largest river, the Oceanus, manifests itself in a wide circle on the Earth's surface. This brings us to the limit of the head, the Earth's skull. It is interesting to note that according to some sources the "kidneys" of the solid Earth are located in the layer of magma on the border of Steiner's air Earth and liquid Earth. It is their function to regulate volcanic eruptions which serve to cast out undesirable impurities from the centre of the Earth, just as man coughs up phlegm. With the help of the anatomy of the Earth that is developed, these kidneys can also be classified as organs for carrying out the commands of the Earth's head organism.

The threat to man of the deadening effect of the Earth's head area is represented in mythology in the Gods of Hades and Hell.

In viewing the chest once more as the connecting system in the Earth, we discover much agreement in recognizing river- and sea–water as the blood of the Earth's heart and vascular system, Poseidon's regions. Some sources also emphasize the essential function of the salt water of the sea as a source of energy for the Earth, though weather conditions are described more as an expression of the Earth's mood than as the heart itself. In Germanic–Nordic mythology, sea–water is seen as the blood of the first giant, Ymir. But the myth of Ymir regards the symbolism of the giant's head differently. As reflected in this myth, the giant's skull is not the Earth's crust, but the starry sky. The teeth in the giant's jaw are the rocks of solid Earth, the brains are clouds and the eyebrows, as a symbol of the nervous–sensory system, are the area in between, the garden of Midgard, where man lives between the mountains and the clouds. It is interesting that the mountains are seen as Ymir's bones, which was confirmed by Mellie Uyldert when she identified the Andes and the Rocky Mountains as the Earth's backbone.[2]

Some sources consider that the ozone layer forms the outer limit of human life, which is confirmed by the classification of the Earth's chest developed in the previous chapter on the basis of anthropological studies. The myths no longer use concrete images for the higher layers of the atmosphere. They refer to these areas by the names of the gods, such as Zeus and Odin, with regard to the chest area, and Chronos and Börr for what I called the belly area, or the Earth's implementation system. The characteristics of these gods reveal that for large areas of the Earth's surface there are other dimensions. Space has not un-folded there yet, and time (Chronos) is beginning to exist. This suggests that what Steiner said in this respect about the limited scope of application of our four dimensional time–space continuum, also has a basis in mythology (see Table 9.2).

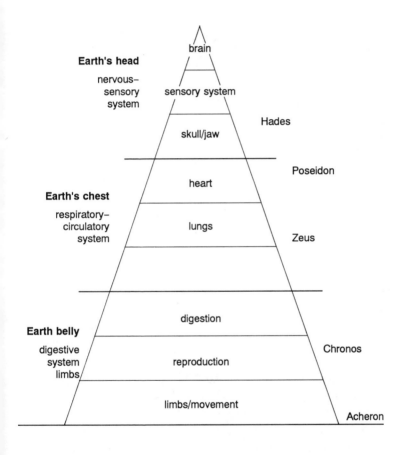

Table 9.2. The area of operation of the Greek gods in the body of the Earth.

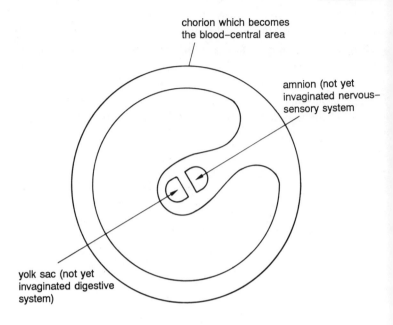

chorion which becomes
the blood–central area

amnion (not yet
invaginated nervous–
sensory system

yolk sac (not yet
invaginated digestive
system)

Table 9.3. The polarity of the head and belly in the embryo during the second week.

9.3   Towards a horizontal classification

The surface of the Earth and the landscapes which can be discerned on it are closer to our own experience than the large scale of the Earth's vertical anatomy. I will now move on to a smaller scale, and try to find out how the principle of the threefold divisions applies to life on the Earth's surface. If man's organization is actually a summary of nature around us, it should not be too difficult to find the same organizational principles in nature as are present in man.

However, this does give rise to some complications, because the connecting system — or chest area — cannot be immediately identified on the Earth's surface. This is also the case in embryology, as Jan Diek van Mansvelt explained to me. In the embryo, the nervous–sensory system and digestive system already exist in the second week in the form of the amnion and the yolk sac, as shown in Table 9.3. However, what is lacking up to the end of the second week is the central area which surrounds the amnion with the embryo as the chorion. Up to that moment the heart still surrounds the head–belly as a central area. After the second week there is a connection between the amnion and the yolk sac from which the central area is formed (see also Table 4.7).

The Earth's surface is now similar to this stage of embryonic development. The continents of the northern hemisphere between approximately 30° and 60° latitude north of the equator form the centre of consciousness because the largest part of solid Earth and of mankind is located there. There is relatively little land in the region between 30° and 60° latitude south of the equator. This region is dominated by oceans, so that it can be seen as the digestive centre of the Earth's surface. The area around the equator with tropical rainforests does not form a clear rhythmic central area. In fact, this is found in the atmosphere which functions as a central area folded outwards like the chorion for the embryo. It is comparable to the stage at which the ethereal body has not yet united with the physical embryo. The spiritual organs of the heart and lungs have not yet been incarnated and, as it were, float outside the embryo. However, this view of the Earth in two parts, and the central area as an enclosing cosmos, is not the only possible view. Its scope of application seems to apply to an observer who has not yet arrived on solid Earth, but observes the Earth from the ethereal sphere. This means that a vestige of the vertical classification remains. Descending further towards a fixed Earth sphere, we should also recall the image of the organs on the Earth's surface briefly outlined by Mellie Uyldert. Her image corresponds with the above with regard to the digestive centre which is located in the southern hemisphere. Adding to this the backbone formed by the vertical mountain chain of the Rocky Mountains down to the Andes in North and South America, we come up with a human figure spread over the entire Earth's surface.

Just as man consists of two–thirds of water, water also accounts for two–thirds of the Earth's surface. In geological terms the Earth is unique among the planets, in that the solid continents rise above the oceans. In fact all the planets consist of basalt which is found on Earth in the ocean bed. The lighter rock, diorite, is formed by the absorption of water and sedimentary layers, after being melted in the Earth's mantle.

The continental plates, which are composed of diorite, are about 40 km thick, while the oceanic plates are 6 km thick. These lighter continental plates float on the underlying magma,

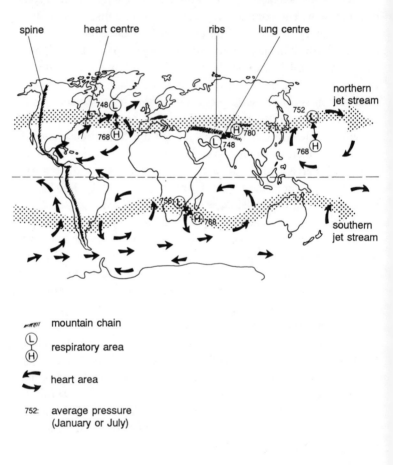

Table 9.4. Skeleton and chest organs of the Earth's surface organism.

and on average protrude 4 km above the ocean bed. Thus without the oceans on our planet the continents could not have formed, nor life on land.

Steiner pointed out how in contrast with the north–south orientation in the western hemisphere, all the mountains in the eastern hemisphere are oriented east–west.[3] Thus mountain chains running from north to south on the American continents form a cross with the Eurasian mountain chains running from east to west. According to Steiner, this structure was transferred to Earth from the Old Moon metamorphosis. He indicated that the forces responsible for this should be sought in the Moon gnomes, the precursors of the Earth gnomes. They transferred the solid matter of the earlier Old Moon into the solid matter of Earth. The cross was made on the Earth in a single movement during the most recent Alpine formation. A band of mountains can be seen in the Pyrenees, the Alps, the Carpathians, the Caucasus and the Himalayas, which is reminiscent of the ribs in the human chest cavity lying across the vertical spine. The axis of the spine lies between 60° and 120° longitude west, with Central America as a hinge at 90° longitude west. Exactly opposite this, at 90° longitude east, is the summit of the mountain range running from west to east, formed by the Himalayas, which rise up to 8800 metres high. In this arrangement, the Urals can be compared to the human sternum. Thus the Eurasian continent forms the chest cavity of the Earth's surface organism. It is therefore clear that the heart and lungs should be sought in this chest area (see Table 9.4).

With the lungs as the respiratory centre, the obvious areas are those where the rhythmic differences in atmospheric pressure are greatest. Hagemann suggested that a small number of respiratory centres could be identified on the surface of the Earth.[4] For this purpose he compared the most frequent high pressure and low pressure areas in January and July (see also his Table 29, plate 4). The area with the largest changes in atmospheric pressure lies between the Persian Gulf and the Gobi Desert. In this area the Earth breathes in and out deeply with a minimum atmospheric pressure of 748 millibars per month, and a maximum of 780. A second important centre is situated above the North Atlantic

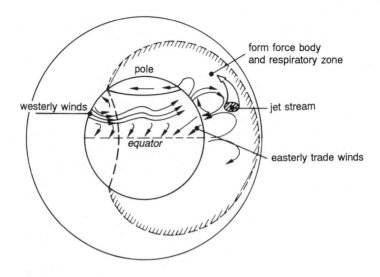

Table 9.5. The three aspects of the circulatory process in the atmosphere.

Ocean with a winter low pressure area to the southwest of Iceland, and a summer high pressure area near the Azores. A parallel breathing centre can be found above the northern Pacific Ocean.

In the southern hemisphere the difference between summer and winter is much less obvious. There is a weak respiratory centre to the southeast of Africa.

Hagemann also indicated that these respiratory centres often fulfil an important function in the history of mankind. The centre near South Africa lies on the site of the former Lemuria, the centre above the northern Atlantic Ocean is where Atlantis was situated. The Central Asian centre was the cradle of the Indian civilization at the start of the post Atlantean era.

Thus, the Central Asian respiratory centre may be viewed as the central point of the lungs, or external transportation function of the Earth's surface. The variation in atmospheric pressure is the result of air circulation on the northern and southern hemispheres. Wachsmuth shows that in both hemispheres three aspects can also be distinguished in the circulation of air with reference to the polar areas, temperate regions and the equatorial regions.[5] In turn, the circulation of air forms an important driving force for the circulation of water in the oceans. The intensity of the air currents is less from the equator towards the poles (see Table 9.5). Another phenomenon plays a role in this, known in meteorology as "jet stream." These powerful subtropical air currents occur on both hemispheres just below the tropopause about 10 km above the Earth's surface, usually at about 30° latitude. The jet stream snakes its way round the Earth's surface, and the air stream can attain a speed of 70 metres per second, or more.[6] A jet stream is maintained by the air moving from the equator to subtropical high pressure areas and some of the air maintains its westerly direction as a result of the Earth's rotation. Jet streams are particularly powerful in winter when there is a great difference in temperature between the equator and the poles. Changes in the path of the jet streams around the Earth can have a great effect on climate and on water currents in the oceans. Some experts even attribute the downfall of the Mycenaean civilization in approximately 1200 BC to a change in the jet stream which led to a reduction in rainfall. When the jet stream is weak, it snakes even more dramatically which considerably affects local climates. When a weak northern jet stream is obstructed by the Rocky Mountains or a high pressure area above the islands of Great Britain, this can result in extreme heat in summer and icy cold in winter.

Before tracing the centre of the heart area, the internal transportation function, it is necessary to give a more detailed description of the movement of the oceans. A strong movement from east to west of the warm upper layer of the ocean can be found directly to the north and south of the equator, both in the Pacific Ocean and in the Atlantic Ocean. These so-called north and south equatorial currents continue to depths of 400–900 metres, in which the water has a temperature of 10° to 30°C.[7] The speed of the current amounts to approximately 1.2 km per hour. The colder layers below move much more slowly. The powerful currents are stirred up by the easterly trade winds which blow in these regions. As a result of the shape of the oceans in relation

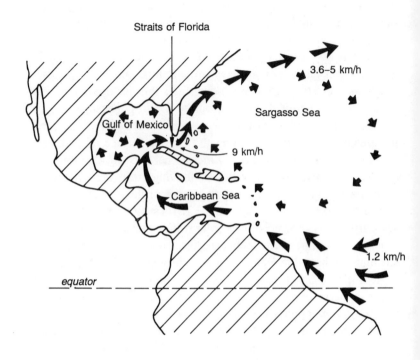

Table 9.6. The propelling force of the Gulf Stream after passing the "heart" of the Earth.

to the continents, the Gulf Stream in the Atlantic Ocean has a special significance in relation to the comparable, though slightly less strong, Kuro–Shio Stream in the Pacific Ocean. Because of the Rocky Mountains, the current in the northern Pacific Ocean cannot exert as great an influence on the land as the Gulf Stream does in Europe. The Gulf Stream is extremely strong and is formed when the south equatorial and north equatorial stream along the north coast of Brazil come together, as shown in Table 9.6. Some of the stream, which extends across a width of 5400 km and is 500 metres deep, feeds into the Caribbean Sea and the Gulf of Mexico. A smaller part takes a northerly direction to–

wards Florida. From the Gulf of Mexico the stream bends eastward and is forced through the straits of Florida. Between the
east coast and the west coast of the tip of Florida, there is a
difference in the water level of the sea of 19 cm. At this point
the water bends to the north through the narrow channel of
Bimini, with a powerful current of 9 km per hour over a depth
of 700 metres. This current is three hundred times stronger than
that of the largest river on Earth, the Amazon. The Gulf Stream
then broadens out and flows up the east coast of the United
States, then to bend away further and further east. This is the
result of the dominant westerly winds supported by the jet stream
and the force exercised by the incoming cold water from Lab-
rador and Greenland.

When it crosses over to Europe, the speed of the Gulf Stream
is still 4–5 km per hour, and then it divides into three. One
branch goes to the south, forming the circular flow around the
Sargasso Sea. Another branch flows northeast to Iceland and
Greenland. The main branch surrounds the islands of Great Britain and travels via the coast of Norway as far as the Barents Sea.
The climate in the whole of Europe as far as the Urals is influenced by the Gulf Stream. About 30% of the solar heat which
reaches the northern Atlantic Ocean is transported to northern
Europe in this way. This results in moderate temperatures, as
well as a relatively high rainfall, which encourages abundant
vegetation. The Gulf of Mexico and the Caribbean Sea function
like a large heart with the centre to the north of Brazil in the
Caribbean Sea. The ventricle is the Gulf of Mexico, from which
the Gulf Stream arises in the Straits of Florida, like the aorta.
Moreover, the two heart centres of the Gulf Stream and the
Kuro–Shio Stream are linked by a current of extra salty water.
This runs across the bed of the Atlantic Ocean to the south,
around Africa, through the Southern Indian Ocean, and resurfaces
in the northern Pacific Ocean. This girdle transporting heat and
salt is caused by the surfeit evaporation in the Gulf Stream area,
which means that salt water flows down to the bottom.[8] Researchers have found indications that rapid climatic fluctuations may
have been the consequence of small changes in the distribution
of surface and deep ocean currents.[9] In Europe particularly,

changes in the Gulf Stream can have a great effect on the climate.

The atmospheric area dominated by the Gulf Stream, which runs from the Gulf of Mexico as far as the Urals and Europe, can be viewed as the main "heart" area on the surface of the Earth, while in Asia the high peaks of the Himalayas are the "lung" area *par excellence*. In the Himalayas the above–mentioned surrounding central area and the respiratory process, which is bound to the surface of the Earth, touch each other.

Having identified the backbone, chest cavity, heart and lungs, the remaining body functions remain to be found. The tropical rainforests, together with the oceans at the same latitude, un–doubtedly form the centre of the digestive and metabolic pro–cesses, the growth of vegetation and the production of oxygen and water vapour. The areas surrounding these, such as the African savannah, offer the greatest variety of living conditions, and accommodate most species of plants and animals. As such, it could also be seen as the present reproductive centre, although in earlier times the origin of the species took place particularly in the above–mentioned respiratory centre in the area where Atlantis once lay. According to Hagemann, the breeding place of the most important plants to be cultivated and animals which are bred for food lay near the Central Asian respiratory centre.[10] However, to maintain a genetic diversity, man is now mainly dependent on the tropical rainforests and the adjacent areas.

According to the principle of the threefold division, the centre of movement may be expected to be near the South Pole. Al–though the South Pole itself, with its large masses of ice, seems immobile to us, geologists have recorded large shifts in the continents, particularly in the southern hemisphere. During the formation and later the break up of Pangaea there was a greater movement of continents near the South Pole than at the North Pole. This applies particularly to South America and Australia, which first moved from the equator to the region of the South Pole, and then moved apart during the Triassic period.

I will now look for the "head" of the Earth's surface in the North Pole area. The polar icecap springs to mind, for its layers constitute a memory in the form of precipitation from many centuries gone by. Like sedimentary rocks, layers of ice bear silent witness to events from the past. Thus the polar icecap is valuable for archaeological research. The ice forms the excretory product of atmospheric processes. It floats in the cold water of the Arctic Ocean, unlike the ice at the South Pole, which lies on the Antarctic continent.

I cannot yet determine the extent to which polar ice, fed by rainfall and dissolved as it melts and crumbles, has an effect on determining the direction of internal and external transportation functions. However, it does not seem unlikely that it contains a crucial steering mechanism, and that the steering function is determined by the amount of ice deposited, the measurement function corresponds with the precipitation at the poles, while the planning function coincides with the separation of icebergs and cold melted water feeding the deeper oceans and also affecting the Gulf Stream and the Kuro–Shio Stream. In this way the North Pole monitors the thermoregulation and climatic processes of the Earth's surface, in which the above–mentioned saltwater current on the ocean bed is an important mechanism.

Another mechanism which supports the steering function of the North Pole is the influence on the climate of the Earth's magnetic field. For example, fluctuations in the strength of the Earth's magnetic field correspond to fluctuations in temperature.

In this process the rotating Gulf Stream and Kuro–Shio Stream can be viewed as electromagnets, and the rotating ocean currents seem to be wound up whenever the Earth's magnetic field increases sharply. As a result the heat is distributed more evenly over the globe.[11] When there is a decrease in the magnetic field, the opposite effect takes place. This mechanism explains how changes in the Sun's activity, and also in the Moon's position, ultimately affect the weather on Earth by influencing the constantly changing magnetism of the Earth. Steiner also mentioned this connection at the beginning of this century.[12]

This analysis produces a picture of the Earth in which the head is formed by the North Pole, to some extent reflected in the South Pole, the chest cavity is spread over North America and Eurasia, with the Gulf Stream and the Kuro–Shio Stream forming the motors of the internal transportation system, and the

Himalayas as the most important external transportation function. The parallels of the heart and lungs are found in other places on the Earth's surface in a less evident guise. The belly, with the digestive and reproductive functions, can be found in the continents on the southern hemisphere, and the tropical rainforests, particularly in Brazil, safeguard the wealth of species of plants, and are responsible for digestion, together with life in the oceans at the same latitude. The essential transformation process of the Earth's surface is the conversion in the tropics of light and carbon dioxide into oxygen and organic matter by means of photosynthesis. Antarctica and Australia are the exponents of the movements in the Earth's crust in the region around the South Pole. The characteristic products of the Earth's surface identifying it as an organism are fossil fuels, particularly coal, which is also found in Australia. Derived from this is the occurrence of coral islands deposited by coral polyps.

Steiner described how man owes the capacity for physical movement to the solid Earth metamorphosis.[13] Metabolism in the body enclosed by skin is possible because of the liquid Old Moon metamorphosis. Earth owes its respiratory and circulatory systems to the air radiated with light of the Old Sun metamorphosis, while man owes his nervous–sensory development to the Old Saturn metamorphosis of the Earth, which was dominated by heat. Thus we find the heat processes in the Earth's head, the light and air processes in the Earth's chest, the liquid processes in the Earth's belly and the solid processes of the movement of continental plates and the formation of sedimentary rock in the limbs. This completes an outline of the north–south anatomy of the globe.

9.4   The east–west classification

With regard to mountain chains, an east–west direction was discerned as well as a north–south direction. In a cultural respect, there also appears to be an east–west orientation in the patterns of the surface organism of the Earth.

Basing himself mainly on the most densely populated northern hemisphere, Steiner divided the Earth into three cultural areas:

the American culture, the Central European culture, and the Eastern culture.[14] He compared these cultures with the spiritual character expressed in the three creatures representing the three aspects of man. For the head this is the creature of height and of thinking, the eagle, which also represents the outer planets. For the chest, the rhythmic processes, it is the lion which also represents the Sun. For the belly, or digestion, it is the bull or cow, which represents the inner planets.

Western culture is particularly sensitive to the character of the eagle. According to Steiner, since the fifteenth century man has been exposed to the increasing temptation to let the head dominate the activities of the chest and belly. This is the period when America started to develop. That which man wishes to retain in the areas between, the rhythmic area of respiration and the circulation of the blood, the light of the atmosphere, is expressed in the ancient cultures of Europe. Finally, eastern civilization is particularly in danger of allowing the heaviness of the cow to dominate, to be dominated by digestion, by analysis with "scales, measures and numbers" as a sort of science of initiation. According to Steiner, the worship of the higher astral processes which take place in a cow, is the real reason for the Hindu worship of the cow.

This cultural east–west division has America as its "head" area, Europe as the chest, and Asia as the belly. Wachsmuth gave a parallel classification according to ethereal climatic regions,[15] as shown in Table 9.7. These are regions in which one of the four sorts of elementary creatures are dominant. These beings, which were discussed in an earlier chapter, are only known to us through fairy tales, but they are still visible to someone with clairvoyant powers. In general, gnomes or root spirits are responsible for the germination of seeds and for plants which grow roots.[16] Nymphs are active in leaf formation, combining and dissolving substances. Then elves bring light to plants so that they are permeated with light. In this way plant figures are woven from light. Finally, spirits of fire bring warmth into the flowers of plants and into the seed which forms from the flower (see Table 9.8). In America the gnomes are dominant. This is the area of ethereal life which gives plants their square–shaped stem.

Furthermore, it is not surprising that the gnomes which are at home in the solid Earth's crust dominate the Earth's backbone. Nymphs are dominant in the region of the Atlantic Ocean and on the west of Europe and Africa. This is the area of chemical ether which gives leaves their semicircular shape.[17] To the east of this area to approximately 100° longitude east, ethereal light and elves (sylphs) are dominant, which gives leaves a triangular shape. The fact that the ethereal light area coincides with the respiratory centre above the Himalayas, provides a fitting parallel with the air and light processes described in the previous para-

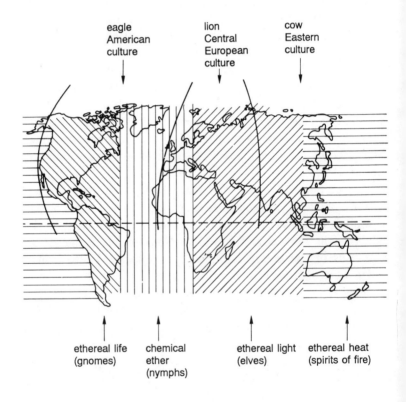

Table 9.7. Ethereal climate and the three cultural areas in the northern hemisphere (see also Table 9.4).

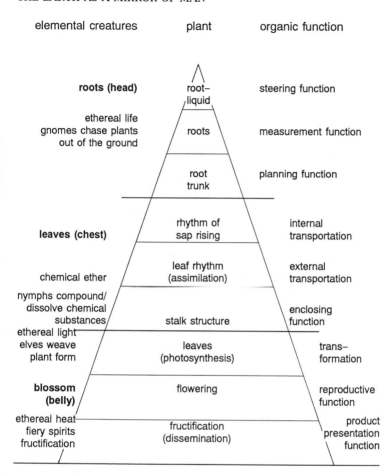

elemental creatures	plant	organic function
roots (head)	root–liquid	steering function
ethereal life gnomes chase plants out of the ground	roots	measurement function
	root trunk	planning function
leaves (chest)	rhythm of sap rising	internal transportation
chemical ether	leaf rhythm (assimilation)	external transportation
nymphs compound/ dissolve chemical substances	stalk structure	enclosing function
ethereal light elves weave plant form	leaves (photosynthesis)	trans- formation
blossom (belly)	flowering	reproductive function
ethereal heat fiery spirits fructification	fructification (dissemination)	product presentation function

Table 9.8. The threefold structure of plants and the effect of elementary creatures.

graph, which form the origin of the chest area of man and the Earth. East of the Himalayas, in the Pacific Ocean, as far as the mountain chains of the American continent, ethereal heat and the fiery spirits or salamanders are dominant. These go with the round leaf shape.

Thus we found the gnome and ethereal life in the head area, which is dominated by thinking, and the fiery spirits and ethereal heat in the Asian belly area. Chemical ether and ethereal light dominate in the European area in the same way that they are dominant in the central part of the plant. The cultural division between east and west actually has a strongly economic character at the moment. The economy is steered in the United States, while it is exercised in Asia, as shown in the labels of many articles: Made in Hong Kong, Taiwan, and so on. This economic classification into three areas is parallel to the physical classification of the west and east in the northern hemisphere into three parts, with the Rocky Mountains as the crown of the skull, and the Malay Archipelago, together with Southeast Asia as the belly area. In this area the product presentation function can be recognized in the wealth of islands which characterize the east coast of Asia, with Japan as a clear example.

The tropical island of volcanic origin is the product in which the physical surface organism of the Earth is revealed. It reminds one of the paradisiacal island in the Garden of Eden. It is curious that the east–west polarity referred to above is reversed with regard to religion. With regard to this aspect, the east is dominant. Again we see that the physical polarity is reflected in the spiritual polarity. I will discuss the deeper causes of this in a later chapter. All these ideas suggest that the heart, the internal connecting organ of the global organism, is situated in Europe when the classifications in the vertical direction, north–south direction, and east–west direction are combined. At this stage of the Earth's development the connecting internal centre is situated there. It is the central area, above all, which must harmonize the east–west and north–south polarities.

9.5   The interaction of the continents

The continents have developed their own organic character, harnessed between the north–south and east–west polarities indicated above. In broad terms, three pairs of north–south areas can be distinguished. In the west, there are North and South America, in the middle, Europe and Africa, and in the east, there is Asia to the north of the Himalayas, and the rest of the Asian continent south of the Himalayas as far as Indonesia and Australia. This rather unusual classification is again based on the

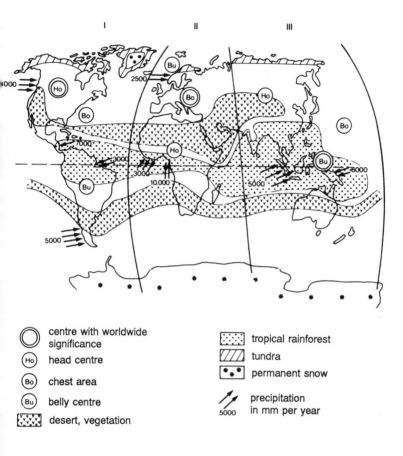

Table 9.9. *The threefold division in the three pairs of continents on the Earth's surface.*

principle of the threefold division. There are two oceans between these three pairs (see Table 9.9).

The shores of the mainland are always seen as a "head" or steering centre for the oceans, while the oceans — dominated by strong currents — are the chest area, and the areas with fewer currents, such as the Sargasso Sea, form the belly centre.

Massive quantities of algae acting as a gigantic digestive

213

system grow there. Hagemann explains how this results in a surfeit of heat, as in the belly of an animal.[18] Comparable systems can also be found in other places in the oceans, forming links between the pairs of continents. The tropical rainforests of the equatorial areas are a general characteristic of the three southern parts of the pairs. The vast expanse of tropical rainforests in a single huge area is most apparent in South America, and least developed in Africa. This phenomenon can also be found in the area stretching from Southern Asia to northeast Australia, though it is fragmented over the numerous islands between these areas. It is clear that where water from the ocean is directly available to feed the vegetation with life–giving blood in the form of rain, the vegetation is much better protected against the encroaching desert. The tropical rainforest is dependent on rainwater, but at the same time it is also an essential factor in areas threatened by desertification, by producing rainfall as a result of evaporation. This process has undoubtedly been most affected in Africa, while it is the most intact in the Malay Archipelago.

In places where radiation from the Sun is no longer compensated for by cloud formation and precipitation, there is a greater danger of desertification. This is found in areas to the south of the tropical rainforest in each of the three southern continents. Their geographical position and the fact that unfavourable prevailing winds and high mountain ranges restrict the rainfall also greatly contribute to this process. The three southern desert areas are located in southern Argentina, Namibia and Central Australia. There are also desert areas to the north of the tropical rainforest area. Because of the changing position of the continents in relation to the equator, the following deserts are found in the southern parts of the three southern continents: the northern desert in the west lies in North America in the states of California, Arizona and Utah at 30° latitude north. In the middle, the desert area is still in Africa at about 25° latitude north, while in the east the northern desert area has developed at 45° latitude north.

As a result of these shifts, the differences in the polarities in the continents in the northern hemisphere are greater than those in the southern hemisphere. In this respect it is particularly noticeable that there is no desert in Europe, unlike any of the other five continental areas. A further investigation of the two American continents reveals that the polarity of this pair consists of the head in North America, dominated by mountains, deserts and ice, and the belly in South America, dominated by the forests of the Amazon Basin. It is not really possible to locate the chest on the land, and as discussed earlier in this chapter, this is found in the drainage area of the Gulf Stream. The central area consists mainly of ocean waters.

In the pair comprising Europe and Africa, the continent of Africa is more dead, dominated as it is by the deserts of the Sahara and the Kalahari. Europe with its temperate climate, countless small and medium sized rivers, and parallel to the prevailing westerly winds and mountain chains, is very much a central area. The digestive centre could be located in the warm sea–water of the Gulf Stream, which ensures a wealth of animal life along the northern edge of Europe, unique at this latitude.

The head of the central pair of continents is situated in a warm equatorial area, while in the western continents it was in a cold area. The chest, which is situated in America in the oceanic waters of the Gulf Stream, lies on the mainland in the central continents. The digestive area, located in the Amazon Basin for the Americas, can now be found in the North Sea and Norwegian Sea. There is yet another distribution of the threefold division in the continents of the east. There, the head can first be found in the north Asian continent with the Gobi Desert and the Hima-layas. The area to the south of this, stretching from the Ganges and Mekong Basin, to Malaysia and Indonesia, and as far as Australia, can be characterized as the digestive centre. As in the American continents, the chest area is to be found in the Pacific Ocean with the Kuro–Shio Stream and the North Pacific Stream leading from this. In the head of North America, the mountain chains run from north to south, but in the Asian head, they run in an east–west direction. In the west, the belly is located on land; in the east, it is spread out over many islands. In this way the polarities alternate rhythmically, going round the Earth from the west to the east. However, this rhythmical alternation is broken when we move from the east to the west across the

Pacific Ocean. This time the same polarity of the head in the north and the belly in the south is repeated. It is striking to see how the Earth seems to compensate for this lack of harmony by the huge expanse of the Pacific Ocean and the folded mountain chain of the Rocky Mountains down to the Andes, rising up from the ocean like a wall from north to south.

Thus the three pairs of continents together, and with the oceans between them, form an organic unit which is a more detailed expression of the north–south polarity which can be discerned in the surface organism of the Earth. Apart from the polarities described above, there are of course other less obvious polarities. I will merely give a general indication of these for the six separate continents.

9.6   North and South America

There is a north–west, south–east polarity in the North American continent, which is most evident at 30° latitude north, as shown in Table 9.10. In the west the landscape is warm, dry and mountainous with cacti, culminating in the Grand Canyon, where the head is situated. Towards the southeast, rainfall increases and there is a moist subtropical climate. The Gulf Stream is largely responsible for this. This polarity decreases towards the north, where the above–mentioned larger scale north–south polarity becomes dominant. The tundra is dominant in the extreme north, while Greenland is largely covered by ice.

In contrast with North America, South America is charac-terized by a north–south polarity. Obviously the Amazon Basin is the digestive centre, while the desert area in the south is the head. There is also an east–west polarity from the Andes to the Amazon Delta. However, for the continent as a whole the north–south polarity is more evident. In so far as there is also a north–south polarity in North America, this is the mirror image of the situation in South America. North and South America form a whole, even more than the other two pairs of continents.

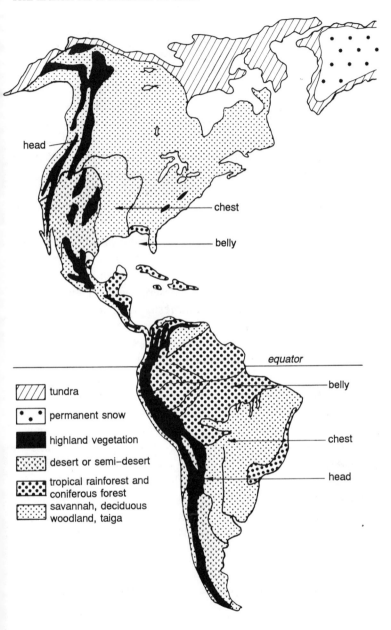

Table 9.10. The threefold division in the two American continents.

9.7 Africa and Europe

The north–south polarity found in South America is even more evident in Africa (see Table 9.11). The dead area of the two deserts in north and south Africa is linked to the living rainforest found mainly in the Congo Basin by the central areas consisting mainly of savannah. Suchantke describes how the characteristic African savannah areas undergo a rhythmic seasonal change. They form the heart of the landscape and change dramatically as the rainy season makes way for the dry season.[19]

During the dry season in winter all life has been breathed in, the trees lose their leaves, and animals hibernate during a period of drought. The air is dusty and full of the smoke of bush fires caused by lightning. However, the vegetation of the savannah is usually able to survive these fires. When the rains come in summer everything shoots up and insects and animals reappear. For many thousands of years the desert has been encroaching upon the savannah and the rainforests. It is characteristic of Africa that the landscapes to the north and south of the equator reflect each other. Unfortunately this means that the desert plays an important part both in North and South Africa.

Europe, which is protected against the encroaching African desert, only reveals a weak polarity, as there are no deserts or tropical rainforests. In general there is a weak north–south polarity. As an extension of Africa, the southern European countries are warm and dry, while most of the rain falls in Scotland and Norway. The central area is dominant in Europe and is characterized from the North Sea as far as the Urals by moderate rainfall and deciduous woodland. The head lies to the south of the Pyrenees, the Alps and the Carpathians. The digestive centre can be found above all in the salt water of the Gulf Stream.

9.8 Asia and Australia

Like Europe, with which it is directly linked, though separated by the Urals, the area of North and Central Asia has a weak north–south polarity, as illustrated in Table 9.12. Again the dead

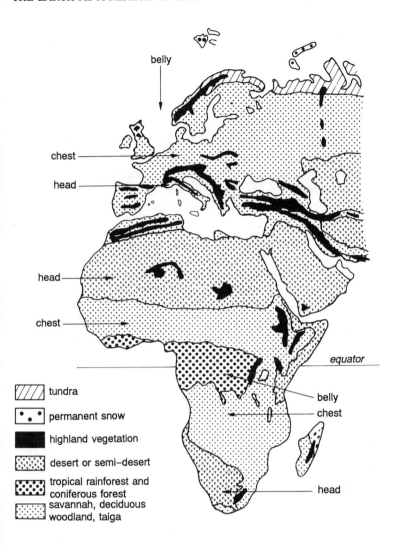

Table 9.11. The threefold division in Africa and Europe.

area is the Gobi Desert and the Tibetan plateau with the Himalayas in the south. Further north, the digestive processes are
predominant and great rivers, such as the Ob, the Yenissei, and
the Lena, carry water to the Arctic Ocean. Although there are

219

greater extremes in northern Asia than in Europe, the average rainfall is clearly lower. The vegetation consists predominantly of taiga, and in the far north, of tundra. This continent can equally be characterized by an east–west polarity. In eastern Asia the rainfall is extremely heavy, as it is in southern Asia in the islands of Indonesia and the Philippines, and on the east of Australia. The rainfall results particularly from the prevailing winds which transport larger quantities of water vapour to the land because the water of the ocean is at hand and temperatures are tropical. It is no exaggeration to view this area, with its average rainfall of 1000–10000 mm per year, and its tropical rainforests, as the most extensive digestive centre on Earth.

In southern Asia a number of large rivers, such as the Indus, the Ganges, the Mekong and the Yangtze Kiang drain away the water. The basins of these rivers, which regularly flood their banks, are very densely populated. This contrasts with Australia, which is very sparsely populated, like most other head centres of continents.

9.9 The threefold division of land and sea

Now that the effect of the threefold division has been clearly shown, and the role of the continents has been roughly outlined, I will reduce the scale even further. To do this it is necessary to review the essential characteristics of landscapes and seas.

Apart from desert areas, the landscapes of the continents are essentially determined by river basins, which can be viewed as huge water organisms. Every large river has its source in a mountainous area where the water from small streams joins together to form a larger one. This is a characteristic process of concentration corresponding with the contraction of the head of the Earth or of a plant. Thus the upper reaches of the river organism form the head. The delta is evidently the belly, often a fan–shaped marshy area where sedimentary processes take place in the shallow water, forming new land. Life and growth take place here. As they flow down to the sea, rivers also have an increasing tendency to move and to meander. The middle reaches of a river often comprise reservoirs in the form of lakes,

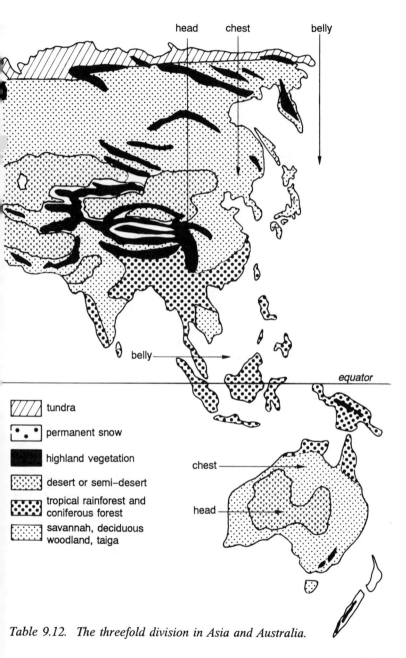

Table 9.12. *The threefold division in Asia and Australia.*

legend:

- tundra
- permanent snow
- highland vegetation
- desert or semi–desert
- tropical rainforest and coniferous forest
- savannah, deciduous woodland, taiga

and storage in ground water, which smooth out and harmonize the differences in drainage levels. The river organism also has other aspects, such as the physical skeleton in which the processes of the flowing water take place, and the life in the water. In fact, there are various systems which all affect each other, just as in man. I will return to this in more detail below. Furthermore, the river forms part of the hydrological cycle.

Steiner extrapolates from the outline given here. He suggests that the springs in the mountains have the same function for the Earth as the eye does for man. The Earth looks at the world through its freshwater sources. The salt sea–water represents something comparable to our digestive organs.[20]

A mountain area can be seen as a steering system for the river, linked by the river itself as a middle area to the sea or ocean. The steering function of mountains in the hydrological cycle consists in causing the air to rise, so that it can then deposit its moisture in the form of rainfall. The course of the river in the air reflects its course on the Earth's surface; it flows in the opposite direction. The function of the sea or ocean is to evaporate the water, maintaining the hydrological cycle by linking the stages in which water is in the form of liquid and water vapour. In this evaporation process, cloud formation is the product presentation function, while the cloud also serves to transport water to the mountains. Clouds are the "limbs" of the evaporation organism, just as rain functions as limbs for the vapour transportation organism and silt for the river organism. The threefold division of the water cycle and the river can be found everywhere on the continent, and is comparable to the threefold structure of a plant.

In salt water there is also a threefold characterization (see Table 9.13). The top layer of water, carrying the river's silt and as an area where photosynthesis takes place, reveals the most intensive metabolic processes and sedimentary formation. The energy contained here is passed on to higher organisms living in seas and oceans as their astral body, via the network of food chains. The digestive centres of rivers and seas converge in the delta area. At a physical level, the conversion function of the ocean organism is actually the formation of solid matter by means of photosynthesis and the sedimentation brought about by

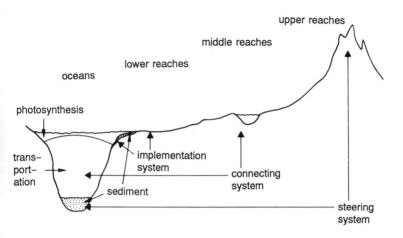

Table 9.13. The mirror image of the threefold classification in river and sea.

rivers. Silt is a typical product characterizing the ocean's belly functions. On the ocean bed there are also sedimentary layers of the mineral shells and organic substances of creatures. The sediment on the deeper ocean bed can be dispersed when gases are released, producing nutrients which stimulate the growth of algae. This gas formation gives form to the steering function of the ocean bed. In contrast with the system of the mountain, the head is at the deepest point of the sea, while the belly is at the surface of the water.

9.10 The landscape

Finally, we need to examine the principle of the threefold classification on a human scale. The village, the farm, the factory and the town can always be identified as elements in mountain and river landscapes. In most modern landscapes a distinction can be made between industrial areas, residential areas and agricultural or natural areas. In a sense these form the landscape's steering system, connecting system, and implementation system.

223

For a better understanding of these three systems, I will first study the components which go to make up the landscape.

In each of the elements of the landscape it is easy to find a core from which the physical processes are monitored and where everything is gathered together. Examples of this are the farmhouse on a farm, the head office on an industrial estate, and the church and town hall in a square. This is surrounded by the production elements, such as a field full of cows, woodland or cultivated land for a farm, factory buildings with their machines and production lines for the factory, as illustrated in Table 9.14. These form the centre of metabolism for carrying out commands. The two centres are connected by transportation and storage systems, such as dirt tracks, a yard, a hayrick or stables on a farm, the asphalt forecourts and warehouses for the factory, and the shopkeepers round the market in a village. In fishing villages the harbour and market square are often found close together. In large conurbations the village square is replaced by high–rise office buildings, while warehouse complexes have taken the place of the market square and agricultural businesses or fisheries have been replaced by industrial estates mushrooming on the edges of cities. This is a physical illustration on a horizontal plane. It is also possible to illustrate each part of the landscape on a vertical plane.

When the landscape consists of vegetation, the vertical polarity consists of the concentration pole in the deeper roots, and the distribution pole in the foliage stretching upwards. In this vertical structure we come across the ethereal element which permeates the horizontal physical organism. The layer of humus forms the central area or diaphragm where forces above and below the ground meet, as we saw in the vertical structure of the planetary organism of the Earth in the hydrosphere and stratosphere. Dead leaves and plants provide information about the previous season for the soil. In fields or woods the soil characteristics and the relief of the land form the physical body. The vegetation is an expression of the richness of the area's ethereal body, while animals, songbirds, deer, foxes, and buzzing insects form the astral body.[21]

This distinction helps us to be aware that we should always

The village and farm

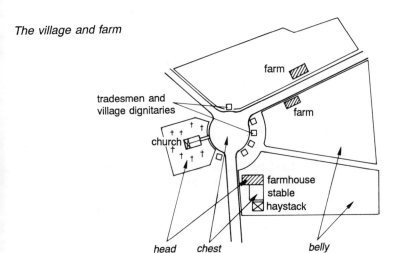

Industrial estate

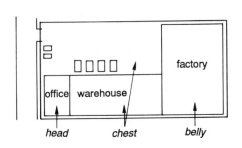

The home

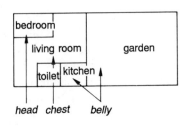

Table 9.14. The threefold classification of elements in the landscape and the home.

see whether a description of an organization is on a physical, ethereal or astral level.

The physical body is actually the "dead" skeleton, just as the chest cavity forms a rigid physical frame for man. Other higher processes take place within this framework, as discussed briefly in relation to rivers. The physical body reveals the ethereal body and astral body of man's individuality. The bearer of the ethereal body is the transportation system of liquid in the form of the heart and circulation of the blood. The bearer of the astral body, the soul, is formed by respiration, the transportation of air. It is a curious phenomenon that the threefold structure of the physical and ethereal organization is reversed for that of the astral organization. The boundary of the physical body lies in the skull, the boundary of the astral body lies in the belly, man's physical body fans out downwards, while the astral body fans out upwards. A more detailed analysis of the threefold organizational structure of organisms again and again reveals this reversal between the physical organization and astral organization, or in other words, the skeletal organization and the functional organization. The ethereal body corresponds to the physical body in its orientation, and can be recognized in the radiation phenomena of the medium which bears the organization's identity. An organization's identity, its Self, can always be recognized in its role serving the larger whole of which it forms a part. An example which came up earlier was the east–west polarity of the northern hemisphere. Its skeletal organization is determined by the continental structure and the nations' position in this structure. The functional organization is determined by the stream of goods and money which form the identity of the economic organism, and which currently has a steering centre in the United States. The astral body which has an effect on all this is still to be found in the spiritual organization of which the steering centre lies in Tibet and the Himalayan region, the belly area of the east–west organism. The economic and cultural poles lie opposite one another.

This reversal of the vertical threefold classification can also be recognized in man's buildings. In one building many organizations are operating together. For example, the physical organization of any building consists of all its rooms in which the temperature is kept constant within certain limits. The transform-ation function in this case consists of creating a spatial unity with a constant temperature. For example, the product may be an of-fice with all its requirements. The central heating installation is the internal transportation function, and the air–conditioning is the external transportation function, which both belong in the middle of the building. The building itself has an enclosing func-tion. The steering system, usually installed in the cellar, measures the temperature, humidity and so on, and when the set limits are exceeded, particular systems switch on and off. The highest steering system consists of changing the set levels themselves. This is a brief outline of the organism of the physical building.

Within this physical building the ethereal or flow organization consists of the people working in the building. These people carry the identity of the organization, the blood of the flow organization. This is clearly illustrated by what happens to visitors. The steering function determines who is admitted and who is not. The porter registers the arrivals and passes them on to the host. He fulfils the measurement function. The host makes the decisions. Then there is a transportation plan for the visitor to reach the host. This consists of the internal transportation function, comprising corridors and lifts. The visitor himself fulfils the external transportation function for people working in the building. The transformation process is a dialogue. The canteen, preferably situated next to a garden, and the physical building, create the conditions for follow–up discussions, fulfilling the reproductive function. The report of the discussion is the present-ation of the product.

In addition, a distinction can be made with the functional or astral organization in the building. The place where commands are carried out, and where the industrial production process is located, is often situated at the bottom of the building. Generally the steering centre, in the form of board rooms or conference rooms, is found on the top floors. This again reveals the reversed direction of the astral organization.

The reversal of the astral organization and the skeletal organization can also be found in the landscape. For example, a river delta functions as the implementation system, while the higher land behind it is the steering system of the skeletal organization. Industry develops particularly in the delta. Man's intervention in the natural landscape has resulted in a reversed industrial organization, when the new astral body ousts the original astral body formed by animals.

The next chapter gives a more detailed account of the landscape, incorporating in an organic way the different elements (city, town, nature and industrial estates) referred to in this chapter.

10. Recreating the biosphere through gaiasophy

> *To which Zarathustra said:*
> *"Almighty God who brings about all things: adorn the earth with fragrant blossom. And give us, the people, pure pleasure."*
>
> Zarathustra, Yasna 29:10

10.1 The task of man in the Earth's cycle

Steiner divided man's life into stages of three periods, each 3 × 7 years long.[1] Up to the age of twenty–one, man's body is developing and his physical body, ethereal body and astral body evolve into a physically adult body and self–conscious individual. During the period between the ages of twenty–one and forty–two, man's soul continues to develop, while his physical functions slowly start to undergo the ageing process after the age of thirty–one. The tissues begin to harden, leading to a reduced flexibility and increased wear and tear. The body is no longer able to perform the same feats of strength, and gets tired more quickly. The slowing down of the digestive processes reinforces the tendency to build up deposits of substances, which can lead to the arteries furring up, an increase in weight, and many other symptoms of ageing. After the age of forty–two the ageing process of the physical body accelerates and man can only continue to develop spiritually. In the present stage of mankind's development this is a preparation for building man's higher Self. I looked at this process in some detail in Chapter 2. For the physical Earth there is a comparable life cycle in each of its incarnations, and also within the individual eras. Chapter 4 indicated how the period of the present Earth metamorphosis is composed of seven small cycles in which the present stage of development is situated in the fourth small cycle. The fourth small cycle comprises seven form conditions, in which the Earth in its present form condition assumes a solid material form, later to become increasingly spiritualized, leaving behind the solid, useless shell. Following the Polar, Hyperborean, and Lemurian eras, which were a repetition of Old Saturn, Old Sun and Old Moon, the Age of Atlantis started as a central era. During this era, the Earth assumed a solid form for the first time, and man was incarnated as a self-conscious being. The middle of the Age of Atlantis can be compared with man at the age of about thirty-one. The physical building processes have passed their peak, and the process of spiritualization has started. The post-Atlantean era, which will last about 15 000 years, has also passed its midpoint. The Earth in its present form is comparable to a man over the age of thirty-one. The ageing process will start to be dominant, and according to Wachsmuth,[2] temperatures will begin to fall in the next millennia, anticipating the new ice age expected after the year 11 000. This will conclude the present post-Atlantean era, and the Seal age will begin (see Table 4.5). According to these predictions, ice ages occur when the spring equinox of the Sun crosses the signs of the zodiac of Libra, Virgo and Leo.

Man's task with regard to the Earth's ageing process which has already started is to ensure that the ageing process does not take place too quickly, and to introduce order where nature itself no longer creates harmony. However, this should be done in such a way that the landscape and the biosphere are treated in an artistic, organic way, according to their character. Nature should not be left to itself, as Jurriaanse and Bockemühl have remarked.[3] After the Fall, which took place in the Lemurian age, the organic unity of man and nature was disrupted. Jurriaanse points out that since that time there has been less and less true natural equilibrium. Up to that time man fed himself through a cosmic umbilical cord, rather like the way in which the foetus feeds. After Lemuria, man fed on fruit and suckled from Mother Earth like a baby suckles at the mother's breast. In Atlantis, man also fed on game he had killed, and used the salt of dead nature. Eventually man increasingly turned to nature for his food. The cultivation of crops, the monocultures of agricultural products, and the breeding of domestic animals became widespread, as did the preparation of bread and wine. Because of the increased gap between man and nature, man felt the need to tame nature and exploit the land. Central Asia, the cradle of post–Atlantean cultures, was mentioned earlier as the centre of the cultivation of plants and animal rearing. In this way man's intervention resulted in a disruption of the landscapes of the central areas on an ever–larger scale, and this was followed by erosion and deforestation. There was an acceleration in the ageing process of the surface organism of the Earth in all areas. Man, placed in the area between the jaw of the Earth's head and the chest area rising up above it, is like the larynx of the Earth, which needs a voice to speak with. It is through man's own voice that the Earth appeals to us to put an end to the injuries and illness, the accelerating breakdown of an organism that should still be at its peak. Which words are needed to show the way to restore harmony to man and the Earth? And which acts should accompany these words? I am holding the keys in my hand, but I will now have to find and open the doors to their practical application.

10.2 Gaiasophy and the principles of disease and cure

In Chapter 7, I mentioned that Steiner sees the cause of internal diseases particularly in the processing of food in digestion. The circulation of the blood as an internal circulation system, and respiration which brings about an interaction with the outside world, are responsible for the healing process. Man develops on this basis.

The Earth is sick. This should allow the Earth and man to develop. Man must help the circulation of the blood and respiration of the Earth's ecosystem to keep the digestive forces responsible for the illness in check, so that there are uninterrupted cycles of substances. It seems very simple, but requires more thought. This is the aim of what I have termed "gaiasophy." Gaiasophy sees the Earth, Gaia, as a living organism, made up of components which each bear a resemblance to human organs. In order to understand this, and act in accordance with this concept, it is necessary to have wisdom, *sophia,* as well as knowledge.

The organisms of man and Earth are seen as the result of a long spiritual evolutionary process in which cosmic relations are reflected and developed.

With regard to the causes of disease in an organism, the hierarchy of bodies or organizations play a part, as well as diet, as outlined in Table 2.4. Disease is often caused by a lack of harmony in one of the higher bodies: the flow organization (ethereal body), the functional organization (astral body), or the identity of the organization (Self) as a link providing a service in the larger whole. In this way our astral body organizes our metabolism. If someone's Self causes him to lead a sedentary life, the astral body may become "lazy," so that the right foods no longer go to the right places and are deposited as waste matter somewhere else, resulting in disease.[4] As soon as the need disappears for a service provided by an organism in our environment, such as a lake, factory or an office, all the subsidiary organizations disappear, the lower bodies become ill and die off. When an office ceases to exist, documents stop arriving and being despatched, the telephone no longer rings, the building is no longer maintained, and eventually succumbs to the disintegrating forces of nature and society, windows are smashed, anything useful is removed, and finally the wind and the weather have free rein.

Diet and disharmony in higher organizations can be responsible for sickness and death. First, we shall take a closer look at food as a cause.

To do this, I will take an easier example than the human organism, such as an aquarium or an airplane, systems which are easy to grasp. In a goldfish bowl the steering centre consists of the surrounding glass, just as the chest cavity surrounds man. The belly, with the living processes of metabolism, is formed by the goldfish. The water acts as the central area, the heart of the bowl, while the surface of the water, where there is an interaction with the air, can be seen as the lungs. In principle, putting too much food in the bowl results in too many fish, which means the water becomes smelly and the whole system becomes sick. This can be counteracted by reducing the food supply and increasing the effect of the heart and lungs. Regularly changing the water produces a strengthening of the internal transportation function, and fitting an air pump reinforces the external transportation function. Obviously the transformation function of digestion will also have to be regulated after some time by limiting the number of gold-fish in the bowl. Too much food causes the system to fall sick. The heart and lungs can make it healthy again within certain margins. The correct level of the system is determined by the bowl, the steering system.

I will now take the example of the airplane. This example is not part of a living system, but a completely artificially created mechanical organization, though the same principles apply to it. The skeletal organization of the airplane also has a threefold structure. The steering function is formed by the panel of instruments in the cockpit. The transformation process, at the centre of metabolism, consists of the cargo space being moved from the point of departure to the place of arrival. The intermediate area is formed by the engines and wings. The engines and fuel tanks are the internal transportation system, which give the plane its power. The wings interact with the surrounding air, so that the plane can be carried in the air. The engines and wings are the heart and lungs, both attached to the body, which is like a chest cavity. The cargo space itself is the reproductive function with which the transformation process, the flight, can be carried out again and again. The tail piece is comparable to legs joined to the belly, and fulfils the product presentation function.

This provides an outline of the physical organism, the skeleton of flight. The flow organization, or "ethereal body" of a flight is related to what happens to the cargo or the passengers from the time that the flight is planned up to arrival at the destination of the flight. The product presentation function is now represented by the passenger, taken to his destination and reunited with his suitcase. Finally, the functional organization (the "astral body") is composed of the personnel of the airline company and their interaction.

In this case "health" can be described in terms of harmony and security, a state of order throughout the system. The functional situation is healthy when the plane is flying on course, according to schedule. The situation is "unhealthy" when the passengers suddenly wish to be taken to a different destination, or if there is more freight on board than was calculated on departure. This results in feverish activity in the cockpit, where the planning function operates to realign the chaotic forces. The sickness can be cured by adapting the speed or altering the course. In principle, the health is best during the flight, from the point of departure to the destination. The flight is under way, and on course, and there is sufficient fuel on board. In contrast, the state of ill health is worst while the plane is grounded. What is the new destination? Are the expected number of passengers present? How much fuel should be taken? What is the weather forecast? How busy is it on the runway? Is the plane still working properly? And so on. As soon as the plane fills up with passengers, starts moving and taxis to the runway, the process of recovery begins and the state of order improves. The cure consists of going to the destination. Sickness results from deterioration or loss in the destination of the plane, the physical organization, in the passengers who give energy and form to the total organization, or in the crew, who animate the plane. When something is wrong with the pilot, the representative of the Self, sickness follows in the crew, the passengers and the plane. Health is restored only when the organization as a whole moves towards the goal, and all levels are working together harmoniously. Life and health are processes which can be described, in Schrödinger's terms, as the accumulation of order from the environment, while sickness and death are characterized by an increasing condition of chaos.[5] This reveals the duality of youth and age.

Now it is time to turn back from these two examples to the sick Earth. What is the matter with the Earth? The metabolic processes are becoming increasingly dominant. Increasing numbers of passengers are stuffed into the aircraft, to use the analogy of the plane, and the stops between flights have become shorter and shorter, without any protests from the pilots. There are passengers who no longer disembark, but travel on and on, because the personnel is no longer checking this and the prices are ridiculously low. For this reason, the support provided by the intermediate area in relation to the weight of the belly is affected, the transformation function is overburdened, and the operational reliability of the whole system is reduced. Sometimes an engine drops off, which corresponds for the Earth, for example, to a period of hardship and drought. When this happens, the sick organism is in danger of dying.

What can be done to effect a cure? Obviously, in the first place the number of passengers should be reduced. The Earth is succumbing to over–population, resulting from the unbridled expression of the reproductive urge. If it is not possible to reduce the number of passengers in the short term, therapeutic steps must be taken regarding the strength and operational reliability of the engines, an increase in the yield of the agricultural sector, as well as to increase the load–bearing capacity of the wings, in other words, reducing the per capita consumption of the population. Furthermore, a great deal can be achieved by taking into account the next destinations when making plans. This will reduce the chaos which occurs after every landing. For the Earth will have to be able to accommodate those who come after us. If there are only flights from Amsterdam to New York, the chance of another flight is greatly reduced. Creating possibilities for many different destinations, creating the conditions for many different solutions to the problems of food, space and control of the environment, will create a healthier situation.

Every example has its limitations. I will return later to the dangers of technology which seeks solutions by enlarging the scale of solutions to smaller problems. The history of flight started with man flying gliders, followed by the Piper Cub, and later the Jumbo Jet. Now he is flying spacecraft to other celestial bodies. The day is approaching when man will have to be capable of controlling without accidents the spaceship which, in a sense, our planet is. To do this the healing functions of the heart and lungs are essential, and a restoration in the balance of digestion, the number of consumers and the bounty of nature. Strengthening the heart function means avoiding waste that cannot be processed, and promoting the recycling of materials. Strengthening the lung function means that materials are only exported from an ecosystem when it is clear that these materials will not destroy the balance of the larger natural cycle. Taking the capacity of nature into account means that man must balance the objectives of his technology with the inner objectives of natural ecosystems, and take these as the starting point for his activities, instead of destroying them in a short time in his passion for egocentric exploitation. These solutions will have to be applied on a small scale with regard to landscapes, river basins, nations and continents, so that ultimately they will also have an effect on a scale comprising the whole Earth. Just as a plant combines cosmic and earthly forces, man must combine the healing force of nature harmoniously with the unhealthy forces of technology. It is technology that is making the Earth sick and at the same time it is awakening spiritual forces in man. Sickness is a strong challenge for us to become spiritually healthy and awake.

10.3 Cell–organ–organism structure

I will merely indicate in general terms how rejuvenating trends can be introduced to the ageing ecosystems of the landscape and the planet as a whole. Basically, this is always a matter of complicated relationships, which often have to be worked out individually. For many people this will be an extremely important task in the future. At this point I would like to compare briefly the principles that have been developed with the Earth's organs described in the previous chapter. In doing this we shall move back from small to large, from the landscape to the planet Earth.

In general, a relationship can be discerned which is comparable to that found in the human body, that is, between the cell, organ and organism. On a small scale, for example, an area of fields, or the farmhouse of a farm, could represent the cell within the organ, the farm. This in turn is part of a mountain or river landscape, the all–embracing organism. Continuing this line of thought, the landscape is part of one of the three components of the river basin, while the river basin itself forms part of a nation or continent. The continents together with the oceans form organs within the organism of the Earth's biosphere. Finally, this forms part of the vertical layers of the planet Earth as a whole. To begin with the organs and cells composing the landscape, it is necessary to make a further subdivision. Therefore I will make a distinction between industrial areas, urban areas, agricultural areas, forestry areas, natural areas, and water areas. For each of these organs in the landscape, I will give a brief description of the processes of sickness and health.

In doing this, my anatomical starting point will be the 3 × 3 classification of man which is revealed in evolution as a mirror image of the cosmos and of our solar system. This structure can be found in every living organization. It is summarized in Table 8.3. In addition, the hierarchy shown in Table 2.4 of the skeletal or physical organization, flow or ethereal organization, functional or astral organization, and identity or Self, also applies. I will begin by turning to the skeletal organization in order to gain an insight into an organic spatial order. In this book it will not be possible to continue this process for higher organizations. However, I will give occasional indications of disharmony in higher organizations as a cause of sickness.

10.4 Industrial areas and urban areas

The industrial area

The industrial area and the urban area are the dominant organs in the landscape. Heavy chemical industries, such as mining industries, blast furnaces, artificial fertilizer factories, textile factories, paper factories, refineries and related chemical industries, are all typical cells of an industrial area. On a smaller scale, traditional industries such as tanneries, and metal or woodworking factories, can be found. Together these form the industrial centre of metabolism. In practice, this takes many different forms, depending on the geographical situation. In principle, this centre of metabolism may be found as a circle surrounding a centrally positioned transportation system, such as the estuary of a river, a crossroads, or a mine shaft. Further in, we find the industrial chest functions where the periphery of the particular geographical location outlines the physical chest cavity. The system of transport routes, such as a sea port, airport, and transfer from rail to road or water transport, constitutes the lungs. The industrial area communicates with the outside world by means of these transport routes. The heart of the industrial area is formed by the infrastructure of energy supplies, water supplies and sewage. In principle, the head can be found nearer to the centre of the industrial area. This receives signals about the functioning of the organs in the belly and chest through a network of measuring instruments and telephone, telex and computer links.

The steering is carried out on the basis of these signals. Apart from steering in the form of commands via this nervous system which can lead, for example, to a selective use of raw materials and energy in the case of air pollution, there is also a more general form of steering by means of a material form of energy, namely, money. Nowadays industrial processes can copy virtually all the physical functions of an organism, from the steering processes in the human head, that is, in the computer, to the product presentation function of the limbs in the form of a car. Table 10.1 shows the structure of the skeletal functions in an industrial area, based on the organization of the human body. In addition, these functions provide a possibility for creating an organic spatial order in the industrial area. The use of heat produced by the waste matter from the digestive processes in the internal transportation function, which was traditionally provided by the public service industries, is very interesting. By means of the so-called heat–energy link, the excess heat produced by a refinery can be used for a chemical industry in the vicinity. In this way some organic cohesion will gradually have to be introduced in the industrial area.

In the industrial area the forces which have a hardening, deadening effect, have free rein. This is expressed by expanses of asphalt, decaying buildings revealing a total absence of imagination, forests of pipes and chimneys, a suffocating stench, steam and air pollution, throbbing engines, screaming sirens, chaotic heaps of rusting scrap metal and structures for storing liquid and solid substances towering over people. The unhealthy aspects of the process of metabolism is often immediately apparent. In the coal mines, the slag is unscrupulously heaped up next to the factory site in hills as large as life. There are clear examples of this in northern France.

In the industrial area, metabolism has assumed a totally dominant position in which a small select number of products are manufactured in quantities for the largest possible market. "Economy of scale" determines whether the industry will survive

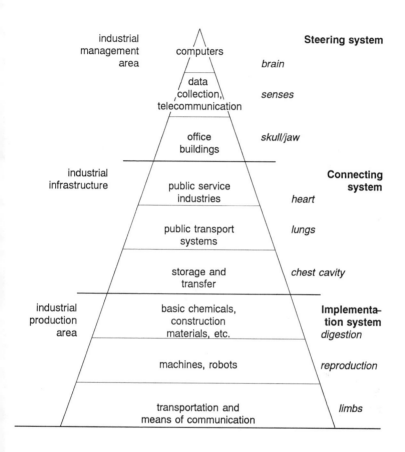

Table 10.1. The threefold skeletal organization of the industrial area.

in the technological jungle. There are monocultures of chemical production in which the chemicals must be prevented from coming into direct contact with nature, or from damaging it. The alienation of technology and nature has gone as far as it can go on industrial estates. This is why men are seen increasingly rarely on industrial estates, where they are replaced by computers and robots. This applies even more to the administration and

239

management of industries and for the engineering offices, banks, accountants and so on, which are working for them. Although the industrial estate is man's "natural" place, he seems to dematerialize in the head of the industrial estate, like matter in a black hole, or in the Earth's core, and then reappears elsewhere in the urban area.

Because of the nature, intensity, and large scale of the processes involved, the insulated, deadening forces of subnatural elements from the centre of the Earth are manifest everywhere on the surface of the Earth. Technology also brings the metabolic processes of the atmosphere to the surface of the Earth without any protection, where they also destroy nature. They are the manifestation of the processes which take place in the belly, revealing what is concealed there. The heart and lungs, which are naturally strongly developed, in places where industrial estates are situated, are unable to curb the digestive violence. Overburdened as they are, they swell artificially to mega–proportions. To provide for industrial requirements, electricity generating stations process gigantic quantities of fuel, thus contributing a major part of the excretion of waste products into the soil, water, and air on a national scale. The landscape is dominated far and wide by furnaces, chimneys and cooling towers belching smoke and steam. They influence the local weather. The same phenomenon arises with regard to the road network, where ribbons of asphalt six or ten lanes wide cover the soil, killing off all local life processes. The chest and belly of the industrial estate have incorporated the deathlike quality of the Earth's head, and are disseminating the misplaced force of death like a malignant cancerous growth.

The urban area
The same process is continued in urban areas. The unbridled metabolic processes are apparent in the ever–larger scale of hypermarkets on the edges of many towns. Apart from government institutions, the centre also contains the head of the industrial areas and the services providing for these, such as banks, organization consultants, computerization firms, and so on. The people who work in one of the two poles settle in between the centre of the town and the industrial estates outside. In resi-

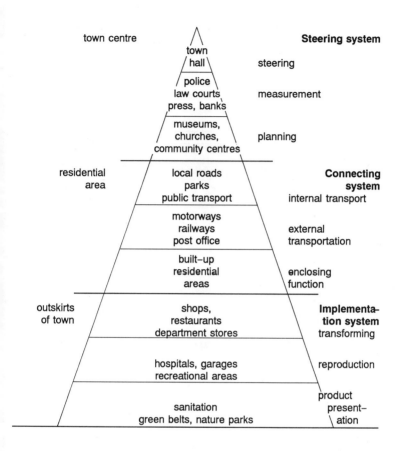

Table 10.2. The threefold skeletal organization of the urban area (with no industry).

dential areas, as much room as possible is left for the rejuvenating force of nature, with sport and recreational amenities on the edge of town, and cultural facilities towards the centre of the town, as shown in the structure for a dormitory town in Table 10.2. Public transport and motorways link the middle area of the town with its centre, and with the periphery.

As in villages, the periphery is characterized by an agricultural centre of metabolism. The original threefold division of the town

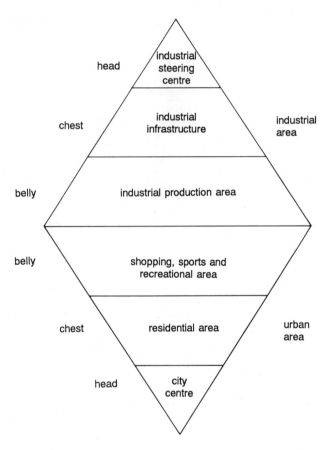

Table 10.3. The living and working areas of urban man between the town centre and the industrial steering centre.

is increasingly replaced by a large–scale industrial centre of metabolism, spreading death and decay (see Table 10.3). Only the wealthiest people can escape the ageing effect that is dominant along the city centre (industrial area) axis, by living in those exceptional areas where the city still has a rural character.

With the growth of the city and of industrial areas the deadening element of the industrial area also affects the living belly centre of the city, and of agricultural and natural areas.

Restoring the health of urbanized areas

Before a city can be cured, the industrial area must be cured. A precondition for this to happen is that the steering mechanism of the industrial area is returned to its proper place, the industrial area itself. Without a head, and the cells related to this, such as offices, shops, restaurants, banks and recreational amenities, the industrial area is an extremely unhealthy and aimless organism. The chest and belly organs should be positioned in such a way that the people working there and in the head can also live in the industrial area itself in an acceptable fashion.

Another precondition of restoring the health of this area is that the "oversized heart" must be cured. Compared with the airplane, used as an example above, to symbolize an organism which needed a stronger heart and lungs, everything in the industrial area is the other way round. There, the heart and lungs have burgeoned and have to be restored to the correct proportions. Regarding the generation of energy, this means applying energy-saving techniques, for example, by means of a heat–energy link, and breaking the monopolies of electricity companies with regard to the distribution of energy, so that small–scale solutions are strongly promoted. In the long term this means turning away from nuclear energy and fossil fuels, where they are needed on an unnaturally large scale, and therefore inevitably cause environmental pollution. Decentralized small–scale energy generators will replace these, such as solar energy, terrestrial heat, wind energy, water power, and — while they cannot be avoided — fossil fuels. Furthermore, we must not give up the search for entirely new environmentally friendly sources of energy and more efficient ways of transporting energy without cables. Has technology really reached the limit in this respect? Was the famous Nikola Tesla (1856–1943) really mistaken when he said that energy could be transmitted very economically without cables, and that solar energy could be used, as well as other forms of energy?[6] The greatly enlarged heart in the industrial area should therefore be transformed into a number of smaller, decentralized "engines" for industry and urban life. Regarding the lungs and the belly, the transportation system and metabolism system respectively, the recycling of waste materials will have to become a determining factor in the nature and intensity of activities. Refuse should only be simply cast on to the ground in very exceptional cases, for looking after this refuse will affect society for many generations to come. Perhaps waste matter should be returned to its place of origin. Everything should be part of a perpetual cycle making life–processes possible in the cells, organs and organism of the landscape. This also implies selective restraint in the mining industry, which Mellie Uyldert describes as the process of emptying the nervous system of the Earth.[7] It is easy to ignore her view, for nowadays we see the mineral world as dead matter, without a specific function for the Earth. But are we on the right track? The lungs, which provide for communication with the outside world by the exportation and importation of goods by land, water and air, will in future also have to give feedback signals about the level of pollution which the environment can tolerate. Nothing can simply be deposited in the environment without causing any harm unless it fulfils a function in the larger organism. Acid rain and climatic change are examples of this.

The balance in the flow of matter must constantly be restored for every cell or organ in the landscape, and the stream of matter flowing in and out should in turn form part of a balance in the larger organism. The best possible balance of matter should be the goal of every cell in the landscape, particularly of farms. For industries this is not possible on a small scale. However, on a larger scale, achieving a balance in processing matter is also essential for industry. The planet Earth as a whole cannot survive if it does not find a balance. We shall examine this more closely later.

In addition, it is essential that the spiritual element is artis-tically expressed in industrial buildings. In this way technology can be spiritualized and humanized. Steiner pointed out that when mineral raw materials are extracted from the natural environment, the elementary beings which held these substances together are driven out and demystified by man. When they are transformed into new substances, these are not without a spirit, but new elementary beings are conjured up. In general, these are lower elementary beings which cause man to forget to be conscious of the spiritual world. The aesthetic value and spiritual expressive power of the form determines the nature of the elementary beings which man conjures up in the substance. In forms dominated by cold technology, demonic elementary beings are conjured up in the substance, exerting a negative influence on man. This is why the design of technological products can be a way to raise them to a higher spiritual plane. In this, there is a challenge in finding artistic forms which correspond with the basic plant, animal and human forms. Art can conquer the dreariness of industrial areas.

Rehousing people in industrial areas, breaking the "oversized heart," controlling cycles of substances by restricting their use and recycling waste matter, as well as providing an organic design for buildings, can all be ways of helping to cure cancerous industrial growth. In the industrial area everything is reversed, in mirror image, just as in the Earth's head itself. The life force of nature must be put into industrial areas through the head and lungs of the industrial organism. By using a spiritual approach to design, the heart and belly can also be cured, provided that the heart and digestion are adapted to the organism's capacity to process waste matter. It is only possible to decide to change to another diet, and find a harmonious balance between nature and technology, at the highest hierarchical level of industrial organizations and the social institutions which supervise the operation. In the final analysis, these are the consumers, in other words, ourselves. Changing the industrial areas begins in the home, and in the last instance, the identity of the service provided by the industrial organism, as well as its planning and consequent procedures and products, are all dependent on consumer wishes. The Earth is sick because the population is not monitoring industry properly, because we are not sufficiently aware of our own responsibility with regard to the mushrooming growth in the direction of large-scale production.

Once industrial areas are restored to health, the step towards healthier urban areas is much easier. The excessive dimensions of the urban head will be reduced by moving some of the offices back to the industrial areas. In the town, saving energy and decentralized generation of environmentally-friendly energy for districts and groups of houses will make a vital contribution to residential areas. In addition, energy will be saved by heating towns in conjunction with industrial areas. In the town the organic, artistic design of buildings in chest and belly areas is also vitally important. This applies particularly to public transport systems which are essential to the heartbeat and respiration of the urban organism. Without good, clean public transport systems, which fit into the structure of the town without disrupting it, the streets become congested with the exhaust fumes from taxis and private cars, and all the attendant unhealthy consequences, such as loss of time and additional air pollution. The inevitable consequence of this development is the increasing use of sound barriers along motorways, ultimately creating tunnels which capture the polluted air and purify it before releasing it back into the atmosphere. Either cars will create less noise pollution and become cleaner and more environmentally friendly, or the environment will be increasingly hedged in by the car. The excessive use of cars and of strongly polluting fuels in houses are the very first ways in which everyone can be aware of how waste products directly affect their own organism and that of the Earth. The use of these will have to be greatly restricted by using and creating alternatives.

A new environmental policy will have to be achieved by self-regulation based on an insight into the functioning of the cells, organs and organisms in the biosphere. By providing a service to the Earth, we are keeping ourselves alive. Moreover, it is self-evident that it is vitally important to bring nature into urban areas as much as possible, particularly on the edge, where rural areas should continue to operate on a viable scale, but also in the chest and head area, where buildings should have a visible, organic link with small surviving natural areas. It is necessary to alternate large and small scales, so that new viable cells, organs and organisms can develop and be maintained within smaller areas of towns. The general pattern in Table 10.2 should constantly recur on a small scale. In principle, every district should present a balanced threefold division with the old town or village structure, consisting of a centre with a church, shops and banks, sufficient room for the chest area, comprising roads, ditches, parks, car parks, and houses, and the peripheral area, consisting of department stores and sports and recreational facilities, instead of farms. The differentiation and individualization of the cells of the urban landscape will improve the health of the total town organism. The large–scale destruction of this threefold structure means that the dead mechanism of technology will become dominant.

Different levels in urbanized areas

A comparison of the structure of village communities in the countryside and modern urbanized areas reveals that the parallel of Table 10.2 is applicable at various levels. A house in a city suburb is like a small–scale reflection of the organization of the town. The nine functions of every living organism can be distinguished. A brief summary is shown in Table 10.4, while the characteristic dimensions of the house, the street, the district, the town, the conurbation, and the megalopolis, are illustrated in Tables 10.5 and 10.6. Table 10.4 shows how the higher levels of the scales have an effect on the lower levels of urban areas. The planning function at a particular level constitutes the steering function at a lower one. We also see how the internal transportation system of the higher level becomes the external transportation function of the lower level. The organic relation between the environment built by man is revealed in this way, and the large–scale organism develops from the component parts of the lower levels. The Dutch conurbation comprises the cities of Rotterdam, The Hague, Amsterdam and Utrecht, while the megalopolis of the North Sea basin with over 100 million inhabitants, is formed by the estuaries in the North Sea of the Rhine, Meuse, Scheldt, Thames and Elba. Comparable areas with a megalopolis character include the Gulf of Bengal and the Yellow Sea, while the Gulf of Mexico is also developing in this direction.

It is interesting to see how, as the level gets higher, its function assumes a wider form. The steering function develops from the bedroom to the village hall, the church, the town hall, the district council offices to the head offices of multinational companies and international controlling organizations. For the external transportation function, there are consecutively the garage, the bus stop, the tram stop, the railway station, the continental airport and the intercontinental airport. The function for

Functions	House	Street	District	City	Con-urbation	Megalo-polis
steering	bedroom	junctions	church	town hall	provincial government head offices computers	transport interchange internat'l. managemt.
measure-ment	meters, larder	pedestrian crossings	police, bank, post office	police, bank post office, press	state police law courts, warehouse	internat'l. law courts
planning	workshop, study	homes	district centres	church, cinema, etc.	city halls, museums, heavy industry	sea-bed mining, internat'l. organiza'ns
internal transport-ation	staircase, storage space	pavement, sidewalk	road network, bus lines, car parks	main roads, tram, bus, metro, park house	gas, motorways, railways, waterways	continental highways, air traffic, express rail
external transport-ation	hall, garage, gas, water, electricity	parking, bus-stops, gas, water, electricity	main road, tramline, gas, water, electricity	motorway, railway, gas	continental highways, sea ports, airports	interconti-nental transport, pipelines
enclosing	periphery of plot, fence	periphery of road area	periphery of district	built-up area	periphery of con-urbation	periphery of mega-lopolis
implemen-tation	living/dining room	lanes for traffic	shops, cafés	department stores, business, restaurant	shopping centres, specialized industry & agriculture	high-tech production
repro-duction	kitchen, bathroom	road signs	service centres, sports field, garages	mainten'ce and sports centres, hospitals	specialist services, recreational centres	popular recreational facilities
product present-ation	toilet, dustbins, garden	manholes, refuse area, green area	sewers, refuse containers, small parks	warehouse, sewage, refuse tips, parks	waterboard, incineration reclamation natural area	chemical waste, islands, waters

Table 10.4. Survey of the functions at the characteristic urban levels.

carrying out commands is represented by the growing trading sector, while the production of basic chemicals and consumer durables develops in the context of the planning function, from the "head" of the vast urban conglomerations. The reproductive function comprises public services and sport and recreational facilities. The product presentation function is characterized by successive steps in the processing of waste matter from toilet to sewage works, and from household rubbish to the specialized processing of chemical waste. In addition, the garden is comparable to the green areas, public gardens, parks, nature reserves, and natural water reserves. A sufficient area of unbuilt–up land is important for the viability at every urban level. Table 10.6 reveals how there are fewer and fewer unbuilt–up areas as we reach the level of the urban house. While the conurbation still contains approximately 80% unbuilt–up land, for the average house this is often 20% or less. The percentage of unbuilt–up land should be an important measure for urban planning at every level, while the functions indicated in Table 10.4 should also comply with the requirements of an organic relationship as regards their location.

Each urban area cannot survive on its own. It functions like a patient in a hospital. From a wide area, food is brought to the urban area to support life. It is only in this way that it is possible to maintain the roughly one hundred times higher population density of urban areas, compared with natural areas. A problem directly linked to this is the large quantity of refuse concentrated at urban levels, which is, moreover, much more damaging than agricultural waste products. The concentration effect of the urban area is clearly shown in Table 10.5, which reveals the parallel between:

farm	house
hamlet	street
village	suburb
landscape	town
river basin	conurbation
continent	megalopolis.

Whenever concentrated refuse cannot be processed in the territory at the urban level, it must be exported to suitable places to be recycled, or to be released into the natural environment in a responsible way. Animal manure from intensive cattle–breeding is a good example of a problem posed by waste products which cannot be solved locally on small plots of land.

The constant enlargement of scale which we find in urban areas is produced by a desire for the instant gratification of needs

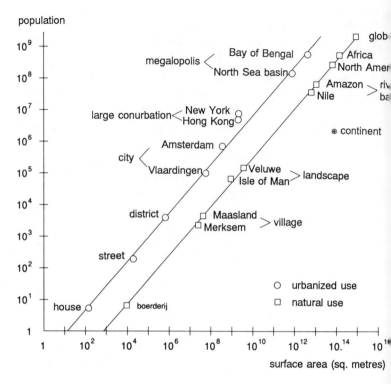

Table 10.5. Population density in natural and urbanized areas at different levels of the scale in about 1980.

at almost any time and place. Production, storage and transport systems are disproportionately related to this desire. If the process is to be reversed, change will have to come about at the level of each household, and facilities for transport and leisure must be modified.

Sometimes I get the feeling that nowadays we are desperately trying to satisfy our souls' deepest needs in a material way, while in fact our souls can only find answers at a spiritual level. The question arises whether there is yet another step in the progressive urbanization of the megalopolis. Will the whole planet yet turn into a gaiapolis?

When we realize that the megalopolis of the North Sea basin can only survive by using huge areas of land in other places to

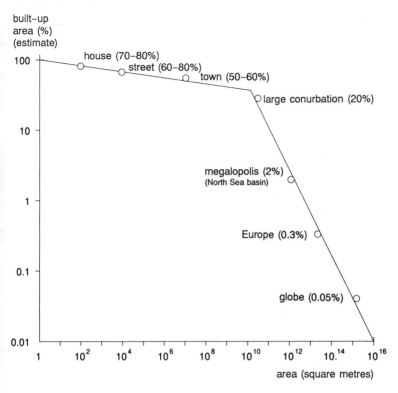

Table 10.6. Estimate in percentage of built–up area or urban and natural areas at different levels of the scale in 1980.

generate its raw materials, it becomes clear that we are facing an urbanization trend which is reaching its natural boundaries, and that in some places these boundaries have already been reached. In principle, every organism must be able to subsist on the raw materials, preferably long–lasting materials, which are available within its own territory.

Moreover, it is interesting to note that at several levels in the centre of the urban area there are natural spaces in the form of tree–lined village squares, the green belt areas of conurbations, or the sea in the North Sea basin, where there is an ecologically healthy development. Without these natural spaces the head of the urban area would become a desert.

251

The design of the growing city

The nature of urban design differs in the city centre, residential areas, and on the edge of the city. In many Dutch cities living in the centre has become more attractive as a result of urban renovation. For this purpose, industries have been moved out of the centre to a location with better opportunities for expansion and improved connections. This is a positive development. Although industry often develops in the urban "head," it belongs in the urban "belly" area. The danger of undesirable development is greatest on the periphery of many cities. There are districts of blocks of flats which are on such a large scale that man and nature have become alienated from each other and are subordinated to the increasing scale of the industrial production process. In the Netherlands, the fall in population growth will largely put a stop to the growth of cities, but in the rest of the world cities will grow enormously.

By the year 2000 there will be more than fifty cities with over fifteen million inhabitants, such as Dacca, Bombay and Jakarta. It is absolutely essential that this growth takes place not only in the large cities themselves, but also in surrounding centres, and that high–rise buildings are avoided as far as possible. High–rise building limits the possibilities of project development, while traditional trades and crafts can survive in low buildings. In large parts of the Earth the city will have to be integrated into the landscape in such a way that the function of the landscape is not really affected.[8] With regard to the expansion of cities, there is a challenge in the need to give form to the constant process of change. Where there is prolific growth, it is particularly important in poor countries to continue creating the threefold organism. The industrial area must develop separately from the urban area, so that there is an acceptable level of growth for both. It is unacceptable for the industrial area to be enclosed by residential areas nearby, and the reverse situation is even worse, as we see in the Netherlands at Pernis and Hoogvliet. If an industrial area has a planned lifespan of twenty to forty years, this means that former industrial areas could be moved in their entirety after a while, and rebuilt to become urban areas. In this case, it is essential that the ground has not been polluted. The dynamic process of the growth of the town is rather like the process described earlier for the solar system, in which the Sun expels the planets from itself. In the same way, a growing town can expel industrial areas, residential areas and shopping areas with department stores from the centre to the periphery, creating satellite towns.

It is urgently necessary to base the planning of the environment on an understanding of the natural relationship between the areas within an organic whole, as indicated by gaiasophy in Table 10.4. This allows for a better development than development based on promoting economic growth, the starting point used in the Dutch government's Fourth Report on Town and Country Planning.

The example of Rotterdam
A good example of harmonious growth during the early stage of a town is the threefold structure which was maintained for a long time in the city of Rotterdam in its so-called "old city triangle," as shown in Table 10.7. Rotterdam was originally an ancient settlement called Rotte, which was swept away in 1164 in the Christoffel flood. The tributary of the Nieuwe Maas was formed when the sea broke through. In the place where the tributary, the Rotte, joined the Nieuwe Maas, the land that was lost was reclaimed. In 1240 the existing dykes at the level of the present Hoogstraat were connected by a dam with six outlets to interrupt the confluence of the Rotte and the Nieuwe Maas at high tide. The elongated polder created next to the Rotte in this way was called Rotterdam, and following its growth it was given a city charter in 1299. The area was later named the Oude Landstad and could be considered as the head and a heart of an imaginary body in which the six outlets for water functioned as "heart valves" with a rhythm of two heartbeats per day. The outer water meadows attracted all sorts of activities, and in 1412 they were added to the city as the Oude Waterstad. In this way an organism was created with a head, heart and lungs, later strengthened into a real chest cavity with a wall.

To function perfectly there was considerable growth at the base of the triangle towards the river. There was a tendency to move out, break through the local cycle and look outwards to the

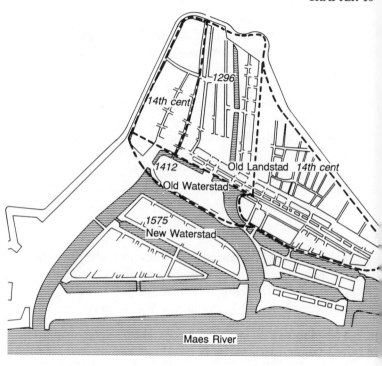

Table 10.7. The city of Rotterdam in the sixteenth century.

rest of the world. From the middle of the sixteenth century the city's belly area developed enormously, and during the time of the councillors Johan van Oldenbarneveld and Grotius, the Nieuwe Waterstad developed, a succession of harbours such as the Leuven Haven, de Blaek, de Oude Haven and the Scheeps-makers Haven. In 1620, the triangle of the city was fully grown. In this way the threefold city structure was perfectly completed. Religious life, with the St Laurens church in the centre, took place in the Oude Landstad, where the waters were still, or flowed slowly. Local shippers passed by, rooting Rotterdam in its immediate environment with the ditches of the polder and the windmills. Between this head area and the economic activity of the harbours there was a connecting system, the above-mentioned Hoogstraat, with the heartbeat of the sluices, which was also the shopping centre and meeting place of the town. The former town hall and weighhouse can also be found there, where a balance was determined for economic life on the basis of spiritual life. Faasse, whose studies as an architect at the Technical University of Delft led to these insights, concluded: "Therefore old Rotterdam was an example of a harmonious distribution and interaction between the three social areas: spiritual–cultural life in the north, economic–commercial life in the south, and social–judicial life in the centre."[9] His classification is aimed at the higher level of human organization in the city. Economic life forms the flow organization in the community, while judicial life forms the functional organization, and the true spiritual life reflects the actual identity, the real meaning of man's existence on Earth. These higher organizations are at a higher level than that at which I am studying the city in terms of city planning and as an environmental system. Furthermore, it is striking that urban man's loss of contact with his spiritual origins is revealed in the fact that the focal point of the church has been replaced by banking. Modern man attributes greater value to his income than to his religion.

This example of the development of the inner city of Rotterdam is an inspiring model for the skeletal organization of a growing city. However, after the Second World War the industrial growth of Rotterdam was so turbulent and uncoordinated that for a while it was necessary to designate the Rhine delta as an area requiring decontamination from air pollution. This situation lasted from 1972 to 1987, and since then the small distance between the industrial area and the urban area has continued to be a problem.

Materialism and spirituality in the urban area
Analogous to the structure of the Earth organism, it is also possible to describe the structure of the skeletal organization of industrial and urban areas. The head, the industrial area, is in the centre, surrounded at a safe distance by the urban area as the chest and rural areas on the periphery, which I will discuss below. On a horizontal plane, man also lives in towns in the chest of the landscape. The health–giving force of nature and the unhealthy forces of technology will have to be co–ordinated in

255

urban development. In towns it is necessary to remove the alienation between man and nature, resulting from technology. In the
town, residential areas form the connection between the out-
wardly directed shopping centres and sports and recreational
facilities, and the inwardly directed administrative and cultural
centre.

When the threefold division of the urban area is compared
with that of the industrial area, it becomes clear that — like the
structure of the Earth — sports, recreation and shopping facilities
occupy a position next to the digestive centre of the industrial
area. The steering mechanism of the city is in mirror image to
that of the industrial area, as indicated in Table 10.3. Like the
Earth, and its mountain chain in North and South America, and
like the planet with its Earth's crust, a robust transition area is
required for the transition from the industrial belly with its production complexes, to the belly of the city. This takes the form
of interruptions in the landscape, such as roads, earthworks or
waterways. The greatest danger threatening the urban area is that
it will be combined with the industrial area to form a single unit.
As for the Earth, protective layers are needed between the living
environment and industrial transformation processes. By calculating the risks involved, it is possible to arrive at a rational basis
for protecting the population and nature, for example, in the form
of protection zones.

The impossibility of uniting the mechanical aspects of industry
with organic spirituality is expressed in city building in various
ways, as both of these tendencies vie for priority in the centre of
the city. The conflict can be seen very clearly in the design of the
highest point in built-up areas. Traditionally the highest buildings
were connected with religious symbols. In ancient cultures they
also had a magical significance and effect. The temples were the
highest buildings in the area and served to connect heaven and
Earth. This was where man communicated with the gods, and
where the power of the light from the Sun and the cosmos entered man and the body of Mother Earth. Examples of this are
the Mayan temples and Egyptian pyramids. The Parthenon on the
Acropolis in Athens is a perfect illustration of the dominant
position assumed by the gods in the city about two thousand

years ago. Many churches and cathedrals built in later periods fulfilled the same role. The church, with its soaring spire, dominates the landscape, connecting that which is below the Earth with the heavens in a mythical sense.

In the fifteenth century there was a fundamental change in the structure of these mythical buildings, the square pyramids from the Egyptian culture and the temples and cathedrals of the Graeco-Roman culture, with the introduction of domes, first incorporated by the Italian architect Brunelleschi (1377–1446) in the Duomo of Florence in 1423. The dome reflects the dome of heaven as a microcosm summarizing the macrocosm. This was the point at which man first became self-conscious and, in the era which followed, he either consciously tried to find the way back to the spiritual world or became increasingly bogged down in materialism. In a city like Paris, this conflict is depicted in the two structures which have dominated the city for a century: the magnificent dome of the Sacré Coeur on a hill which is difficult to climb, and opposite it, the hundred year old Eiffel Tower, the pride of technology, with a lift to take you to the top.

Man always looks for a view from the highest point of the city. Approaching the centre of the city, buildings and people are crowded more closely together per square metre. It is as though we are drawn into the centre rather like a black hole, a whirlpool in which every man undergoes a metamorphosis or initiation. This initiation can merely take a physical form, like going to the top of the Eiffel Tower in Paris or the Empire State Building in New York, or the numerous even higher buildings which have gone up recently. It is true that from these towers there is a view which seems to remove the limitations of space to some extent. From a height you can see two cars driving towards each other at a crossroads and crashing before the drivers notice themselves. It makes for fascinating theatre, but is based on technology, and not on spirituality. Modern man tries to storm the heavens with towers to imitate the infinity of space and time which is characteristic of heaven. We still build towers of Babel and fall prey to the temptation in the desert, described in the Gospel according to St Matthew (4:1–11). First, the Devil suggests to Jesus, who has fasted for forty days, that the stones be turned into bread. Then he takes him to Jerusalem, places him on the roof of the temple, and says: "If thou be the Son of God, cast thyself down: for it is written, He shall give his angels charge concerning thee: and in their hands they shall bear thee up, lest at any time thou dash thy foot against a stone." Finally, the Devil took him up to a very high mountain and showed him all the kingdoms of the world and the glory of them, and said to him: "All these things will I give thee, if thou wilt fall down and worship me." As we stand on our towers of Babel, these words are still being whispered to us. Wouldn't anyone be entranced by the spectacle of a large city, flickering with millions of lights as evening falls?

However, in the centre of the city there is another way out of the whirlpool, the spiritual centre which reflects the cosmos, and in which man learns to know himself as a microcosm. A striking symbol of this can be found in the west of the Netherlands with its squat church towers, such as the Laurens church in Rotterdam and the churches in Den Briel, Goedereede, and Zierikzee. These towers seem to invite people to climb them, to stand on the tower so that they themselves become the dome reflecting the macro-cosm. Perhaps our large cities will once again make room for this spiritual function of the centre, despite the high price of land there, rather than demonically vying with each other as the hundreds of skyscrapers in Manhattan seem to do. There, the centre of the urban conglomeration provides a glimpse of hell.

10.5 Agricultural and forest areas

In many places in the world the farmer is the main controller of the environment. Even in the densely populated Netherlands, farmers control over 70% of the land. I mentioned before that farming can be divided into horticulture, arable farming, animal husbandry, and forestry. I will choose a few characteristic examples from the extensive literature on the ecological crisis in agriculture, and the solutions offered by organic farming. Manfred Klett points out how the four agricultural cultures which developed separately in Europe in the pre–Christian era, such as the culture which developed when man started to till the fields and herd sheep, started to become interwoven and interact.[10]

For the first time, these four separate activities were combined in one person. From approximately the eighth century this combination formed the basis of agricultural development in Europe. This resulted in an organism in which the belly area of the deep woods was permeated with the chest area, consisting of arable farming, animal husbandry, horticulture and forestry. The head centre, where cathedrals were built, was situated in this chest area. In this way the Gothic cathedrals of Rheims, Ulm and Chartres can really be considered as artistic structures which form the head of an organic unity with the surrounding landscape. According to Uyldert, many of the old towns of Europe are also Indo–Germanic sacred places, where the Earth's force lines cross each other and springs have their sources.[11] They developed as a result of the special relationship which man experienced there between cosmic and earthly forces. The cathedrals in these cities serve as a challenge to our present culture to give the industrial centre an identity in the same way.

The medieval village, as an organ in the landscape, clearly reveals the living arrangement of the four agricultural activities as part of an organic spatial skeleton.[12] Table 10.8 reveals how tradesmen, craftsmen and farmers settle around the church. They are surrounded by a strip of market gardens for horticulture. Beyond this there is a ring of orchards, and then the open land of fields and meadows for arable farming. This reaches to the edge of the woods. The woods form the invisible boundary with the neighbouring village, and are the outward face of the village, fulfilling the product presentation function. The cattle live with the people under the same roof. This example can be seen as a parallel with the suburb of the town, which was discussed above.

In broad terms there is a threefold division, man–cattle–crops, in which cattle represent the internal transportation function between man as the head and the command centre, which runs from the fields to the edge of the wood. The fields form the area where the characteristic agricultural transformation process takes place in the form of the cow producing milk. Once again, we have a 3×3 structure, with the church, tradesmen and farms as the steering system, the barns, stables, market gardens and orchards of farms as the connecting system, and the

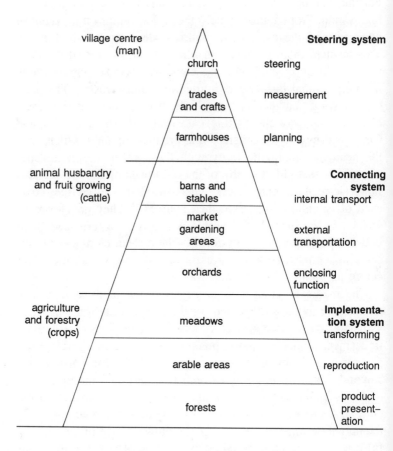

Table 10.8. The threefold division of the spatial skeleton of the medieval European village.

meadows, fields and edge of the wood as the implementation system.

The domestic animals, with their "heart function," enable man to survive the rhythmic changes in climate or the inhospitable nature of some landscapes.[13] In the cold steppes and mountains of the north these are reindeer. In the dry desert they are camels, in other steppes, sheep, goats and cattle. In the wet areas where the cold and snow limit or prevent arable farming, cattle and buffalo are the creatures through which man makes use of the vegetation, and he lives on their meat and blood. The Masai of Central Africa also use the blood of animals as an important source of food. In this case, the heart function of the animals in the organism of the agricultural community is expressed very directly. Man constantly acts as the creator of the relationships which are found in the landscape around him.

In the modern agricultural economy the organic structure of medieval European village communities has disintegrated. A century since the petrifying effect of technology first manifested itself in industrial areas, the same deracination has also started to appear on farms. The goal of modern agriculture consists of maximum short–term yields, and the awareness of the life–giving function of cultivated land as an organism in itself, and as an organ in a larger system, is in danger of being lost. The service function of this organ has become too one–sided, so that it leads to disharmony in the larger landscape organism. In addition, farmers have increasingly specialized; one will cultivate only sugar beet and corn, while another will concentrate on intensive pig and poultry breeding. A third may specialize in growing horticultural crops such as tomatoes and cucumbers in modern greenhouses. This disintegration has the effect of destroying life on Earth. The mirrored surfaces of the greenhouses, the stinking pigsties, fields which are artificially fertilized every week, are all ways in which the landscape is being made as inhospitable as industrial areas.

We are now far removed from the ideal of a farm which constitutes a closed cycle of products.[14] The digestive processes have mushroomed unchecked, encouraged by the temptations of technology and large–scale production. As a result, chaotic, health–destroying forces have gained the upper hand. As in the industrial area, agriculture now has an oversized heart. When the yield is insufficient to feed animals, large–scale production is encouraged by means of artificially irrigating the land and im-porting animal feed, for example, in the form of American soya pellets. Animal manure has a naturally stimulating effect on life in the soil, and brings about harmony in the agricultural cycle by returning the nutrients absorbed by the plants to the soil in another form. This manure has now become a health–destroying factor. The harmonious role of cattle which live on what the land has to give, and return their manure to the land in an enriched form, thus forming a cosmically influenced cycle, has been destroyed. The farm as an organism has been completely ravaged. The sick animals and crops have to be treated with hormones, insecticides, weedkillers and the like, in order to maintain production. The excessive fertilization of the land is comparable to high blood pressure in man.

In order to restore the health of agriculture, the healing forces of the chest area will have to be restored. The closed cycle of the whole agricultural system must be reintroduced in individual farms or comparable units. Starting with the chest area, it is clear that a healthy agriculture does not allow for intensive animal rearing. The animals should be fed, as far as possible, with what the land produces, and the land should be fed only with compost and animal manure and with vegetable waste matter. The amount of green fodder and hay determines the number of animals that should be kept. Even in the past, keeping too many animals led to the death of animals because of food shortages at the end of the winter, or famines, such as those which occur nowadays in the African savannah. On the other hand, the amount of manure to be spread on the land is also a limiting factor. By following this cycle the well–ordered and life–enhancing mechanism is restored. If more animals are kept anyway, the manure must be exported to other areas.

In the last few decades, artificial fertilizers have seriously impoverished and aged the land. Artificial fertilizers cause the roots of plants to grow more in the moisture of the soil, rather than dissolving the minerals in the sedimentary layers themselves with the help of acids that are secreted. In addition, animal manure also contains additional organic nutrients for plants, and together with worms and insects, it forms a rich and nutritious soil for parasites, which otherwise turn to the crops themselves.[15] These then have to be combatted with all sorts of insecticides.

It is only by returning to a less intensive form of farming in which the animals can move about naturally, and by suppressing the use of artificial fertilizers, insecticides, weed–killers and so on, that the chest function in agriculture can be restored. The fertility of the soil should not be replaced by chemical products, but should be stimulated by the correct amount of animal manure.[16] By taking these measures, a great deal of tension can be removed from the belly of the agricultural system. It is important that man now continues to support the natural order of the landscape organism, and does not subordinate nature to his own social order. This means that grass should not be artificially fertilized. Although it increases production, it drastically reduces the variety of grasses. A spiritual management of the landscape entails above all the creation of possible incarnations for as many different spiritual beings as possible in a correct relationship to higher hierarchies. In addition, Lovelock and Margulis pointed out the stabilizing effect of a diversity of species on physical fluctuations in the environment, such as fluctuations in temperature.[17] Arable fields fulfil the intermediate function between grass and woodland. The application of manure must be related to the principle that life must be restored to dead matter in which the life–processes have been lost. By rotating crops and ensuring a diversity of crops, it is possible to achieve the harmony which existed for centuries with the three strip method. Every village cultivated one strip of winter crops, one strip of summer crops, leaving one strip lying fallow. In this way the strip was used in a different way every year. The belly processes in agriculture must be restored to the minimum necessary to restore the health of the whole organism. The unrestrained one–sided Earth forces must also be held in check in arable farming by differentiated cosmic forces. For this it is necessary to reintroduce mixed farming and crop rotation.

Forestry comprises the border area between agriculture and natural areas. In the forests the vertical element is emphasized, which means that vertical polarity is more apparent than in fields. In this area the layer of humus acts as a diaphragm supporting the growth of plants, and depositing particles to form new soil. This layer of humus is a shrivelled remnant of the albuminous atmosphere which existed in the Lemurian age. Jurriaanse describes how the ethereal body of a wood is less of a closed unit than in man.[18] The trees together form an all–encompassing ethereal body which promotes growth and health. Thinning it out too drastically will disturb this. Not all trees have this group effect or morphogenetic field. The oak tree is a world in itself. Other forms of higher unity develop as a result of the symbiosis of fungi and toadstools with the roots of trees. However, these lower organisms are very sensitive to atmospheric pollution. Apart from their highly organized ethereal body, woods also have an open, astral body. This can be seen in the animals which often move freely in and out. In this they differ from the ideal centre of an agricultural system, as described above, which should function as a closed entity. No manure or foodstuffs have to be bought in, and the surplus produce is sold as food. The domestic animals stay within the boundaries of the farm. In principle, the woods are more open, and form part of a larger unit. Deer, wild boar, birds and rabbits move in and out. Nevertheless, foresters leave almost as great a mark on the woods as the farmer does on his farm.

Just as man owes his consciousness to the fact that the Self and the astral body to some extent kill off the ethereal and physical body, animals, as representatives of the astral body, feed on plants and twigs, or bore into them. For example, if the wood is unhealthy because of a one-sided composition of trees and undergrowth, the astral body kills off too much. This can take the form of plagues of insects, or cattle which graze on the new green shoots in the woods, rather than in the fields, which may not lead directly to the death of the wood, but will cause it to die off completely after a few decades when the cattle have eaten all the new shoots. Foresters have to think a century ahead. Their imagination must prevent uniformity and one-sidedness in replanting areas that have been cleared. In small woods, there is no large game, the function of which — according to Jurriaanse — is to be taken over by hunting.

By means of sensitive reforestation and an understanding of selective felling and hunting, forests can be protected against disease. The spiritual relationship between man and the forest will gradually become apparent when a healthy equilibrium is achieved. In this way, forests require the same spiritual guidance that is required for designing urban and industrial areas. A healthy balance can be attained in forests, as long as the health is not disrupted by harmful substances in the air that blows through them. Unfortunately this is the case throughout most of Europe at the moment. The only remedy is to reduce the amount of pollution from agricultural, urban and industrial areas to acceptable levels, and to develop stronger species. In this way, by means of a synthesis of science and spiritual science, man can create woodland, both to produce timber, and to serve as a healthy, natural area.

10.6 Rural areas and water areas

In natural rural areas, attempts are made to prohibit the exploitative influence of man altogether. They are islands where soil fertility is permanently regenerated. Because of the diversity of physical geography and composition of the soil, and the existence of micro–climates, numerous species and varieties of plants and animals have developed. Everywhere in the world, areas with a unique position and significance have been declared protected areas. In these areas, trees which fall, natural fires, and so on, are left to their fate, and there are strict limits on their use as recreational areas. Nevertheless, in many cases it is clear that these natural areas cannot be left entirely to themselves. Nature is ageing, and is developing the symptoms of old age. New infectious diseases, such as oak mildew and poplar disease, are developing. There is no natural balance, as became clear, for example, in the Swiss National Park in Unterengadin. This may express itself in an unbridled proliferation of species which have no natural enemies. In high places crops are in danger of becoming overgrown and drying out, so that they no longer contribute to forming a layer of humus. Man is needed here to supervise nature by participating in an organic way and ensuring that pollution of water, the soil and the atmosphere is limited to acceptable levels. Natural areas are often situated near watery areas. Marshes, dunes and water meadows are typical examples of this. On the other hand, the tropical rainforests are excellent examples of natural areas. However, they are on such a large scale that they are not covered by the unit of the landscape, as I

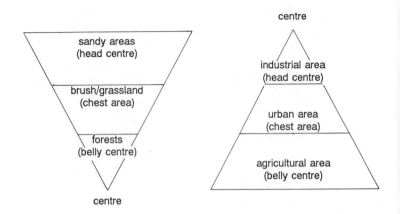

nature: belly is central   technology: head is central
large scale of centre: stimulating effect   large scale of centre: deadening effect

Table 10.9. The reverse orientation of landscapes formed by nature and those formed by technology.

see it. I will return to this later. In smaller, natural forests, the same threefold division is found as in the wood. The physical belly area is near the ground. If the forest is part of a landscape with low–growing vegetation, such as heather or brush and grass–lands, the lower grassland — particularly when there are sandy areas — forms the dead head centre which can be very extensive. The brushland and heather form the intermediate area and the forest itself, the belly. It is interesting to note that this is the reverse of the situation in industrial and urban areas where the head is central, as indicated in Table 10.9. This table indirectly assumes that there are several towns surrounding the large–scale industrial area, which is more desirable than the reverse situation. In this way vulnerable natural areas are protected by towns and by man's wisdom from the harmful effects of industry.

There is another striking phenomenon in natural forests. Un–like the vertical threefold division of the physical body or skeletal organization of the forest, there is a reverse vertical threefold division in the astral body. The reversal in the order of the astral body compared with the physical body was discussed above in the previous chapter in relation to the organization of man, a building, and a river. Crawling creatures of the belly, such as worms and toads, live in and on the soil, the physical head centre of the forest, while birds, creatures of the head, live in the treetops, the belly of the forest. As remarked earlier, the predators are often absent. These represent the heart of the forest's astral body, so that the correct balance can no longer be achieved naturally. In order to give these "creatures of respiration" a chance of life, it is often necessary to establish an even larger scale for the organism concerned. In this way the natural area in which the higher hierarchies operate benefits from as large a scale as possible leading to a differentiation of species. This is in contrast to technology, where the large scale of things leads to diseases (see Table 10.9). The remaining contrasts between urban and industrial areas, on the one hand, and natural areas, on the other, can be mutually reconciled by means of farms and forestry.

It is difficult to retain natural areas in densely populated river basins, because man needs to remove the dangers of flooding and drought. Engineering projects such as dykes, canals, dams and locks have been built as a result. Reservoirs have a very large destructive effect on their immediate environment. They are artificial hearts in the natural area, and they seriously disrupt the silting process. This is currently an enormous problem in the Nile Delta. A natural area which is characterized precisely by a large number of very small-scale threefold divisions, is seriously affected by these large-scale works. A small scale in these engineering projects is even more important for strengthening the health of natural areas than in towns and industrial areas. In this respect, the 1986 decision of the Dutch State Water Board to break through the summer dykes along the large rivers in the Netherlands was a step in the right direction.

Nevertheless, it is sometimes difficult to avoid large-scale solutions because of the size of the sea arms and the strength of the water. In this case, it is necessary to adapt to the nature of the water area as far as possible. An example of this is the dam which allows the tidal water of the East Scheldt to pass through, although raising the dykes would be a more obvious solution. In the landscape of the lower reaches of a river basin, like the characteristic Dutch landscape, the delta and the coast along the sea and the ocean form the beginning of an almost immeasurable surface area of water which man has only recently been affecting on a large scale. Intensive shipping, the dumping of waste matter, over–fishing, and accidents with oil rigs and supertankers are the first signs of the way in which natural water areas are affected. This is most serious in the shallow seas along the continents, where concentrations of waste matter are highest, and the natural digestive processes are most intense. The excessive stimulation of the belly function, localized in the shallow waters, results in the spread of disease. The solution here is to restrict the flow of waste matter and prevent what I would call "hyperventilation." Hyperventilation is the result of the worldwide transportation of raw materials in bulk. In order to save our natural areas and save the energy that is needed for transportation, raw materials should be processed where they are found.

On the other hand, the premature damming up in reservoirs of river silt means that the ecosystem of the river delta is starved. It is only the ocean depths that do not seem threatened. Mountain landscapes with bare outcrops of rock and permanent snow constitute a natural area comparable with the depths of the ocean, but situated at the opposite end of the scale. Infinity stretches in a vertical direction and there is a marked drop in the direct influence of human activity. On these chilly, lifeless mountain tops, nature seems least vulnerable. Nevertheless, a small change in the climate can result in an enormous increase in glacial ice, or the ice can melt away altogether. Therefore the snow–capped mountains are essentially much more vulnerable than water areas. The depths of the oceans are the last hope with regard to main-taining a natural balance.

The threefold division of water areas consists in principle of the water itself, the waterline, which is determined by the movement of the water, and the permanent position of the land. The essential transformation process for the skeletal organization — which is my main concern — takes place along the water-line where new land is formed. This can be seen along the beaches and in the water meadows along river banks. The new

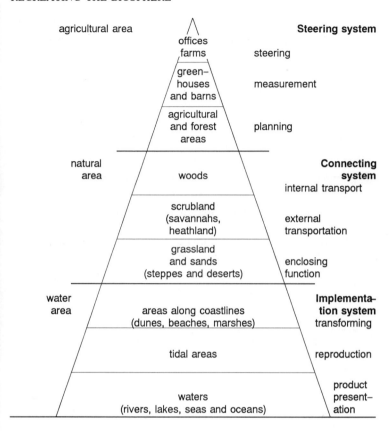

Table 10.10. The threefold division of the skeletal organization of the agricultural area, the natural area and the water area.

land is formed in the belly. Like the humus layer on the land, the seas and oceans are a reminder of the ancient albuminous atmosphere during the second half of the Lemurian era, when minerals rained down. The rhythmic movement of the tides and the submerged bank of the river is the central area rich in life and reproductive processes. The actual water area has the most mobility, and in an "invisible" form it contains the product of the transformation function: the particles of silt from which new land is formed. The eternal movement of yin and yang can be seen here. In fact, the watery area is all belly and limbs, as summar-

269

ized in Table 10.10. When it becomes diseased, the landscape behind seems lost; nothing remains to move out to. The central function of the natural area is to form new land and to safeguard the diversity of species. In this way it reveals a relationship with man's reproductive function. When the flow organization of the water area is examined rather than its skeletal organization, the central function seems to lie in receiving the river water, and the formation of the "atmosphere" in which the "river plant" can flourish, as described in greater detail below. This is at the same time the end and the new beginning of the hydrological cycle.

10.7 The landscape organism in the Netherlands

The above description reveals that the city and the modern land-scape can be structured in a way that corresponds entirely with the ninefold structure of man and of the planet Earth. The head of the landscape consists of the industrial system, the underlying factors of production, and the industrial production processes themselves. The chest is composed of the area containing the recreational facilities, the residential area and the city centre. The belly is represented by the digestion of agriculture, land for-mation and the reproduction of species in natural and water areas. The principle of the threefold division in all the organs com-posing the Earth organism is unmistakable as a life principle.

In this way the Earth, or Gaia, can be understood and sensed in the function of its organs and cells, so that it becomes possible to identify the processes which cause disease and restore health. The aim of gaiasophy is to develop the insight and wisdom needed for man to do this. Table 10.11 shows a summary of the full extent of a threefold division from the urban area down to natural areas and water areas. Examining this table from the bottom upwards, it reveals the whole development of the land-scape and of society. The result of this development can be recognized in the Netherlands in the present provinces of South and North Holland. The land rises up from the water and is cultivated and inhabited to an increasing extent. Room was created for agricultural activities, and this led to the development of villages, sometimes with harbours, to be followed by the process of urbanization and the need for sports and recreational facilities. Means of transport were developed, followed by the first machines, and the industrial production of basic materials, public service utilities, and finally, offices with their computers, like the brain of a gigantic edifice. This brain — and in fact the whole head — wishes to subject the rest of the body to it, and enters into conflict with the controlling organs in the chest and belly area. A closer look at Table 10.11 shows that there is a danger of a control vacuum developing at the industrial head. When an industrial centre is surrounded by several towns, it really needs a separate controlling layer; this was actually created in Rijnmond for a number of years in the form of the Rijnmond council, but in 1986 it was transferred to the province of South Holland. Industry's attempt to operate on a large global scale has a chaotic effect on existing local control centres, which find it difficult to respond appropriately. The danger is that the level responsible for control does not counterbalance industry at a sufficiently high level. The worldwide importance of some businesses actually requires a response which exceeds even the national influence of a government. It is only when each of the parts of the large urban organism is prepared to serve rather than dominate, that the total landscape organism can exist. Moreover, an essential starting point in this system is that each cell, each organ and each organism must itself be healthy.

On the basis of this view, I will attempt to isolate the processes which cause disease and restore health in an ecosystem made up of a river basin, an ecosystem which sometimes represents the territory of a single nation, but which is often more or less than one nation. Before examining the river basin in greater detail, it is interesting to look at the composition of landscapes in the Netherlands by way of example. The Netherlands is a nation with too little territory to comprise the basin of a large river, but it does contain very different landscapes, and some large conurbations.

In a sense, the skeletal organization of the Netherlands is a miniature mirror image or photograph of that of England. The Thames corresponds to the Rhine, which is larger, London to the urban triangle of Rotterdam/The Hague/Amsterdam. In England

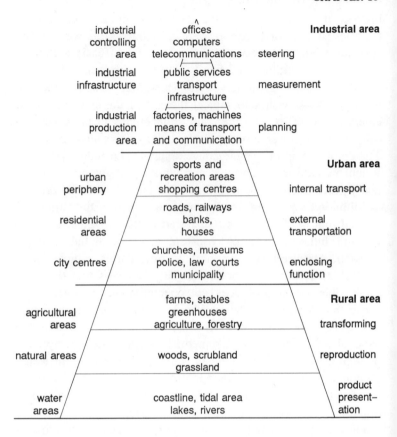

Table 10.11. The threefold (3 × 3 × 3) skeletal organization of the landscape surrounding a large conurbation.

there is a northwest–southeast polarity with the mountains in the northwest and the largest ports in the southeast, while in the Netherlands there is a southeast–northwest polarity.

The physical head can be found in the higher areas of the country. Areas higher than 50 metres above sea level are shown in Table 10.12. There are hardly any of these higher areas in the Netherlands, the only ones being around Enschede, Arnhem–Nijmegen and Maastricht. The peculiar appendage of South Limburg, which has the only Dutch land higher than 100 metres above sea level, is suddenly shown in a different light. Without

Maastricht and the surrounding country, the Netherlands would not have a physical head. At the same time, the three areas mentioned are the points where the rivers — the reason for this delta area's existence — flow into the country: the Meuse at Maastricht, the Rhine at Arnhem/Nijmegen, and the Dinkel, later known as the Overijsselse Vecht, at Enschede. In many respects the umbilical cord, the national stopcock, the monitoring of the entire national water system, is situated in the Arnhem/Nijmegen nexus. At this point the Rhine and the Meuse change from a system which receives water to one which gives water. It forms a diaphragm in the river organism. This is reflected in the fact that the Ministry of Waterways' alarm system for river disasters on the Rhine is situated in Arnhem. Arnhem/Nijmegen serves as a monitoring system for the organization of the flow of water. Maastricht is an old cultural centre now squarely oriented to-wards the European Community, with its prominent position facing Belgium and West Germany. With its industry, Enschede has more of a controlling character. Although these urban centres can be distinguished in the head of the geographical Netherlands, this part as a whole is weakly developed. Because of its nature as the delta of the Rhine and the Meuse, the emphasis on acti-vities in the Netherlands must be found in the belly area. All the area that was recently reclaimed from the water can be identified as the belly area in the natural skeletal organization, as indicated schematically in Table 10.12. This includes the dunes, numerous polders, the Friesian islands and the islands of Zeeland. The dunes and polders form the natural product presentation function of the Netherlands. The image of the triangle expanding at the base, which applied to the old centre of Rotterdam, is repeated at a national level. Limburg is the physical head. The area where the large rivers, railways and motorways criss cross the country like the arteries of an organism, from North Brabant to Drenthe, is the connecting system, and the whole coastal area with its direct hinterland is the growing belly area. The centre of gravity of the connecting system or chest area is formed by Utrecht, which is supported by 's–Hertogenbosch/Eindhoven in the south and Zwolle in the north. The largest part of the population and industry has settled in the implementation area of the Netherlands,

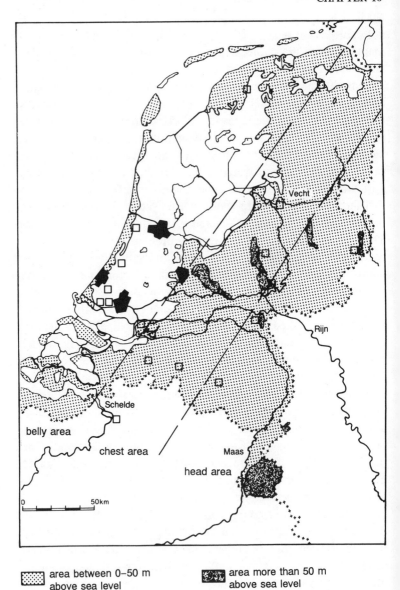

area between 0–50 m
above sea level

area more than 50 m
above sea level

Table 10.12. A schematic representation of the threefold skeletal structure of the Netherlands.

behind the dunes of the mainland of Holland, situated between the two groups of islands.

A summary of the skeletal organization of the Netherlands shows that the head and steering system of the national organism is in the south east. Silt, which is essential for the transformation of water into land, and water, which is essential to ensure the necessary flow, enter the country at this point. In the central area the silt is taken to its destination in the southwest or northwest by tributaries. Sediment is deposited and land is formed in the implementation area and this process is artificially speeded up by man.

The flow organization or "ethereal body" of this skeletal organization is dependent on the rivers which cross the border. Their characteristic steering centre is in Arnhem/Nijmegen, the connecting system in the central area where locks and dams have been built as mechanisms for regulation and the implementation system in the belly area. This ethereal organization of nature is reflected in the vegetation with the tallest growth in the south and east, which are higher, and the lowest growth in the fields and dunes of the low–lying provinces. On the other hand, the wealth of bird life, which represents the natural astral body, is greatest in the watery belly areas.

Obviously this brief outline of the natural areas in the Netherlands is only a small part of the total national organism, and it is often difficult to identify. Other components of society — including complete urban organizations, as summarized in Table 10.11 — also have to be fitted into this picture. However, it is quite clear that the typical Dutchman lives and works in the belly of the national ecosystem.

The functional social organization has its industrial steering centre in the geographical belly area, its urban connecting link in the chest, and its agricultural hinterland in the head of the landscape. In the functional or astral organization of the Dutch economy there is another threefold division in the steering system behind the Dutch coast, which is reflected in the three major cities. In this division, Amsterdam — as the commercial and business centre — has a steering function, and new developments are initiated and planned there. As an industrial port of worldwide importance, Rotterdam clearly fulfils a more executive function. The role of The Hague for the organization of the national economy lies in its function of registering, harmonizing and co-ordinating. More in general, The Hague is the city which is the legal centre and deals with taxation, just as Amsterdam is identified with spiritual and cultural life, and Rotterdam with economic life. Obviously there are many ways of viewing the social and spiritual classification of a country like the Netherlands. The role of Limburg in the natural skeletal organization, the role of the locks and dams centred in Arnhem/Nijmegen for the hydrological flow organization, and the steering function of the three cities — Amsterdam/The Hague/Rotterdam — for the functional economic organization in the physical belly of the Netherlands will suffice to illustrate our thesis at this point.

What are the greatest threats to the health of the organism of the Netherlands? There is a great deal of material on this subject in the report *Zorgen voor Morgen* (Concern for Tomorrow) which was published at the end of 1988 by the Dutch National Institute for Public Health and Environmental Protection (RIVM). Obviously the pollution of water and air from across the border resulting from excess consumption play an important role, but these will be dealt with in the discussion of larger-scale ecosystems. At the national level the effect on the head of the mining industry and chemical industry in South Limburg and the Achterhoek (the east of the Netherlands), are significant. In the head and chest area the industrialized agricultural sector has a very harmful influence, and intense cattle and pig breeding on the poor sandy soil of The Peel and the Veluwe form a serious threat. What is the maximum number of animals that the Netherlands can cope with to put an end to over-fertilization? It is only a fraction of the present number, unless the manure can be processed and exported in a dried form. In 1990, there were as many pigs as people living in the Netherlands. The annual amount of animal manure has increased since 1900 by a factor of seven to about 700 million kilos (phosphates and nitrates), and every year almost the same quantity of largely superfluous artificial fertilizers are added to this as well. This is an untenable situation. However, the core of environmental concerns and planning lies in the belly area. How can the new land be incorporated in the surrounding countryside? Does the expansion of centralized urban growth and the industrial area take place according to an organic plan in which the capacity of the natural landscape to assimilate waste matter is respected? The unique seriousness and extent of the problem of soil pollution, which is most extreme in many places in the belly area, emphasizes the need for a responsible — and eventually total — recycling of waste materials, and an end to the practice of dumping. Examples of severe cases of soil pollution in the belly area of the Netherlands can be found in Lekkerkerk, Volgermeer, Gouderak and Maassluis. Apart from the pollution of the land, the lake and river beds, which have an essential steering function for aquatic life in shallow waters, are also under threat from the harmful substances accumulating in the silt, such as cadmium and PCBs. With the tendency to reclaim more and more land from the sea it is important to consider whether the larger ecosystem of the North Sea can do without the reproductive function of the tidal waters in the Westerscheldt and the Waddenzee. In Zeeland and the Ijsselmeer this function has already been considerably eroded. There is also a great danger of over-fishing in the North Sea because of the over-large capacity of national fishery fleets. Excessive fertilization, poisoning, severe organ transplants, the over-exploitation of land and sea, are all characteristic of the Netherlands as part of the Earth's organism.

It is not surprising that the Dutch Earth organism is sick. All three systems and all nine functions are under threat. If it is to be cured, it is necessary to adjust the size of the population, the standard of living, the use of space and the intensity of industry and agriculture to correspond with the limited natural capacity. The discussion of the three pairs of areas in the landscape gave some suggestions for objectives to achieve this. Obviously the real cause is the lack of harmony between the gigantic economic organism and the limitations of the natural skeletal organization and flow organization. This will have to be the starting point for the harmonization of these elements.

10.8 The river basin

Following the discussion of all the aspects of the landscape organism, it is appropriate to examine the river basin at a higher level of the natural scale. The large river links not only different countries, but also air, land and sea. It is like a plant spread over the surface of the Earth, with its roots in the mountain slopes like the veins in a hand. The paragraph on the threefold division of land and sea, and the illustration of Table 9.13, referred to the place of the river in the hydrological cycle. It was shown how the river's skeletal organization and the flow organization were overshadowed by the organization of the transportation of humidity, which goes in the opposite direction. Rainfall gives life to the river and its capacity to flow, while the flow organization gives form to the skeletal organization of the landscape by means of erosion, silting and sedimentation. According to Steiner, there was also some transportation of salt below the river bed, moving in the opposite direction from the mouth to the source of the river, and resulting in deposits of layers of salt under the river bed.[19] The deposits of salt form the food for the roots of plants. In the river basin the vertical dimension has a clearer function than in the landscape. The river is a real form force organism with a "water head" where the water is collected, while its true nature only becomes clear in the delta through its own movement. It grows in the delta, which is comparable to the flower of a plant, where the process of assimilation makes way for blossoming. The rhythmic meanderings in the lower reaches are like the petals of a plant, and when the river flows into the sea, this is like the seed being scattered over the land. Just as the astral body is found in the flower of a plant, the fish in the river's mouth embody the astral body of the river represented in the animal world. They go towards the wealth of food in the river flowing towards them, just like insects make for the honey in a flower.

Depending on the size of the river, some or many of the landscapes described are combined in an organic way in the river basin. All the pollution resulting from the digestive processes the atmosphere, drainage system and soil, finally to reach the delta area via the river and its tributaries.

It is usual for the landscape at the mouth of the river to be strongly dominated by industry, while natural areas are dominant at the source. The Rhine, the Mississippi and the Mekong are all typical examples of this. However, there are numerous variations and exceptions to this rule, for example, when the delta is very inaccessible, and the hinterland is therefore cultivated first. This is the case with the Orange River in South Africa, which flows into the sea in a desert area. By contrast, the Ganges and the Yangtze Kiang flow through densely populated urban areas virtually from the source.

Rivers also become sick as the result of an imbalance in the higher organization of the water circulation system, which leads to periods of drought and flooding, and to excess production of waste matter. The cause of disharmony in the organization of the water transportation system is usually climatic changes in the larger organism of which the river basin forms part. This applies to a lesser extent for excessive fertilization as a cause of disease, which is expressed in the high consumption of oxygen needed for bacteria to mineralize the degradable substances, so that the water reeks of putrefaction and fish die through lack of oxygen. A respiratory rhythm is revealed in the oxygen content of a river and to an even greater extent in lakes. The oxygen content is lowest in the morning in summer, and highest in the afternoon as a result of the oxygen produced by algae. If these fluctuations are too great because of the wealth of nutrients for the growth of algae, and the water is almost without oxygen at the end of the night, large numbers of fish can suddenly die on a summer morn-ing. The sporadic dumping of poison can also deliver a death blow to algae, crustaceans and fish. The chemical accidents at Hoechst in 1969 and at Sandoz in 1986 are examples of this for the Rhine. It is clear that such a river system is seriously ill. The digestive processes should be restricted. It is characteristic of a river that the chest function and the heart and lungs can achieve a great deal in this respect. To make this clearer, I will describe the river system in greater detail, as illustrated in Table 10.13.

A distinction should be made between the skeletal organization and the flow organizations. In the river system as a whole the mountains form the head. The steering function lies in the mountain tops which cause rainfall by forcing currents of air containing moisture to rise, so that the water falls, forming layers of snow and glaciers. Mountains and topography to a large extent determine the flow of the river. The memory of snow which has fallen in earlier times is preserved in the layers of a glacier. At the same time, the amount of snow and ice monitors the distribution of water. The water on the mountain slopes melts in proportion to the solar radiation, functioning as a thermostat, and this forms a transition to the programming of the distribution of water, the transportation of water and the silt formed by erosion. This planning function can be seen particularly in the upper reaches of a river basin. Another expression of the measurement function is the level of ground water which influences the flow of ground water, as well as evaporation of moisture by vegetation. The head of the river skeleton is strongly developed in rivers in cold areas, such as the Yukon in Alaska and the Lena in the USSR.

The heart and lungs are expressed in the middle reaches, while the chest is comparable to the enclosing boundaries of the river basin. The river's heart function is determined by the subterranean supplies in the layers of rock carrying the water. These ground water reservoirs which feed the river have a levelling effect on the flow, so that heavy rainfall takes a while to increase the flow, and in a drought, water continues to flow for a long time. In fact, the largest volume of water in the river basin can be found in these underground streams of water, which therefore fulfil the internal transportation function. The ground water often flows more slowly, as it is deeper below the surface. Very deep ground water may be thousands of years old, while shallow ground water flows away within a few months or several decades, depending on the porosity of the substrata. The vegetation on the surface generally ensures that this porous layer remains in place, for otherwise erosion would soon cause it to be flushed away, leaving behind bare rock. On the other hand, the vegetation contributes to the evaporation of some of the rainfall. Therefore when woods in the mountains are not properly managed, this

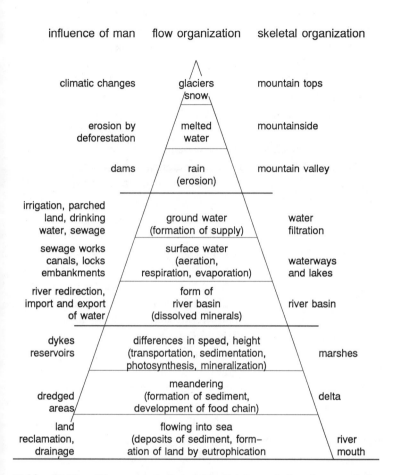

influence of man	flow organization	skeletal organization
climatic changes	glaciers / snow	mountain tops
erosion by deforestation	melted water	mountainside
dams	rain (erosion)	mountain valley
irrigation, parched land, drinking water, sewage	ground water (formation of supply)	water filtration
sewage works canals, locks embankments	surface water (aeration, respiration, evaporation)	waterways and lakes
river redirection, import and export of water	form of river basin (dissolved minerals)	river basin
dykes reservoirs	differences in speed, height (transportation, sedimentation, photosynthesis, mineralization)	marshes
dredged areas	meandering (formation of sediment, development of food chain)	delta
land reclamation, drainage	flowing into sea (deposits of sediment, formation of land by eutrophication	river mouth

Table 10.13. The natural threefold division of the river and the influence of man.

can result in deforestation and floods in the mountain valleys. The lung function of a river is performed by the surface water in the form of lakes and river tributaries and the vegetation. Here the water is aerated and evaporated. It is the external transportation function of the larger subterranean body of water. When the water is aerated, the oxygen and so on is dissolved in the water and carbon dioxide is released into the atmosphere. Waterfalls form the lungs of the river *par excellence.*

The belly function of the river has already been discussed. The transformation function is the transportation of water. In addition, sedimentation, mineralization and photosynthesis take place in the water. In these processes sunlight is stored in chemical energy, which assists the food chain: algae–water–flea–fish–predator. An intensification of these reproductive processes takes place in the water meadows and delta areas. The meandering river deposits silt, and sometimes floating islands are formed by vegetation. Finally, the silt and plants form banks and islands in the mouth of the river; the ultimate dead remnants of the river's whole course. The new land and fertile soil are a by–product of the river. The chief product is the water, which is returned to the sea.

The health–giving role of the heart and lung function consists of stimulating the flow of water, and providing sufficient time for mineralization and the supply of oxygen. Man almost always has to strength these functions artificially as the population grows, because a great deal of waste water is inevitably produced in urban landscapes by drinking and industrial water, and this has to be processed by the river. Waste water has to be caught in the reservoirs of sewage purification plants and artificially aerated to speed up the process of mineralization. Further upstream, small reservoirs are sometimes made where the water can be artificially aerated by blowing in compressed air at sufficient depth. It is only returned to the main river after this process. Reservoirs primarily have a planning function for the regulation of waste removal from the river. Table 10.13 schematically shows this sort of human intervention in the river's skeletal and flow organiz-ation. In the sewage purification plants which, together with the sewage system, can be viewed as the heart and lungs, silt con-taining metals is also removed from the water, as well as the phosphates which contribute to excessive plant growth. In this way it is possible to restrain the rapid accumulation of land in river deltas. This solid waste matter can be used again in agricul-ture, from which it originated in the first place, in so far as it came from food. This does not apply to phosphates which are produced by household detergents and what is washed away from artificial fertilizers used on agricultural land. In order to restore the health of river life, it has been necessary to change to phosphate-free detergents and to reduce the use of fertilizers to a minimum, as indicated above. Because of the present over-use of fertilizers and the high concentration of toxic metals such as copper, the use of sewage silt in agriculture is not very feasible. Recently silt has therefore been burnt in a number of places. In addition, it is necessary to stop completely the production of chemical waste matter which is not easily degradable, and is therefore harmful in principle. These substances, such as insecticides like DDT and bentazon, are often found on lists of dangerous substances which are a threat to the environment, though this does not mean that their use will be prohibited in the short term. In order to restore the health of the river system, strengthening the heart and lung function on a small scale and reducing over-consumption and pollution are of central importance. Fortunately these processes have been applied for some time, and some badly polluted rivers in Europe, Japan and America are in a much better state than they were in the 1970s. However, by no means all the problems have been solved, such as the pollution of metals and the persistent organic poisoning of river and sea beds.

In characterizing the skeletal and flow organization, I have only partly described the true river organism. We should not forget the importance of the migratory fish, such as the salmon and the sturgeon, which have their breeding grounds in the upper reaches of rivers in the early spring. For these fish the upper reaches of a river are like a belly opening out, a sort of womb, or a reflection of the much larger outside world of the sea and ocean. This reversal of the orientation in the threefold division is also found in the economic significance for the larger environment of the river basin. The mouth of the river then acts as a steering centre for the river basin behind it, as shown in Table 10.14. The real transformation function consists in the storage and transportation of goods from areas overseas and vice versa. In this way the river perfectly reflects the complexity and interrelated nature of human and natural organizations.

It is clear that when landscapes come together in a river basin, a new organism is created. Unfortunately this organism is often so seriously diseased that it is comparable to a patient in inten-

Flow organization

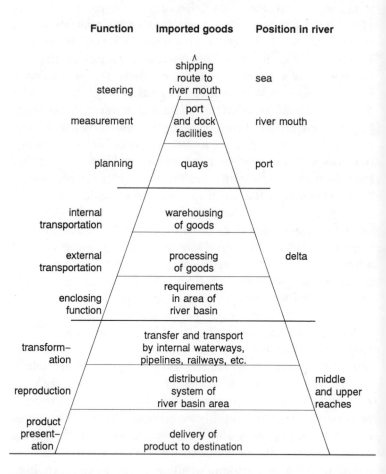

Table 10.14. The organization of a river basin from the perspective of the transportation and storage function for the surrounding area.

sive care on a heart and lung machine, who is kept alive by intravenous drips, artificial kidneys and drugs. I have shown that the river as an organism obeys the same principles as man, and that it can fall sick and be restored to health in the same way. This is encouraging when considering even larger-scale and more complex organisms, such as continents, on the basis of gaiasophy.

10.9   The continent: Europe and Africa

There is no room here for a discussion of the organizational principle of the life organism of every continent. This will have to be done for all the continents at a later stage in more detail. I have chosen Europe and Africa as examples, and will elaborate these in outline in different ways.

In Europe the organism is determined by numerous river basins with countless lakes, a few important inland seas and the Atlantic Ocean with the Gulf Stream. The most important mountains are the Pyrenees where the Ebro and the Garonne have their source; the Alps, where the Danube, Rhine, Rhône and Po arise; the Carpathians, which feed the Oder and the Vistula; the Turkish Anatolian highlands, where the Tigris and Euphrates arise; and finally the Urals, which provide part of the water of the Volga. In the mountain chains of Scandinavia, there are dozens of short rivers, which are partly connected to tens of thousands of lakes. Europe is a continent where there is a fine balance between water and land. The diversification of land and water is found even on a small scale throughout the continent, so that vegetation can thrive everywhere.

The threefold division of Europe has already been mentioned. The southern areas of the countries bordering the Mediterranean Sea, the Black Sea and the Caspian Sea, are driest and most arid, particularly in summer. The head lies here. The plain enclosed by the Pyrenees, Alps, Caucasus, Urals and Scandinavia can be viewed as the chest area. The digestive centre is located primarily in the shallow Irish Sea, the North Sea and the Norwegian Sea warmed by the Gulf Stream. From the point of view of gaiasophy, a continent is an even more complicated organism than a river basin. If the river as a flow organism is dependent on the organization of the transportation of moisture, which is essentially an air organism, a continent is concerned with this heat transference organism itself. The transfer function of a river is the transportation of water and the product is water enriched with minerals. The transfer function of the European continent is the transportation of air, which is dominated by the Gulf Stream, and the product is an exceptionally temperate climate with predominating wet westerly winds. Table 10.15 shows how the European organism is built up as a skeletal and flow organization.

The sweep of mountains from the Scottish Highlands to the Scandinavian mountain chains and the Urals, forms the chest, which encloses the most important river basins and inland seas. Above these river basins the internal continental circulation of air in Europe takes place, while the external exchange — with the Atlantic air and water circulation — takes place more in the area of inland seas. In Europe the role of the mountain system running from east to west is particularly interesting. This is the rib cage in the chest of the Earth's surface organism. These mountains fulfil the planning function of the European organism for the circulation of air by forcing air brought by westerly winds deep into the chest area to fall as rain on the mountain slopes. In this respect the Alps form the most important centre for the origin of the European rivers, the Rhine to the north, the Danube (which is by far the longest) to the east, the Rhône to the south and the Seine/Loire to the west. The Alps seem to have taken over from the first centre of the development of mankind, which was called the Garden of Eden. Four rivers, which were mentioned in an earlier chapter, also arose there. In this light, the Rhine can be seen as a counterpart of the Nile.

Apart from these mountain chains, the head of Europe consists of the sensory function of the Mediterranean Sea which registers the tidal movements and the sea level of the great Atlantic Ocean on a small scale like an instrument of measurement. This is possible because of the extremely small opening at the Straits of Gibraltar. In fact, the whole head area of Europe is protected from the oceanic influences bringing rain by the Iberian plateau.

Finally, the steering function of Europe, the climatic programming, can be seen in the combination of the Gulf Stream and east–west mountain chain. The Alps were formed by volcanic activity, which is now greatly reduced, but is still present in this area in active volcanoes, such as Mount Etna in Italy. The head of Europe, like the head of a reincarnated person, is a reminder of an earlier period in the development of mankind, when this area was the centre of activity for four thousand years during the Egyptian/Chaldean and Graeco–Roman cultures.

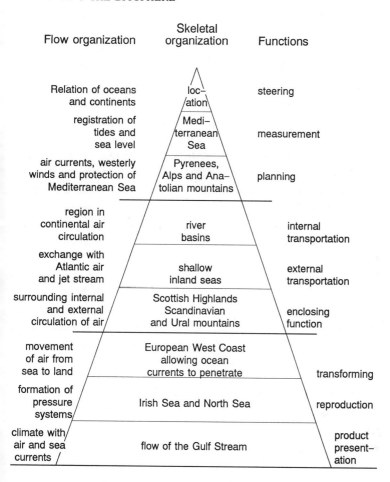

Flow organization	Skeletal organization	Functions
Relation of oceans and continents	loc-ation	steering
registration of tides and sea level	Medi-terranean Sea	measurement
air currents, westerly winds and protection of Mediterranean Sea	Pyrenees, Alps and Ana-tolian mountains	planning
region in continental air circulation	river basins	internal transportation
exchange with Atlantic air and jet stream	shallow inland seas	external transportation
surrounding internal and external circulation of air	Scottish Highlands Scandinavian and Ural mountains	enclosing function
movement of air from sea to land	European West Coast allowing ocean currents to penetrate	transforming
formation of pressure systems	Irish Sea and North Sea	reproduction
climate with air and sea currents	flow of the Gulf Stream	product present-ation

Table 10.15. The skeletal and flow organizations of the European continental organism.

Having outlined the skeletal and flow organizations of Europe, it is useful to consider the processes of disease and the possibilities of curing this organism.[20]

The increasing intensity of excessive consumption is expressed on a continental scale in the growing pollution of shallow seas, such as the Adriatic Sea in the head and the Irish Sea and the North Sea (with the Waddenzee) in the chest area. More and more frequently the water smells of spilt oil or putrefying algae. Animals such as seals, which are at the end of the food chain, are most exposed to the increasing quantities of toxic substances, such as cadmium and PCBs, and are threatened with extinction. This is exacerbated by the fact that the fish on which they feed are all caught by man. For example, in 1986 there were 60% fewer harp seals in Spitsbergen on the Norwegian coast, and on some islands there were 90% fewer guillemots. The cause of this is believed to be the too intensive fishery on smaller fish species on which these seals and birds feed. The herring catch in the North Sea has been disturbingly low for many years as a result of over-fishing. Spawning grounds along the coast and in parts of the river upstream have disappeared or have become inaccessible as a result of hydraulic engineering projects, such as sea walls, canals and dams. Even Europe's belly, which is much less vulnerable in principle than the water of the stagnating Mediterranean Sea, is succumbing to disease. This is exacerbated by the increasing erosion of woodland and agricultural areas. The acid rain in the chest area is threatening to destroy large areas of forest, so that the topsoil is in danger of being washed away, particularly on mountain slopes, leaving only bare rock. The jaws of the head area are rapidly expanding at the expense of the health-restoring chest area. The agricultural practices described above also lead to sickness and therefore have an erosive effect. All the silt that is taken by rivers to coastal waters means more fertilizers and more poisons. Apart from this process of disease spreading in Europe's belly, there is another danger which is found to an even greater extent in other continents: the land is drying out. As a result, the area surrounding the head expands, while the steering function which feeds the rivers declines, so that deposits of ice and ground water reserves shrink. The head grows at the expense of the chest, with a deregulating effect. In many southern European countries and in England the time is approaching when the water supply for agriculture and industry, as well as the population, will not be able to meet the demand. This has been the case in Israel for some time. Tourism in the dry summer season has aggravated the water shortage in Southern Europe. Because of this the so-called "water barrier," the point at which supply and demand are balanced, will become an important factor in future economies. This critical point will be exceeded in many of these countries by the beginning of the next century. It will be necessary to find solutions by recycling waste water and introducing far-reaching measures to save water, and ultimately the only answer will be the energy intensive desalination of sea-water. This results in an entirely artificial heart function, and it would not take much for a serious disaster to occur.

In the next century, Europe will also be confronted with the phenomenon of desertification unless alternatives are found to maintain a balance between the chest function and the belly and head. In view of the enormous annual flood of tourists from Europe's chest area to the head — to the ski slopes in winter and the beach in summer — this problem becomes even more difficult. It will be necessary for tourists, on the one hand, and the Earth organism on the other, to make many sacrifices. The steady waves of tourists have a deadening effect on the natural organism of Europe. It is as though the European population is subject to the same sort of process as spawning fish which seek to return to the "womb" every spring in the upper reaches of the river, its physical head. In the same way tourists seek their recreational escape every year in Europe's shrinking head area. It will be necessary to take measures to restrict tourism and pass the agricultural measures suggested above. These consist above all in restricting mobility, and limiting the use of artificial fertilizers and intensive cattle breeding in agriculture. In this way it will be possible to halt the erosion of agricultural land and stimulate the soil to form a new layer of humus, the real product of the natural landscape. Far-reaching measures will also have to be taken to combat acidity and deforestation and to initiate reforestation. It is essential to reduce the emission of sulphur dioxide and nitrous oxide from large power stations and refineries. In addition to limiting the numbers of cars, it is also necessary to further reduce the emission by vehicles of nitrous oxide and other gases harmful to vegetation, such as hydrocarbons, tetraethyl, lead and soot. Furthermore, it will be necessary to reduce drastically the emission of ammonia from the surplus manure produced by intensive animal rearing. A healthy farm contributes to strengthening the continent's chest function in two ways. Apart from retaining the layer of humus and keeping the subsoil alive, cultivated land and woodland has another essential function with regard to health — to stimulate the circulation of water on land.

Combatting acidity in Europe also means fighting encroaching desertification. Southern Europe has a great deal to learn from irrigation projects in Israel. A careful programme of planting and good forestry management is the preventive way of strengthening the continent's heart and lung functions. In this respect it should be remembered that irrigation projects based on natural ground water entail the risk of sickness through the use of technology. Artificial irrigation and agricultural activity based on this, which is much more extensive than the natural ecosystem can cope with, will sooner or later end in disaster. The current catastrophes in the Sahel are the direct result of grazing flocks which are much too large and which were artificially built up by the people with the help of ground water pumped up temporarily. As soon as there was a period of drought and the wells dried up, the land was first grazed bare, and then the animals died, leaving only desert.

Apart from stimulating the heart in a natural way by constructing decentralized supplies of water, and by encouraging the circulation of moisture in the atmosphere by forests, governments will have to have the courage — and people the wisdom — to limit the number of people and animals in an area to its natural capacity. This is the greatest challenge facing the European communities in 1992; to find a true cure for the sick organism of the continent. Plans for the future will first have to take into account the capacity of nature, the transformation functions of the landscape, the river and the continent to form humus, transport water and circulate air. Otherwise the process of ageing and dying will gain the upper hand, as has been the case in Africa for a long time.

Life in Europe is also threatened by dangers other than acid rain, surplus manure and the landscape drying out. These dangers are related to the functioning of the belly. The metabolism can be slowed down artificially, as in the Scandinavian lakes. In these lakes, which have little resistance to acid, acid rain resulted in aluminium being released in the sediment, which is harmful to fish. This means that the fish can no longer reproduce. In shallow seas other metals accumulate in the silt, and eventually stifle life. Nature has a defence mechanism against this process based on the conversion of metals by bacteria into volatile, organic metal compounds. Lovelock points out that the lung function can contribute to the detoxification of sediments by evaporating these volatile metal compounds which are formed, and distributing the substances over the land via the atmosphere in less harmful concentrations.[21] However, man will have to learn to release these harmful substances into the environment in a far more selective manner.

Recycling waste matter and retrieval processes are essential to restore the health of the continent, particularly in view of the scarcity of many raw materials in the long term. Materials should only be removed from circulation in exceptional cases. Everything should be assimilated in the constant stream of life processes in a controlled way, so that it is carried by the cells and organs, the urban landscapes and river basins themselves.

Finally, the health of Europe is extremely dependent on the Gulf Stream, which to a large extent determines the character of the climate and landscape, and the intensity of the air transportation organism characteristic of Europe, as we have already seen. The same applies for the jet stream in the higher troposphere. Small changes in its direction and in the composition and temperature of the water of the Gulf Stream will have far-reaching consequences for Europe. I will return to this again in the discussion of the Earth's biosphere.

At the moment, desiccation is only a threat to Europe, but in Africa it is a cruel fact of life. Africa is almost entirely in the tropics, and does not have a clear structure demarcated by mountain chains, as in Eurasia and in North and South America. It is really almost a single large plateau. In East Africa there is a volcanic area with the continent's highest peak, Mount Kilimanjaro, which is almost 6000 metres high. Africa's largest lakes are also found here, such as Lake Victoria and Lake Tanganyika. The largest rivers are the Nile, the only river to cross the Sahara

Desert, the Congo (Zaire), the Niger, the Zambezi and the Orange River. The chest function has been receding in many areas ever since the last ice age, so that dry landscapes and desert areas dominate the continent. Approximately a third of the land has no drainage, and in these areas the organism has died. Thus Africa is not merely sick, but dying. Cutting down tropical rainforests for hardwoods and creating agricultural land, as well as the above-mentioned over-use of the savannah, where the heart function was artificially strengthened with water pumped from underground, are speeding up the process. I will not describe the skeletal organization and the exact drainage system of Africa — as I did for Europe — but I will consider some typically African phenomena in general. Table 9.11 shows a general classification of the twofold continental organism of Africa.

In Africa the aspect of metabolism which is responsible for the sickness is expressed in a different way — in the fact that the land is starved and exhausted. In order to combat this exhaustion it is first necessary to reduce man's intense exploitation of the land, which implies that the patient, the continent of Africa, needs additional feeding. The tropical rainforests, the greatest supplier of water for the continent, must be maintained as far as possible.

Almost as much water evaporates from the tropical rainforest as from the same area of tropical ocean. It is this production and circulation of water in the atmosphere which comprises the continental heart function of the rainforest. In this way the tropical rainforests largely produce their own circulation of water. Cutting down the forests is like closing Africa's aorta, which means that the heart function itself dies off. When this happens the metabolic process can no longer take place, and life dies out. The head, a splendid crystal world, with the desolation of aridity and the monotony of mineral waste, takes possession of the land. Suchantke describes how the rainforest grows on soil which is very poor in minerals and on an extremely thin layer of humus.[22] All the minerals required for life are contained in the life cycle. Trees can only grow when the seeds germinate in the rotting wood of fallen trees. When this is forgotten, the consequences are disastrous.[23] When the trees are cut down and agriculture in the open spaces is very productive for the first few years. This soon changes, as the soil is no longer protected by the canopy from being dried out by the heat of the Sun. The humus disappears and the soluble nutritious minerals are washed away by heavy rain. After that, the disturbed land can only feed less demanding vegetation such as grass, and is therefore lost forever, both to man and to the forest. Therefore the tropical rainforests should only be cultivated by opening them up in a way which leaves the forest itself intact.

In the forest (see Table 10.16), the vegetable world and the digestive processes are extremely dominant.[24] It is a purely ethereal world, which also penetrates the astral aspect of the forest.

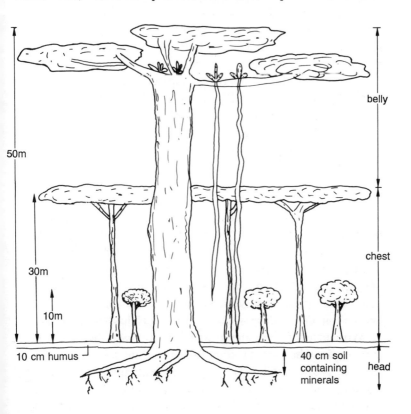

Table 10.16. The composition of the tropical rainforest (using Suchantke's model).

Everything in this belly area is concerned with digestion and metabolism, as in deep sleep. This means that all vegetable matter is strongly expressed, as are the insects which live on the plants, which reveal a range of shape and colour which matches the stages in the different crowns of trees extending up to 50 metres high. The actual belly area of the tropical rainforest, with ferns and spreading liana vines, is 40–50 metres above the thin layer of humus and minerals on the ground, which is only about 50 cm thick altogether. The head of the rainforest has been considerably reduced and assimilated entirely into the life-processes. In the dark rainforest of sleeping consciousness, animals and man whose consciousness is higher than that of plants, cannot take root. There are fewer men and animals than in the savannah, and those that do live there are less developed. In the tropical rainforest animals such as buffalo, dwarf antelope and chimpanzees are smaller in size than related species in the savannah. In the dark forest, man's development has also been arrested at a more childlike stage. Pygmies develop to sexual maturity but this is not followed by further physical growth.

The savannah is a typical rhythmic chest area. Next to the desert, it is the most characteristic landscape of the African continent, where light and dark contrast strongly, as do drought and rain, and aridity and luxurious growth. Man and animals are more fully developed. The astral mammalian world of the savannah reveals its greater wealth in the many different species of antelope, gnu, springbok, buffalo and zebra, which coexist and graze in groups. In addition, there are giraffe and elephant which feed on leaves. These species eat different types of foliage, so that they are complementary and help to determine the shape of the African landscape. Zebra eat young fresh grass, gazelle graze on the remaining stubble, and giraffe specialize in thorny plants.

Without disturbing the growth, in this way the savannah is protected against spontaneous fires which would otherwise have a much greater effect. Although their numbers are not striking, the predators — with 0.6% of the animal biomass — are essential to keep the numbers of grazing animals below a certain upper limit. If this were exceeded, it would result in over-grazing, food shortages and disease. Lions, hyenas and jackals, together with birds of prey like the eagle, are important for maintaining a balance. As a chest creature, the lion is perfectly adapted for the central area of the African landscape, where it rules as king. There is also a much greater wealth of bird life in the savannah than in the jungle. Vultures, falcons and storks are typical inhabitants of the savannah. In this way the astral animal world is dominant in the savannah between the ethereal world of plants in the tropical rainforests and the physical world of the mineral desert. This includes: the lion, as lord of the astral savannah; the eagle, which nests in the transitional area between the savannah and the rainforest; and, on the other hand, the cattle, which live on the edge of the desert with the camel as their typical representative. Once again we see a reflection of the astral world in relation to the physical world. The eagle, a creature of the head, lives in Africa's physical belly, while the camel, a creature of the belly, lives in Africa's physical head. The final element of the astral world of animals is formed by the indigenous population, which embodies the continent's Self-awareness, as illustrated in Table 10.17.

There is also a horizontal threefold division in the savannah itself. On the one hand, there are areas with many trees and shrubs with cultivated fields, which mark the surround of the remaining chest area. Then there is the central area, where every acacia tree stands alone, surrounded by grassland. The acacia tree is the sign that the horizontal and vertical planes are interconnected, and it stylistically symbolizes the external transportation function. Finally, there is the steppe, as the part of the savannah with the least vegetation, consisting mostly of grassland. In Africa, everything turns into its counterpart because the head of the continent is dead. Thus the internal transportation function of the steppe is barely recognizable as a result of drought. The grass is the final reminder of the organization of a drainage system which should encompass the whole continent. The grassland is grazed by wandering herds of cattle; the Masai steppe at Arusha in Tanzania is an example of this. The Masai, and other nomadic tribes such as the Iraku, travelling around in the treeless grassland, demonstrate a cultural isolation and warlike aggression. The self-awareness of the African has reached its peak in those who

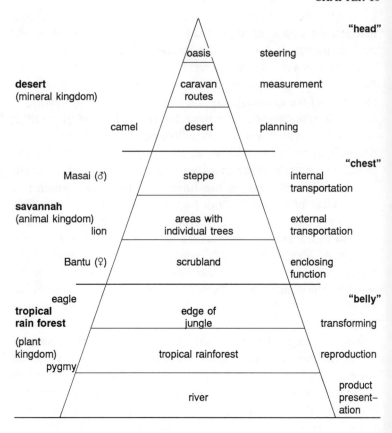

		"head"
	oasis	steering
desert (mineral kingdom)	caravan routes	measurement
camel	desert	planning
		"chest"
Masai (♂)	steppe	internal transportation
savannah (animal kingdom) lion	areas with individual trees	external transportation
Bantu (♀)	scrubland	enclosing function
eagle **tropical rain forest**	edge of jungle	"belly" transforming
(plant kingdom) pygmy	tropical rainforest	reproduction
	river	product presentation

Table 10.17. The general structure of the skeletal organization and representatives of the natural astral body of the African continent.

live at the edge of the desert. The negroes, such as the Bantu and Sudanese negroes, stand between the pygmies, bushmen and Hottentots, who live in the jungle, and the Masai who inhabit the steppes. They have a much more feminine character than the masculine Masai herdsmen. They are skilled at cultivating the land, and they have succeeded in transforming the landscape into cultivated woodland in a natural way. There are tall, individual jungle trees between the banana plantations and papayas, so that the landscape has a varied character. The Giriama have planted an attractive landscape of slender coconut palms round mango

296

trees and other trees in the monsoon area on the East African coast. This landscape is an example of co-operation between man and nature.

The general African continental organism has another curious aspect with regard to the dead head area. In an area where everything has dried up, the oasis has a steering function and serves as a final reminder of the luxurious growth of the tropical rainforest. The oasis has lost its steering function in the continental organism, but serves as a sort of seed, leaving a last small imprint of the larger whole behind it. The transformation function of the skeletal organization of the African landscape in the tropical rainforests is found on the edge of the jungle, the transition between the arid plain and the moist world of the plant kingdom. Just as new land is constantly being created in the wet landscape of Europe, the African landscape requires rain and plants to grow to form humus. Both the oasis and the tropical rainforest express this product in their springs and rivers.

In Africa, the land creates water, while in Europe, land is created from water. This is because the continental organism has not developed beyond the chest function because of the lack of water, and the belly function — which has developed in Europe — is absent.

According to Suchantke, all hope is not yet lost for Africa if monocultures are avoided in farming and the herds on the steppes are kept sufficiently small, while the tropical rainforest is allowed to complete its natural cycle of water and minerals.[25] The land on the African continent originates virtually entirely from the Pre-Cambrian era, and is therefore the oldest of all the continents. Man can learn from his mistakes here. Africa is most vulnerable to the unhealthy effect of over-intensive digestive processes in relation to its natural capacity. The elements which could stimulate the continental heart function lie in the cultivation of fields and animal husbandry which have been practised by the indigenous population for centuries. Together with an insight into the functioning of the complex, delicate organism of the African continent, which is constantly on the edge of an abyss, it is necessary for man to take the first steps to co-operate with nature rather than exploit it.

In Europe, the chest area is surrounded by water, while in Africa it is surrounded by desert. This most clearly expresses the completely different orientation and situation of the two continents. It also leads to the reversal of the characteristic transformation functions of the two continents, which was noted above. In other words, while the river functions in Europe as a link with the vital belly processes, the African organism is halted at the stage of the river. In Europe the belly area lies in the water, so that the organism is threatened by toxication as well as by an excessive wealth of foodstuffs. In Africa, the poorly developed belly lies in the centre of the tropical rainforest, so that all the foodstuffs available are part of an intensive cycle which is therefore much more unstable.

It is necessary to restrict the growth of the population in order to reduce the demands on scarce food supplies. The tropical rainforest as a supply of water will also have to be spared by ensuring that land is cultivated without destroying it. This is also essential to maintain the continent's heart function. Furthermore, a small-scale pattern of integrated arable farming and animal breeding in the savannah to expand the capacity of the heart function is an important ingredient of the essential therapy to help to cure the chronically sick continent of Africa.

The main aspects of the continental organism in the light of gaiasophy were discussed in relation to Europe and Africa. There are big differences between every continent. Each requires an individual analysis and approach to its symptoms.

10.10   The globe

In Chapter 9 I examined the surface organism of the Earth, or biosphere of the globe. The global organism is the heart of planet Earth (see Table 9.2). The skeletal organization of the globe was indicated in Tables 9.4 and 9.5. Table 10.18 shows a brief summary of the system developed on the basis of the principles of gaiasophy.

The vertical dimension now plays an even greater role, extending from the lithosphere to the tropopause. This means that the direct link to specific points on the surface is becoming less clear. The head and chest can be found above the northern hemisphere. The steering function is determined by the Earth's rotation on its axis, symbolized in the North Pole, the fluctuation in the Earth's axis, which determines the seasons, the melting polar ice and the Earth's magnetism, which influences the distribution of heat by ocean currents and volcanic activity. This helps to determine the location of mountains and the albedo (the ratio of the diffuse light reflected by a body to the amount of incident light falling on it). The planning function lies in the position of the oceans and continents and the location of mountain chains on these. The internal transportation function is responsible for the exchange of the processes taking place above the tropopause, such as ozone formation and solar radiation. In this the albedo has a regulating effect. The enclosing function is exercised by the tropopause, which forms the boundary for the transportation of evaporated water. The characteristic transformation function of the globe is the conversion of radiation into heat, in which light is first absorbed by the surface of the Earth and the heating is the result of the returned heat radiation. This heating system is repeated in the rhythm of day/night and summer/winter, which is determined by the steering function. The result is that of a greenhouse in which life flourishes. In this greenhouse or biosphere the northern hemisphere has more solid land, while the southern hemisphere is mostly covered by water. This is reminiscent of the duality in the global organism between hard and soft, giving and receiving, male and female, parallel to the northern and southern hemispheres. The north and south poles of the magnetic field reinforce this image of a globe composed of a male and a female half. With the help of the ethereal body, the mineral kingdom of the globe carries the plant kingdom, the astral body carries the animal kingdom, and the human race constitutes the constant Self within this system. Just as man's blood regulates the heating system and carries the Self, the biosphere and its heating system carries mankind, and therefore the globe's organization of its Self.

When the Self interferes in an unharmonious way with the lower kingdoms or organizations of the biosphere, it becomes sick and increasingly out of balance. With the help of the higher forces within him, man must restore harmony to the globe. If he fails to do so, the higher hierarchies may be forced to interfere to save the Earth at the expense of many human lives.

Man has not yet had any direct visible influence on the globe's steering function. However, the sensitive interaction of the lung function is becoming unbalanced because of the industrial waste gases accumulating in the troposphere and stratosphere and the resulting change in the heating system.[26] A similar phenomenon could occur in relation to the heart function when floating blankets of algae develop on the surface of the sea as a result of the accumulation of mineral salts in the seas and oceans. These could change the reflection of light and the evaporation of water,and therefore the internal heating circulation system. An increase in the amount of nutrients in the oceans and a decrease in the amount on land are developments which are expected in the future. In the northern hemisphere, there are extensive areas where intensive farming and the generation of energy greatly exceed the natural level. This applies for the east of the United States, the whole of Europe and parts of China and Japan. Crosson summarized some of the anticipated trends in population growth and urbanization.[27] In the period 1950–2050 the population of the world could increase from 2.7 thousand million to 6.8 thousand million or more, and it is also expected that the percentage of the population living in urban areas will rise from 40% in 1975 to almost double in a hundred years' time. This illustrates the strength of the driving force behind technology referred to previously, which will have to be adapted everywhere in the world to the living organism of the Earth's surface. In rural areas human exploitation of the rainforests and woodlands could lead to reduced local evaporation and precipitation. Every year $360\,000$ km^3 of water evaporates from the surface of water on the Earth, while $70\,000$ km^3 evaporates from the land surface, the lion's share being produced by areas of vegetation. The development of high and low pressure areas, areas of rainfall and the related winds and oceanic currents, are to a large extent determined by the process of evaporation in the belly area. The delicate balance in the biosphere could first be disrupted by man in the tropical rainforests, as shown in the continent of Africa. Although there is a programme of reforestation in North America

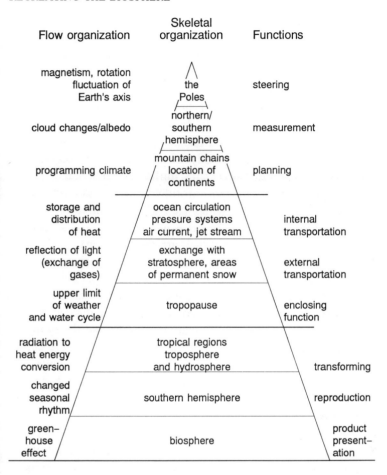

Flow organization	Skeletal organization	Functions
magnetism, rotation fluctuation of Earth's axis	the Poles	steering
cloud changes/albedo	northern/ southern hemisphere	measurement
programming climate	mountain chains location of continents	planning
storage and distribution of heat	ocean circulation pressure systems air current, jet stream	internal transportation
reflection of light (exchange of gases)	exchange with stratosphere, areas of permanent snow	external transportation
upper limit of weather and water cycle	tropopause	enclosing function
radiation to heat energy conversion	tropical regions troposphere and hydrosphere	transforming
changed seasonal rhythm	southern hemisphere	reproduction
green-house effect	biosphere	product present-ation

Table 10.18. The skeletal and flow organization of the global organism.

and Western Europe, the process of deforestation worldwide is almost unstoppable. During the period 1955 to 1980, it was leading to the desertification of the Earth at a rate of 70000 km² per year.[28] There will be further desertification and increasing erosion of the Earth in future, and the capacity of the heart function to restore the health and rejuvenate the Earth will therefore decline. Richards estimated that worldwide, soil erosion caused by man increased from approximately 16×10^9 tonnes per year

301

before agriculture was practised to 91×10^9 tonnes per year in 1978.[29]

Apart from deforestation and erosion, there is also a rapid decrease of marshlands in river deltas and coastal areas as a result of the reclamation of land. Although this reclamation can to some extent compensate for the consequences of erosion, and is the result of a natural process in the landscape organism, rapid reclamation affects the continental reproductive function, so that the continental astral body no longer works successfully. Richards estimates that almost 100 million hectares of marshlands in tidal waters has disappeared worldwide during the last century in order to meet the growing need for agricultural land. The consequences of this for the geo–chemical cycle of substances have not yet been listed, but they are not difficult to imagine. It is more difficult to assess whether man is capable of having a real influence on the distribution of air pressure which is essential for rainfall and temperature control. It is clear that the globe's heart function has been affected. Europe in particular is very sensitive to this. Other air circulation systems and the changing rate of melting of the icecap of the North Pole as the result of rising temperatures could change the Gulf Stream so much that the mild climate of Europe would be altered. This could lead to an acceleration of the ageing process in Europe for which there is no immediate remedy.

The belly processes and heart and lung functions of the global organism are greatly interwoven, which shows how important it is for man to learn to respect the smaller scale of the continent, river basin and landscape from the perspective of gaiasophy.

10.11   The planet Earth

For the Earth as a planet the vertical dimension is predominant. Tables 8.2 and 8.5 outlined the skeletal organization of planet Earth. Table 10.19 gives a survey of the skeletal and flow organization of the planet Earth.

On the basis of the principle of the threefold division, the health of the planetary system depends on its food in the form of hydrogen and radiation rich in energy, which are absorbed and converted in the thin belly and chest layers. The Sun sends a total of 342 watts/m^2 of energy to the Earth, of which 46% reaches the Earth's surface.[30] There is a relatively low uptake of radiation of 4% by what I described as the Earth's lungs, the ozone layer, where ozone is formed by the effect of UV radiation on oxygen. Finally, as we saw at the global level, the radiation reflected by the solid and liquid areas of the Earth is converted into heat in the troposphere, which functions as a greenhouse.

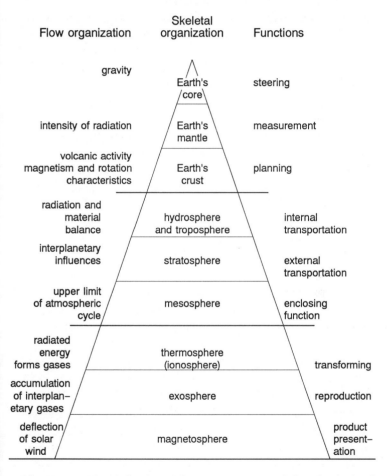

Flow organization	Skeletal organization	Functions
gravity	Earth's core	steering
intensity of radiation	Earth's mantle	measurement
volcanic activity magnetism and rotation characteristics	Earth's crust	planning
radiation and material balance	hydrosphere and troposphere	internal transportation
interplanetary influences	stratosphere	external transportation
upper limit of atmospheric cycle	mesosphere	enclosing function
radiated energy forms gases	thermosphere (ionosphere)	transforming
accumulation of interplanetary gases	exosphere	reproduction
deflection of solar wind	magnetosphere	product presentation

Table 10.19.   The skeletal and flow organization of the planet Earth organism.

303

There is a total of about 240 watts/m^2 available for the climate. A change in the supply of radiation and hydrogen from the Sun to the Earth would have grave consequences for the biosphere. The proportion of solar radiation reflected into space by the Earth is called the planetary albedo. As the planet Earth is a delicate organism filtering streams of energy, I will briefly examine the various ways in which this can be disturbed.

As mentioned in the discussion of the heating system of the global organism, which fulfils the heart function of the planetary organism, the "light–energy" available for heating may change as a result of altered cloud formations, changed reflection characteristics of the Earth's surface, and so on. To some extent the Earth can monitor these itself to adapt to long–term changes in the intensity of solar radiation. Lovelock pointed this out in connection with his Gaia hypothesis.[31] Man also has an increasing influence by extending the area of land on the Earth's surface and accelerating the process of desertification. Nevertheless, the Sun continues to function as the most important steering organ for the Earth's balance of energy. However, this concerns the larger organism of the solar system, which will not be dealt with here. The Earth's head itself steers through gravitational fields emanating from the core. Gravitation determines the relation of the Earth with the Moon, the Sun and the other planets and stars, and therefore the effect of their influence on Earthly relations. Is there a connection with the periodic volcanic activity and mountain formation? Steiner clearly indicated that there is.[32] It is obvious that volcanic activity and the resulting pattern and relief of the continents and oceans has a great influence on the biosphere and reflects the measurable result of former impulses from the centre of the Earth, just as the level of the sea says something about rainfall, ice formation and temperature on the globe. Apart from the steering effect of gravitation and extra–terrestrial bodies, the planet's planning function is exercised by the characteristics of the Earth's rotation, combined with volcanic activity and the magnetic field, which have a great influence on the weather, as described above. For example, many of the climatic changes that have taken place since the pre–Cambrian era could be explained by volcanic activity and the emission of particles which led to a cooling process.[33] The heart and lung functions have already been discussed. The enclosing function is exercised by the mesosphere, which serves as a diaphragm for the atmospheric circulation in the characteristic composition of the Earth irradiated with light. The planet's characteristic transformation function can be found in the thermosphere. Here the Sun's radiation of energy is converted in co-ordination with gravity, creating — as viewed from space — a composition and distribution of gaseous molecules in a ratio which is characteristic of the Earth and essential for the biosphere. From Earth it is seen as the complete diffusion of gases, but from space it is seen as an enrichment and ordering of gases which begins in the exosphere, the area of ethereal life.

The magnetosphere is the magnetic field with which the Earth manifests itself in solar wind. It is important to know to what extent man disrupts the balance of the planet's higher chest and

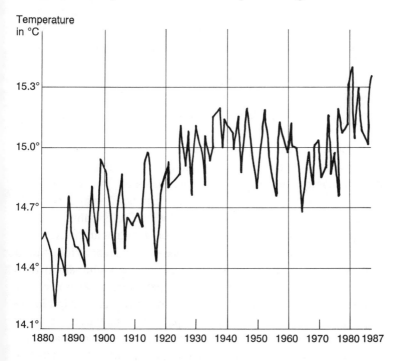

Table 10.20. Rise in the average temperature during the last century (New York Times, March 29, 1988)

belly functions. It is clear that in the past century there have been important changes in the heating system of the chest area and possibly also in the energy system of the Earth's belly. Since the nineteenth century the carbon dioxide content of the atmosphere has risen from 0.028% to 0.034%. According to Dickinson,[34] a further rise may be expected to levels between 0.05 and 0.2% in the year 2100. The content of other trace gases, such as chlorofluorocarbons (CFCs), which are used as propellants in aerosols, has mushroomed since the Second World War; between 1975 and 1985 the average content of CFCs rose by 100%. There will be a considerable rise in the concentration of CFCs in the troposphere and stratosphere, even if their use is terminated immediately. Dickinson expects that dichloro–difluoro–methane will increase from 0.3 ppb (parts per thousand million) to between 2 and 10 ppb by the year 2100. Together with other gases, such as methane and nitrous oxide, which accumulate in the Earth's chest, this can lead to an increase in heat at the upper level of the troposphere from 3 to 15 watts/m^2, and a rise in temperature from 2° to 10°C (see Table 10.20). The rise which occurred during the 1980s is particularly remarkable in view of the 0.2% annual decrease in solar radiation intensity, and the long–term expected decline in temperature related to an anticipated ice age.[35] Atmospheric pollution by the above–mentioned gases is a probable explanation. This influence on the climate of trace gases and carbon dioxide released by the energy generated as a result of the combustion of fossil fuels, is much greater than the amount of heat released by the energy extracted, which amounts to approximately 0.02 watts/m^2 worldwide. Furthermore, a global change in climate could be brought about by nuclear war.[36] The smoke produced as a result of large–scale fires which would follow nuclear explosions could cause summer temperatures to fall by 15°C over the entire northern hemisphere, as a result of sunlight being screened out. This would cause a drastic fall in the potential yield of agricultural crops. Obviously even if these crops did grow, they would be contaminated with radioactivity, as was clearly shown throughout Europe following the much less serious nuclear accident at Chernobyl in 1986.

The differences in the organization of energy as a result of climatic changes will disrupt the hydrological cycle and cause shifts in the frequency of storms and patterns of rainfall to which the organizational infrastructure for water is not adapted. A rise in sea level of up to 1.3 metres is expected in the next century as a result of the expansion of the waters of the oceans as they heat up, and the possible melting of polar ice. This could also lead to the disappearance of glaciers in the Alps in the next century. If the planet becomes approximately 2°C warmer, this will be a greater change in temperature than has ever taken place since the beginning of man's history in approximately 5000 BC.[37] Man is experimenting with the Earth's biosphere without any idea of the outcome. Surprises are likely in the next few years, as man's knowledge increases.

Apart from these climatological effects, there has been growing concern since 1985 about the hole forming in the Antarctic ozone layer during the months of September and October. This causes a rise in harmful UV radiation on the Earth's surface, and indicates that the Earth's lung function is affected by substances containing chlorine which are produced by the above–mentioned propellants and which catalytically destroy the ozone.[38] In the years from 1975 to 1985 the ozone content above the South Pole fell by approximately 50%. In 1988 the hole was not as large, which is explained by the weaker vortex of the east–west stratospheric winds at that point and the higher temperature of the air in the vortex, so that the chemical reactions between chlorine compounds and ozone do not take place so easily.[39] In the next few years the hole may become still larger. Apart from the effects of CFCs on the ozone layer in the stratosphere and the increasing carcinogenic UV radiation on the Earth's surface, a change in the stratosphere's balance of heat could also result. This means that the stratosphere will become colder, and in turn there would be a change in the Earth's wind and weather patterns.[40] From these examples it is clear that the Earth's heartbeat and lung function are being disrupted by man at a planetary level.

There are also influences from outside planet Earth. Without discussing the functioning of the organism of the solar system in detail, it nevertheless deserves a mention, as interesting discoveries have recently been made. Francesco Paresche and Stuart

Bowyer, for example, describe how the Sun's eleven–year solar spot activity results in a respiratory phenomenon.[41] At its peak, solar activity results in hydrogen atoms being flung into space by the radiation pressure from the Sun. When solar activity is low, the Sun's gravitational attraction overcomes the pressure of radiation, and hydrogen atoms move towards the Sun. This process of breathing in and out has an eleven–year cycle and can also be discerned in the direct supply of radiation to the Earth. It is even more important that interstellar gas clouds can float through our solar system in which the density of hydrogen can rise to 10 to 1000 atoms per cm^3, instead of 0.12 atoms per cm^3. It has been calculated that in the last 4.5 thousand million years the Sun has encountered at least one hundred gas clouds with a density of over 100 hydrogen atoms per cm^3. When the Sun encounters an interstellar gas cloud, which is passed in an average period of approximately 100 years, and when this has a density of approximately 150 hydrogen atoms per cm^3 or more, this can lead to a supply of hydrogen to the Earth up to 2000 times greater than that present at the moment. Presumably this extra amount of hydrogen would result in reactions with free oxygen radicals in the thermosphere and ozone layer resulting in a stream of water vapour aimed at the Earth. This water vapour condenses into clouds which reflect solar radiation. This would cause the temperature on the Earth's surface to fall, and after thousands of years would lead to an ice age. In this way an excess in the hydrogen supplied to the belly could also lead to disease by influencing the heart function.

In addition to the example of a change in the belly process, this area of the planetary organism is still unexplored territory. It is very easy for man to inflict damage in this thin atmosphere. Perhaps the effect of piercing the layers of the belly with rockets which emit large quantities of heat and gases in the highly subtle and rarefied atmosphere, is comparable to firing a cannon in a bedroom.

These changes in the planet's implementation system and connecting system, which are caused by man and his technology, are of great importance in the long term. The rise of the carbon dioxide and other gas levels in the atmosphere by 30% over the last century, the anticipated climatic changes, the possible accelerated melting of the polar ice-caps and the annually increasing hole in the ozone layer above Antarctica during the months of September and October, all these constitute more than mere writing on the wall. If the heart and lung functions of planet Earth are affected, this will mean greater instability in the biosphere. This in turn results in a greater vulnerability to periodic cosmic changes in the interstellar medium, and to uncontrolled disasters on Earth. Furthermore, society is increasingly vulnerable to natural disasters which can — at a stroke — immobilize the entire infrastructure of electrical installations, gas pipes, water supply systems, dams and locks, dependent on technology, thus paralysing the whole of society. How strong is the dam of a reservoir or of a nuclear power station against earthquakes or a reversal of magnetic poles? Where should large-scale development be replaced by small-scale development? Although our understanding of the planet's regulating mechanisms is still in its infancy, it is clear that human interference with these global functions — and unfortunately man's capacity for such intervention is constantly increasing — can bring about great risks of accelerated change for the biosphere and the death of the chest and belly organs. It is therefore particularly urgent to set up an effective controlling agency with supranational powers, greater than those of the present United Nations, based on an understanding of the Earth's anatomy and physiology. Twenty-four countries voted in favour of such an agency in the Hague Declaration of 11 March 1989.

10.12   Organizational levels for the Earth organism

Now that the Earth's anatomy and physiology are clearer, I will look back and examine the relation of the natural components of the planetary organism. What are its most characteristic cells and organs? What changes take place in the transition from a lower to a higher spatial organizational level? Which functions are most sensitive to disruption by man? I will then discuss the problem of improved controlling organs for natural and social organisms. First, it is important to understand the Earth's — or Gaia's —

309

carrying capacity. Many initially invisible organizations operate at different levels on our singular planet Earth. Some reinforce and monitor each other; others are in conflict with each other. In order to establish which organizations have a steering function, and which are steered, I will first arrange these different organizations in ascending order of size. In doing this, I have not always separated the natural organism from the social organism. Even a farm is a part of nature that is strongly influenced by man.

Table 10.21 contains a survey of the organization of nature, based on the system outlined above. Five characteristic organizational levels of the Earth organism are distinguished, following from the survey developed in Table 10.4 for urbanized areas:

the landscape
the river basin
the continent
the globe
planet Earth.

This series can be extended upwards and downwards, but it is sufficient for our present purposes. The component parts of the landscape in particular are often the subject of scientific study. Therefore the landscape organism requires some elucidation. A landscape is part of a river basin, and may in turn be composed of smaller units, such as woods, lakes and fields. However, a more detailed analysis of the natural components of a landscape shows that in principle it has the same characteristic life function in the flow organization. The flow organization of the natural landscape is characterized by rainfall as the steering function, the composition of the soil as the planning function, and the vertical transportation of water and nutrients in the roots and plants, which carries out the essential transformation function. Plants are the highest form in which the drainage system expresses itself as a living organism. In the landscape solid matter is dissolved in the soil and is transformed, via the growth and decay of plants, into humus, a new life-giving layer of soil. There is also a limited amount of erosion and silting. In the landscape the vertical dimension is dominant in solid matter and the characteristic transformation process consists of dissolving and depositing solid matter.

In the river basin the characteristic transformation function is the transportation of water from land to sea, a combination of the vertical and horizontal dimension on the mainland. On the continent both transformation functions play a natural role, but the characteristic additional transformation process is the

Functions	Landscape	River basin	Continent	Globe	Planet
steering	rainfall, fire	height profile, tornados	location and geographical structure	magnetism, volcanic activity, rotation	gravity, movement in space
measurement	groundwater level	snowline, water level of river	sea level, temperature	cloud formation, albedo, salt content of sea	radiation and volcanic eruptions
planning	composition of soil	rainfall, fire	size, location of mountain chains	location of continents, mountains, ocean current	pattern of magnetic and volcanic activity, etc.
internal transportation	vertical flow of groundwater and nutrients	horizontal flow of groundwater and drainage	hydrological cycle of the continent	heat storage and distribution in hydrosphere	balance of radiation and matter in troposphere/ stratosphere
external transportation	horizontal flow of water and nutrients	evaporation, aeration	exchange of oceanic pressure systems	exchange of radiation and gas with stratosphere	energy and hydrogen exchange with interstellar space
enclosing	periphery of geographical area	periphery of river basin	periphery of continent/ ocean system	tropopause	mesosphere
transformation	solution and deposit of solids	transportation of water from land to sea	transportation of air from sea to land	transfer of heat from strato- to hydrosphere	transfer of energy from interstellar space to stratosphere
reproductive	vegetation	river bed	coast	surface of Earth	exosphere
product presentation	humus, silt	running water	wind	climate	atmospheric composition

Table 10.21. Survey of the nine functions in the five characteristic organizational levels of the Earth organism.

transportation of air from sea to land which makes the two former processes possible. At the global level the essential additional transformation is that of light in warmth, while in the planetary organism, light and the structure of chemical elements in the atmosphere are formed from radiating energy. "Light" led to the creation of Earth. This gives a fascinating insight into the combination of the five spatial and organizational levels in Gaia's body and the related phenomena. These five visible phenomena can also be found in the human organism.

The "Earth's flow" is found in the renewal of the physical body every seven years and in the excretion of the faeces, the flow of water in the passing of urine and in perspiration, the transportation of air in respiration. Heat is transported by radiation, the highest phenomenon in which the human Self manifests itself physically. The light radiated by man cannot be directly physically observed, although it is well-known that some people have a greater "radiance" than others, a quality that is related to man's higher bodies. As man follows the path of initiation and becomes more "enlightened," his radiance increases. The higher organizational levels of the Earth's body are characterized by the transformation process becoming less and less physical than in the lower processes. The light from the Sun, filtered through the Earth's belly and chest organs, controls the Earth's climate. This determines the flow of air over the oceans and continents in which the river's organization for transporting water is embedded. The product of all these organizations is the formation of humus and the deposits of silt from dissolved matter on the solid surface of the landscape and at the bottom of the sea.

This means that there are many lessons to be learned regarding the sickness of Gaia and restoring it to health. The landscape is sick when too much humus is created; the river is sick when too much water is transported; too much wind makes the continent sick, too much heat makes the globe sick and too much "light" makes the planet Earth sick. Of course, sickness can also be the result of a shortage rather than an excess. All these symptoms can be cured by the heart and lung functions. The landscape of marshland and jungle can be cured by the proper regulation of ground and surface water, a good flow organization. Conversely, irrigation can restore harmony in an arid area. Excessive vegetation in lakes can be limited by preventing too much erosion and the discharge of plant nutrients. A river in which the rainfall flows away too quickly can be restored to health by planting woods on mountain slopes, creating ground water reservoirs, and constructing protective dykes as a temporary measure. The occurrence of strong winds is not yet one of the fields in which man consciously intervenes on a scale of continental significance. To do this, it would be necessary to intervene in the hydrological cycle — although this does occur in many places for other reasons, such as the construction of reservoirs, the reclamation of marshlands and the destruction of tropical rainforests. The distribution of oceanic pressure systems as a regulating factor is important in this respect. These heart and lung functions are exposed, often unintentionally, to changes which can lead to an undesirable increase and shift in the transportation of air.

Changes in the transportation of heat are the surprising result of the global climatic changes expected in the short term. It is well known that the disruption of the exchange of gas and radiation between the stratosphere and the troposphere is responsible for this. Man has no short-term remedy for this disruption of the balance in radiation which is the inevitable result of the dumped substances finding their way into the larger organism of the planet through the lung function. The disease will have to run its course, even after the cause — the emission of gases such as carbon dioxide and chlorofluorocarbons (CFCs) — has been considerably reduced. Finally, the area of the transportation of energy and the formation of light still lies outside the attention of scientific research and society. Very little is known about the possible causes of a disturbance in the balance of energy in the planetary organism. However, this possibility should not be excluded if man influences the planet's heart and lung functions. This is an important area for further research.

In addition to the sickness of the Earth organism at one or more levels as a result of excessive or inadequate feeding and the lack of balance in the heart or lung function at one or several spatial levels, the steering and planning functions also play an important role in the complicated process of disease. If the

313

steering function, the intention and the planning function (the programme for implementing the intention) are not adapted to the capacity of the transformation process of, for example, the landscape or continent, this results in an unhealthy lack of harmony. If the soil is polluted, the plants are sick. The size of the area determines the maximum extent of the vegetation, just as the amount of rainfall determines the average capacity of the river and the amount of water and minerals which are available for the growth of plants. The composition of the soil has already been greatly influenced by man. For many years experiments have been carried out to increase the rainfall, which fulfils the steering function in the landscape and the planning function for the river. For example, in the Soviet Union experiments have been made with scattering silver iodide crystals. Sooner or later we will have artificial rain or sunshine. Changes in the water level of rivers can be traced back to reservoirs and dykes. In this field much more advanced structures are also conceivable for influencing rainfall. The steering functions of the higher organizations, such as the position of continents, the dynamics of the Earth in space, volcanic activity, magnetism and gravity, are still beyond the reach of human technology. Table 10.22 gives a summary of the "five scale model" for the natural ecosystem levels. It is clear that interference in the Earth's higher organizational levels would be most damaging, just as disrupting a top level steering function in an organization is more effective than disturbing a lower executive function. All high-level changes affect the lower levels. Substances which escape from the cycle at one level of the scale because they are "breathed out" to a higher level by the lung function will sooner or later leave problems there, if they are not easily broken down. CFCs pass through all the levels and accumulate in the stratosphere with the well-known harmful result.

We now have a better understanding of unhealthy factors and where they operate in Gaia's spatial organism. In addition, the connection between the Earth's lower organizations and higher organizations is quite clear. The steering function of the lower body, when multiplied, becomes the planning function of the higher body. In this way the height of mountain chains forms the continent's planning function and the steering function of the river basin. This is the connection in the head area.

There is another connecting mechanism in the chest area. The external transportation function of the lower spatial organizations forms the internal transportation function of the higher spatial organizations.

The connecting mechanism in the belly was mentioned above. Moving from a higher organization to a lower one, the density of the transformation process and product increases at the same time that the extent of the enclosing function decreases. Light is condensed into earth via heat, air and water. Here we encounter the classical elements: light, also known as *quinta essentia* (ethereal life), fire, air, water and earth. This also illustrates the fact that the head or steering functions are to a large extent anchored in the past, that the belly or executive functions prepare for the future, and that the chest functions represent the present. The field in which gaiasophy operates is very fertile for giving a better insight into planet Earth's anatomical and physiological

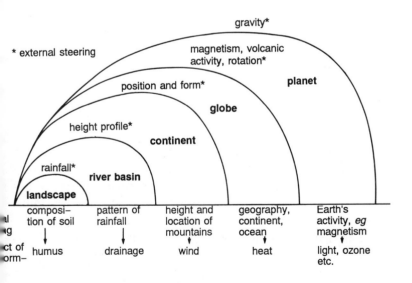

Table 10.22. The five scale model for natural ecosystems.

characteristics. Before man began to interfere, the interplay between the Sun, the Moon and the Earth was in harmony, but this was disturbed by man while he was freely learning to develop morality. During this process, man incurred a debt towards Gaia and the natural world, and the sooner man begins to pay this debt, the better for him and for the Earth.

10.13   Gaiasophy and ecology

It is not enough merely to describe the flow organization for the five hierarchical spatial levels which can be distinguished in the planetary organism. The reality is even more complicated. Apart from the skeletal organization and flow organization, or physical and ethereal bodies, higher bodies can also be distinguished at each of the five spatial levels of the planetary organism. As the description of the African landscape showed, the animal world should also be considered as the astral body of the landscape, river basin or the Earth's higher spatial levels of integration. Incorporating the animal world provides the link with what is scientifically known as the ecosystem. Ecosystems comprise a particular territory and hold their own as living entities for a certain time. Depending on the specific problems, many hierarchical levels of the ecosystem can be distinguished in lakes and landscapes. In this, the distinction is often based on the degree of organization, the transformation of energy or characteristics of the climate and microclimate.[42] O'Neill c.s. gives an important summary of the hierarchy in ecosystems.[43] In general, the animal kingdom is an ecosystem comprising many sorts of species in classes fulfilling the same procedural function in the ecosystem. Several classes together form a community. Finally, the ecosystem is the collection of various communities containing many predator/prey relationships, which are maintained by the primary production of vegetation. Therefore the natural body of a landscape or ecosystem is a very high level pyramid of predator/prey relationships. This organization was described earlier as a functional organization, but in a sense it is a "combative" organization which feeds on the energy generated by the flow organization from sunlight, water and nutrients. Just as man's desires vie for priority, animals in the ecosystem vie for dominance and, in doing so, maintain a dynamic balance within certain limits. It is because of this dynamic activity that an ecosystem can survive through time, accumulating and storing energy, recirculating nutrients, and aiming towards a maximum constant biomass.[44] John Moore and William Hunt distinguish "channels of energy" in this process, within which the predator/prey relationships may vary, though they function as individual "entities."[45]

Within one spatial organizational level of Gaia it is possible to distinguish at least three sorts of bodies: the skeletal organization, the flow organization and the combative organization. Ecology divides the ecosystems into smaller units than the landscape, within which these three types of organizations can always be discerned. O'Neill c.s. pays particular attention to the flow or process organization, which is aimed at the cycling of energy and nutrients in an ecosystem, and the types of organization encompassing predator/prey relationships. It is a classic ecological problem that the two views are difficult to reconcile, and each stands on its own. O'Neill c.s. shows that they are both relevant for a description of reality in which they unintentionally confirm the separate operation of the ethereal and astral body. Table 10.23 gives a preliminary outline of the functions of the combative organization which is itself based on the underlying flow and skeletal organizations of the landscape. Wherever possible, the functions are described in terms of comparable concepts from ecology. It is interesting to note that there are many points of correspondence, and that ecology distinguishes its hierarchical levels in ecosystems in the belly functions of the flow and combative organizations.

Ecology uses the capacity to adapt to intervention as a criterion for the existence of an ecosystem. Interventions always come through the higher organization, and according to O'Neill c.s., they are not a terrible disaster (cataclysm) but fulfil a useful steering function. For example, a fire may be a disaster for the forest, but for a larger area it can be a means of maintaining the spatial diversity of the landscape. Thus the importance of a fire in terms of the correct hierarchical level is what was earlier called a steering function.

An important characteristic of hierarchical ecosystem organizations is that higher levels can influence lower levels, while changes at a lower level have little effect at a higher level. In addition, more phenomena occur in a higher system with a longer timescale than in a lower system.[46] This concurs completely with the connecting mechanisms for the steering functions

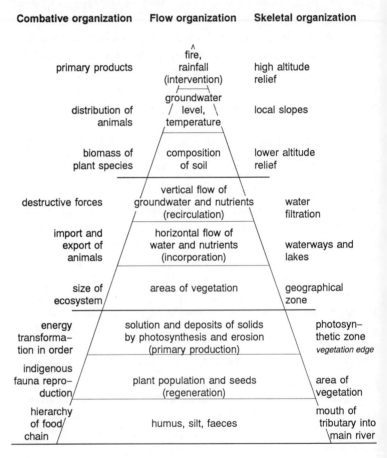

Table 10.23.   Skeletal organization, flow organization and combative organization (physical, ethereal and astral body) of a landscape (ecosystem).

distinguished for the five levels of the Earth's natural flow organization. For the ecologist, another important characteristic of the ecosystem is that it ensures that photosynthesis — or the nutrients for the primary production process — is as independent as possible of the supply of nutrients from outside. We described the internal recirculation of water and nutrients as the heart function. In the astral body decomposing mineral organisms are closely involved in this. The humus and silt which is formed also constitute an important method of storing and stabilizing energy for the ecosystem. The lung function or external transportation function is at least as important. This ensures a certain degree of climatic regulation in a large forest, and in this way something that is described in ecology as the "incorporation of external, uncontrollable factors." The lung function is responsible for the interaction with the higher hierarchical layer, resulting in a certain level of influence of the steering function, such as the formation of rainfall and changes in temperature. Thus the phenomenon of homeostasis, mentioned by Lovelock in connection with the Earth's stable biosphere, is to a significant extent maintained by the lung function. The earlier conclusion that the lung functions of the lower level of the flow organization constitute the heart function in the flow organization of the higher spatial level completely accords with this idea. For the combative organization or astral body, we see that the lung function corresponds with the entry and exit of animals. It was mentioned earlier in relation to forest areas that the astral body of a landscape is not a closed system. Many animals wander in and out, so that the astral body is part of higher spatial organizational levels. For example, predators, particularly birds of prey have a wide radius of activity, and consequently the combative organization of the landscape is connected to that of the river basin or continent. Many species of migratory birds and fish even link continents, forming the globe's astral body. The astral enclosing function consists of the pyramid of grazing animals with the final predator at the top. The essential transformation function in the combative organization has a more spiritual character than in the flow organization. The energy accumulated by photosynthesis is used to build up an order in the predator/prey relationships, often in a complicated ecological

hierarchical structure. The product presentation function is fulfilled by the waste products of the transformed parts of plants or
the faeces of predators which steers the flow organization in the
form of new land.

If it is possible to indicate a direct steering relationship
between a higher and lower organizational level of the flow
organization, this is less clear for the relationship between the
combative organization and flow organization of a landscape, for
example. The combative organization is inconceivable without
the flow organization. On the other hand, the combative organization does have a steering effect on the flow organization,
for example, by the selective eating of certain plants and animals
and the spreading of faeces. The interdependence which applies
on a broader level for the relationship man–animal–plant–Earth
is complex in this respect, but is defined by the skeletal and flow
organizations.

Thus, step by step, we arrive at an increasingly complete picture of the five natural, spatial, organizational levels of Gaia, and
the three ecological hierarchies which can be distinguished within
each spatial level, at the very least. Several additional conclusions
may be drawn from the last type of ecological hierarchy. In the
case of interference with ecosystems, such as earthworks or inci-
dental pollution, it is essential to check that sufficient types of
organisms survive to fulfil the characteristic transformation functions of the ecosystem. As soon as a particular transformation
function is carried out by only one species, the situation is much
less stable than when a whole class of species is available for the
transformation function. In addition, we should be more aware of
the power of the connecting mechanisms which can have a back-
lash effect on the ecosystem via the lung function. One example
is deforestation, which can lead to desertification by causing a
reduction in rainfall. The lungs not only restore health, they also
bring out internal problems so that the enclosing system functions
differently: a boomerang effect. An ecosystem has peripheral
steering conditions in its rainfall, the frequency of forest fires, the
availability of nutrients, and the frequency of the entry and exit
of animal species. When there are changes in these factors, it is
important to ascertain whether this affects an essential transform-

ation function, which can cause the whole organization to change from a highly ordered system to a low–level system for a long period of time. The most characteristic sorts of a particular heart, lung and transformation function may serve as important indications in this respect. Edward Goldsmith points out that ecologists can see the influence of an ecosystem level on the smaller component parts, but that for many of them the larger whole is taboo.[47] Yet organisms can only survive within a hierarchy if they respect the peripheral conditions imposed by the higher level. On the basis of 67 principles, Goldsmith brilliantly constructed a gaiasophical analysis of the ecological crisis facing the Earth.[48] He indicated that it was not the Darwinian "survival of the fittest" principle which ensures the continuity of life, but that the biosphere only exists because of the principle of co-operation. Man is starting to learn this lesson in relation to the survival of Gaia and of mankind. Hopefully man will learn the lesson soon enough to slow down the process of planetary and global destabilization in good time.

As the fourth ecological hierarchy, and as the organization of consciousness, man has a responsibility to adopt a healthier approach to ecosystems, landscapes, river basins, continents, the globe and planet Earth. The next chapter will take a closer look at the significance for man's activities of the insights described in this chapter.

11. The heart of the matter

For there is nothing, Lord — no order, no goodwill that does not originate from you alone. Therefore have mercy on both the Earth and on us, the people. May the fresh dew revive the Earth and make our souls receptive to pure joy.

Zarathustra, Yasna, 29:11

11.1 The alienation of nature and technology

With the arrival of technology man has become alienated from nature. Until the Lemurian era, when man still existed in a non-physical state above the Earth's surface, man and nature were one, just as the embryo is one with the mother. They form a whole. As described in Chapter 4, the process of feeding began during the Hyperborean era. Man's fine, ethereal body was fed by directly taking in and excreting the surrounding substance. In this way bodies were joined together through feeding. This is comparable to the fusion of the sperm and ovum. During the second half of the Hyperborean era man was fed through the umbilical cord connected to the lap of the Earth full of light. This is similar to the first stage after the fertilization of the egg, with the formation of the trophoblast and the embryoblast. Then the Sun broke away and the Lemurian Era started. Man had first fed on the inner core of the Earth, but now he was hanging by cosmic umbilical cords, rather like the foetus in the womb. In the middle of the Lemurian Era the Moon broke away and man had to start to obey the laws of nature outside him. His own circulatory system developed, consisting of the lungs and heart, comparable to the moment of birth. At the end of the Lemurian Era man bred animals and cultivated plants for his food. Man had been born and lived in harmony with nature without being wholly taken over. This situation is rather like that of the breast–fed baby. During the Age of Atlantis, man started to exploit nature by cultivating plants and seeds for food and as a source of energy for their means of transport. Trees were encouraged to grow in such a way that they could be used as houses. This was the toddler stage.

Man's capacity for magic declined at an ever–greater rate, and there was a process of solidification. Consequently man had to turn to tools and fire. In the post–Atlantean cultural periods, man was engaged in mining activities to obtain stone and bronze, and in about 1000 BC, iron. In addition, he started to make wine and bread. Because of his increasingly sophisticated tools man was better able to exploit the Earth's treasures. When the sciences were developed in the seventeenth century after many thousands of years, there was a dramatic turn of events. Industrialization appeared on the scene, first in England, then on the European continent in the nineteenth century, and later in New England on the American East Coast.[1] The steam engine was discovered, the textile industry was established, and the conveyor belt was introduced. The production process, which takes place invisibly in the human belly, was externalized in a stormy development, stimulated by people like the Scottish economist Adam Smith (1723–90). The factory developed relentlessly with irrepressible monotony. Tenant farmers were driven from the land, and women and very young children were put to work in the factories.

The English economist David Ricardo (1772–1823) foresaw a constant increase in the working population, which would never receive more than the minimum required to sustain life because of the competition for work and distribution of food. Attempts to save people from poverty would conflict with the laws of economics.

With the factories came factory towns and the labourers who lived in them. The digestive process of the belly, which initially took place within the natural boundaries of living organisms, developed on an increasingly large scale, spurred on by the coal–fired power of steam. Society reached the stage of the seven–year–old child who has learned how to think. In 1825, steam power brought about a new stage in the externalization of internal processes in the form of the steam locomotive. With the coming of the railways, transportation processes acquired a completely new dimension in terms of speed. The chest processes of the heart and lungs were externalized. This period is comparable to the emotional development in youth up to the age of fourteen. The invention of the steam locomotive was succeeded in 1885 in Germany by the first petrol–driven cars, and in 1903 in the USA, by the first manned flight by the Wright brothers.

It was not only means of transportation that took off, but in the second half of the nineteenth century, public services also spread their wings. Town houses had mains water, gas and electricity. In this way technological products gradually replaced their centuries–old agricultural counterparts in households everywhere. Because of the growing comfort of home and travel, everyone enthusiastically accepted these new "blessings." Moreover, Smith and Ricardo's predictions did not seem to have come true. In America, with its infinite expanse of land, European immigrants found that there was a great demand for labour. In addition, the land was fertile. In Europe, it was not only trade unions and the influence of the German socialist Karl Marx (1818–83) which caused the condition of the working classes to improve gradually. The world wars, with their need for advanced war machines and the considerable reduction in the birth rate, both led to a gradual increase in income, so that the population had access to the products of the industrial revolution.

In the middle of the twentieth century, there was another leap forward in technology with the large–scale introduction of artificial sensory equipment, such as the telephone, television and computer. These externalized the processes of the human head. The telegraph (1844) and telephone (1864) were developed in the nineteenth century. The first television was made in about 1928. However, it was only with the computer that all these means of communication came into their own and there was a new wave of mechanization in households and factories, as well as agriculture. The puberty of mankind is before us, as well as the need to reach adulthood, for every new technological break-through influences all the earlier stages in the sense of an increased alienation between nature and technology. Electricity is increasingly generated in nuclear power stations, the bills are automatically paid by direct debit, factories are increasingly monitored by computers and manned by robots, farms are changing into bio-industries with intensively reared calves, high-yield cows, battery hens and greenhouses in which the crops no longer grow in earth, but in fibreglass fed with nutrients. There are still some traditional farms where man and nature live in harmony, and there are still areas of tropical rainforest where man is assimilated in nature. However, these farms and areas are rapidly decreasing in number.

Just as thinking, feeling and the will are woken in man as he grows up, and are separated upon initiation, the same process occurs in the physical world around us. In the last two centuries the processes of the belly (the factory), the chest (the office) and the head (the computer) have been externalized and become visible in the physical world by means of the technology developed by man. These processes surround us like three wild horses which must be tamed and bridled by man's wisdom to avoid death and chaos in the environment and the biosphere, and to reverse the accelerated process of ageing and death of our planet and of mankind. Using another image, on one side of man there is the belly, with everything that nature still provides us with: minerals, animals and plants. On the other hand, there is the artificial organism of technology, which arose from our thinking processes as an artificial head, and which consists of computers with data communication systems, public services and transportation systems, and industry. Man lives amongst all this — as shown in Table 10.11 — unaware of the divine nature operating within him, and swallowed up by the technology which sprang from him. In this way man is placed between the good from which he was created and the evil by which he is tempted. He must unite these two worlds, so that they become interwoven and harmony is restored. This must be done with respect for the spiritual beings behind natural phenomena, and with moral wisdom to restrain the brute force of technology within human proportions and allocate everything a meaningful place in the Earth organism.

Only man as an adult conscious of this polarity will be able to function as the connecting heart in the technological/natural organism which characterizes our society.

11.2 The effects of gaiasophy on society

Man has given form to technology, which rises to the surface from sub-natural regions, on the basis of the principles which can be distinguished in his body and in nature.

Table 11.1 gives a survey of social organizational forms developed by man in Gaia's body on the basis of technology. Three main organizational levels can be distinguished in this respect, although there are many conceivable intermediary forms. These are:

the farm, as an example of an enterprise;
the agricultural community, as an example of a community;
the megalopolis, as a model of an urbanized centre.

In the farm we see all the functions which also play a role on a smaller scale in a smaller unit, such as a woodland producing timber, or a field of cows. The farm could also be replaced by another unit, such as a factory. There is another stage when we move from the small-scale establishment to a community comprising a number of companies and houses. We find another level of control and procedure for control with the town hall; the market square appears as a primarily inward-looking exchange centre; there is a variety of processing possibilities for local products and the result, the compost heap, which develops into a refuse tip, is undeniable. The megalopolis described above, in which companies operating worldwide developed from simple crafts as a result of large-scale technology, reflects another leap forward. International industries have taken over in many respects, imposing their wishes on local governments. All too often these are eagerly accepted with a view to the employment situation and for the greater glory and prestige of those in power. In this way the government at the local and national level often finds itself in a position which is less one of government than of negotiation between conflicting interests and monitoring the situation. The planning function, which is still exercised by

Functions in the flow organization	Farm	Agricultural community	Megalopolis
steering	farm and acreage	town hall, building programme	multinational head offices, international commissions
measurement	livestock	land, population registers, police	international taxation & law
planning	industrial capacity, distribution of land	budgets and development plan	national governments
internal transportation	supplies of hay, seed, manure, water, etc.	houses and road system, market square	continental highways, pipelines
external transportation	buying and selling of raw materials and products	provincial roads, post office, bank	intercontinental seaports, airports, pipelines
enclosing	farm boundary	town limits	conurbation limits
transformation	preparation of products	processing of products, services	agricultural and industrial products, vehicles, etc.
reproductive	land, cattle	industrial plant	industrial plant, expertise, information, popular recreation
product presentation	bulk-packaged agricultural products, compost	processed products and services, refuse tip	artificial products, high-tech services, chemical waste, natural area

Table 11.1. Survey of the nine functions in three characteristic social organizational levels on Earth.

governments, indicates the boundaries within which decisions are carried out. As in the case of Gaia's organizational levels, connecting mechanisms can be distinguished for these three social levels. The planning function of the megalopolis serves to steer the community. The development plan of the community steers the local company. Thus the mechanism is the same as for Gaia.

The transformation functions reveal a development in the preparation of natural products, ever greater levels of processing, and finally, increasingly sophisticated services available through technology are used for these artificial products. This survey shows that the harmonization of social development and the living organism of Gaia must aim at the head of industrial society and, in the first place, at its steering functions. It is essential to influence the steering function of the megalopolis, international industrial strategy, which consists of a complex interrelationship between a variety of distinct factors. Furthermore, we must become aware that a higher organizational form will evolve from the megalopolis, an organization which already exists in name. The United Nations of the Earth will have to steer industry at an international level, for it is not right that the "captains of industry" are operating at a global level while there is no worldwide government to implement an effective environmental policy for our planet. The control of the environmental management of the planet should be carried out by a world authority, as stated on 11 March 1989 by twenty–four government leaders in the Hague Declaration.

This would put forward the objectives and the control of worldwide human activities which have an influence on the environment, in harmony with Gaia's health requirements. This world authority will have to be based on the principles of gaiasophy if it is to achieve anything to improve the present increasingly chaotic situation in which urbanized areas are devouring natural areas, as shown in Table 11.2. On the basis of the idea outlined above, the principles of gaiasophy mean that for every level of the scale and the corresponding problems of an accumulation of waste matter and a lack of raw materials, there is an effective controlling organ. With regard to the landscape, it may be the council which is responsible for urban development, town and country planning, garbage disposal and the processing of waste matter. With regard to the continent, a continental government should draw up objectives for combatting acid rain and supervising the implementation of these measures by governments at lower levels. For the planet as a whole a similar government is necessary to deal with planetary problems, such as restricting changes in the climate by reducing the emission of carbon dioxide.

11.3 Improving the Earth's steering mechanism

Many ideas have been put forward to steer our planet in a way that can achieve harmony between man and nature. We will not give an analysis here of the views of society in the light of their contribution to the solution of the environmental problem, although this sort of analysis is of essential importance elsewhere. Some of the issues at stake, for example, include the freedom to use natural resources as required, the right of every person to prosperity when this is at the expense of the developmental potential of future generations, and the need for economic growth which constantly requires more raw materials. Perhaps socialism and liberalism should be modified so that society will deal adequately with the scarce resources of the environment, space and raw materials, both at the local and world levels. How can we prevent policies which restrict activity that pollutes the environment from turning into a kind of "ecofascism"? What is the best stimulus for leading technological innovation towards a society which uses a minimum of raw materials? The nature of these questions shows that the environmental question presents mankind as a whole with new challenges and new views on the deepest social principles. In this context it is relevant to consider the views of Rudolf Steiner on the social threefold division of society into spiritual life (the level at which people co-operate voluntarily), legal life (in which people enter into agreements on the basis of equality), and economic life (in which people fulfil each other's needs on the basis of brotherly love).[2] The principles of the French Revolution particularly apply to these fields, in the sense of creating a social revolution: liberty in spiritual life, equality in legal life, and fraternity in economic life. Although Steiner's attempt to introduce this threefold social division was not as successful as he had hoped at the beginning of the twentieth century, there is an urgent need for further attempts at social renovation and finding a solution for the environmental problems inherent in the present social system. In this respect it

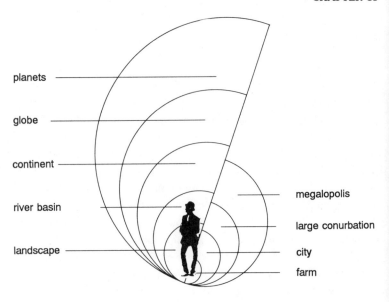

planets

globe

continent

river basin

landscape

megalopolis

large conurbation

city

farm

Table 11.2. Man on the border between the natural environment and the urbanized environment.

is essential for man and society to decide once again to act on the basis of morality, rather than on the basis of short-term profit. Fundamental new economic principles, such as the introduction of interest-free money, a taxation system which taxes raw materials and energy more than labour, and creating a division between labour and income, are all ideas which are relevant in this context. Until the cost of polluting nature is built into the pricing of our products, our society will continue to develop parasitically on Gaia and move towards ultimate catastrophe.

An illustration of future society based on vaguely comparable principles can be found in *The Coming Race* by the Englishman Edward Bulwer Lytton (1803-73), and in the extraterrestrial civilization described by Stefan Denaerde. To develop in this direction, a step-by-step approach will have to be adopted by groups of people who are prepared to act as true social beings on the basis of their spiritual growth, and to distil feelings which may arise, such as envy, dissatisfaction or jealousy, into a feeling of brotherly love.

330

Below I will concentrate particularly on the technical aspects of the organization of environmental management.

The organization of the environmental management of the planet should consist of the steering function of a democratically elected and effective world authority, as indicated in the Hague Declaration. The executive or planning function would be composed of continents and nations, while the measurement function would be represented by an independent world environment service which could be formed by a considerably strengthened "Earthwatch centre" of the United Nations Environmental Programme (UNEP). In his ideas about the organization of decision-making, Gerard Endenburg showed that these three elements — steering, execution and measurement — are always necessary for a properly functioning regulation or healthy head organ at any level.[3] The greatest threat to Gaia is the disruption of the planetary organization. Therefore there is an urgent need to establish a planetary management organ to ensure better steering of the Earth.[4] But it is quite clear that such an organ has not yet been established either for the globe as a whole, or for any continent, and was only established with many problems for particular river basins. The Rhine is a poignant example. Table 11.3 gives a summary of the relevant controlling organs at every level of the scale. However, many people consider that the creation of an effective controlling organ for the planet is not feasible. The Hague Declaration turned a dream into a necessity. During the eighth session of the InterAction Council in May 1990 in Seoul, a meeting of ex–government leaders including Helmut Schmidt (West Germany), Takeo Fukuda (Japan), Miguel de la Madrid Hurtado (Mexico), Valéry Giscard d'Estaing (France), Andries van Agt (Netherlands), and Pierre Trudeau (Canada), it was proposed that the Hague Declaration should be urgently implemented and it was recommended to "establish a High Authority to set an internationally binding policy framework with regulatory powers." Separate levels of control for the management of land-scapes, rivers and continents will be needed as a counterweight to the high demands of exploitation imposed by technology and the agencies governing urbanized areas. In the Netherlands the water authority is a precursor of a controlling organization at the

natural level	number of examples	controlling organizations
planet	1	United Nations Environment Program (UNEP)
globe	1	United Nations Environment Program
continent/oceans	10	EFTA, EC, Council of Europe, Lomé Conventions (Europe and Africa)
river/sea	10^3	Int. Rhine Commission, Oslo Convention (North Sea)
landscape/lake	10^5	state, provincial water authorities

Table 11.3. Examples of controlling organs for the different levels of the natural ecosystem.

level of the landscape. There are many examples of controlling agencies for national rivers, for example, in France *(agences de bassin),* the US and England (river authorities). Gaia's ecological health at different levels of the scale must be safeguarded against every incursion on the landscape by urban development, and every intervention into the river basin and Gaia's higher organizations by the activities of the urban conurbation and megalopolis. It is only if there is a realization of the therapeutic programme drawn up to cure Gaia that society will be able to develop further. This was the profound conviction expressed in the report published on 27 April 1987, *Our Common Future,* by the United Nations World Commission on Environment and Development, under the leadership of the Norwegian prime minister, Gro Harlem Brundtland. In 1988, the Dutch government supported the main objectives of this report. The Brundtland Commission addresses the world's leaders with the message that economic growth can only be sustained if it is aimed at continuity. In addition, it notes that young people are most critical with regard to the lack of an effective planetary steering mechanism.

Conclusion 2 states: "From space we can see and monitor the Earth as an organism whose health depends on the health of the component parts. We have the capacity to ensure that human activity accords with natural laws." Conclusion 4 reads: "The time has come to take the necessary decisions to safeguard natural resources for the life of present and future generations." Conclusion 11 reads: "The environmental crisis, the developmental crisis and the energy crisis are not unrelated. They are all the same crisis." Conclusion 103: "All nations will have to play a role in changing the developmental trends and reversing an international economic system which increases rather than decreases inequality and leads to a rise rather than a fall in the number of poor and hungry people." Conclusion 104: "The next decades are crucial. The time has come to break down traditional patterns." Conclusion 109: "We are unanimously convinced that the security, the well-being and the ultimate survival of the planet depends on such far-reaching changes, now."

However, this good intention will have to be converted into a plan with concrete objectives and thus a controllable reality. It is only when the threat of a seriously sick Gaia results in localized — or possibly global — catastrophes, that mankind tends to wake up. In this respect the Brundtland Commission Report reveals a necessary level of relativity. Conclusion 104 continues: "However, we are aware that such a reorientation on a constant basis is simply beyond the scope of the present decision-making structures, and of national and international institutions." Nevertheless, entirely new initiatives are being developed to enable the sustained development of mankind on Earth. Between 27 and 30 June 1988, the first international conference of ministers, politicians and scientists was held in Toronto about "The changing atmosphere, implications for global security." This led to a plan of action for the atmosphere and the establishment of the World Atmosphere Fund, in particular to provide information for developing countries to reduce the emission of greenhouse gases such as carbon dioxide and methane. In the next century, developing countries like China will actually overtake the present industrialized countries of the west in their atmospheric emissions.

In the autumn of 1988, an Intergovernmental Panel on Climate Change was set up under the auspices of the United Nations Environment Programme (UNEP). This forum was entrusted with the preparation of a convention on climate following the UNEP protocol drawn up in September 1987 for the protection of the ozone layer. Many initiatives followed, including that of the Dutch minister of the environment, Ed Nijpels, who organized a successful first ministerial climate conference in Noordwijk in November 1989, at which agreements were made regarding the stabilization of carbon dioxide emissions by most industrialized countries by the year 2000, in relation to the 1990 level. But there is considerable reluctance with regard to translating these initiatives into concrete measures at a world level. The need of the developing countries to catch up economically, and the poverty of the majority of the world's population, both play an important role in this respect. Is it necessary for higher hierarchies to intervene in a hard and uncompromising way in order to help mankind over the threshold to sustainable development? The French–Dutch–Norwegian initiative which led to the Hague Declaration on 11 March 1989 and the United Nations conferences on Environment and Development in the 1990s are a very hopeful sign that it is not yet too late for a new approach.

The former Dutch minister of the environment, Pieter Winsemius, also took a number of important steps to improve environmental policy.[5] For every environmental intervention there is a "chain of regulations" to be followed: legislation granting licenses, execution, and maintenance. These steps are a sophisticated version of the triad: steering, execution, measurement. On this basis it is possible to set up a controlling organism which also complies with the principles of gaiasophy. Table 11.4 shows the organizational structure for integrating social activities into an organizational level of Gaia. The steering consists of objectives established at the highest level and relating to a therapeutic programme for Gaia. I will return to this question below.

The measurement function serves to determine the state of the environment at a particular organizational level, from a landscape to the planet, and to show whether it is in accordance with the policy objectives and whether the existing regulations are adequate for continuing to comply with the objectives. The planning function is the regulation which operates in the requirements contained in licences for the purification or protective process. The purification process is the executive function which is reproduced by the purification installation. The product of this control

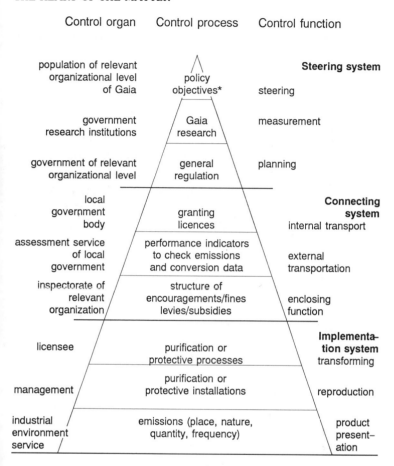

Control organ	Control process	Control function

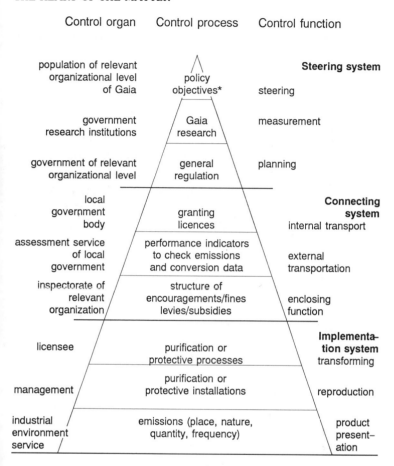

Control organ	Control process	Control function
population of relevant organizational level of Gaia	policy objectives*	**Steering system** steering
government research institutions	Gaia research	measurement
government of relevant organizational level	general regulation	planning
local government body	granting licences	**Connecting system** internal transport
assessment service of local government	performance indicators to check emissions and conversion data	external transportation
inspectorate of relevant organization	structure of encouragements/fines levies/subsidies	enclosing function
licensee	purification or protective processes	**Implementation system** transforming
management	purification or protective installations	reproduction
industrial environment service	emissions (place, nature, quantity, frequency)	product presentation

* based on gaiasophy

Table 11.4. The organization of environmental control based on the principles of Gaiasophy within a spatial organizational level of Earth.

organization is a purified — or better still, a completely recycled — stream of waste matter. This organization works best when the licensee himself, the polluter, is concerned with restoring and maintaining Gaia's health, as well as with the company's economic objectives. This process, referred to by Pieter Winsemius as the "interiorization of environmental policy," a system of self-regulation based on a sense of responsibility and rewarded with financial incentives, is the best guarantee that the therapy for curing Gaia will be successful. It is the responsibility of the environmental inspectorate, together with local government at provincial or municipal levels, and in certain cases, together with the state, to make sure that plans are executed. In this respect, a licence serves to represent the identity of the control organization. The application of peripheral conditions for the licence in the form of controlling, punitive and stimulating measures, should be in the hands of the legislator and the environmental inspectorate. In this way it will be possible, where necessary, to ensure that economic interests conform more closely with the principles of gaiasophy than they do now. With this process of control it is possible to ensure that economic activity corresponds with the objectives of gaiasophy at every organizational level. It is necessary to examine these objectives more closely.

11.4 Objectives of gaiasophy

Table 10.21 showed that the steering function of Gaia's organizational levels corresponds with the planning function of a higher organizational level. Gaia itself has a steering effect in these organizations, as we saw, in gravity, volcanic activity, the geographical shape of continents, the relief of the land and the pattern of rainfall. Man has a great many goals to satisfy his needs, and these have a disruptive effect on Gaia. The essential question, which should be examined with regard to environmental planning and policies, is what may be considered to be a healthy situation. When can the controlling body for the environment be satisfied? At the moment, environmental policy has a qualitative nature. Guidelines are given in existing policies with regard to, for example, insecticides and agricultural policy, but no one can determine exactly what is the desirable result. There is no proper frame of reference for this purpose, nor the insight into the health and physiology of Gaia itself. As long as the existence of Gaia as a living organism is not recognized, there is no basis for what can only be described in terms of ecological objectives. Gaiasophy can be helpful in this respect.

In the first place, we must relearn the ability to make use of the inspiration and strength of the spiritual world which help man to develop in our search for solutions. Secondly, we must learn to manage the living Earth in accordance with the living organs and cells of the continents, rivers and landscapes which comprise it. Every cell and every organ should function as a self-sufficient system with a minimum of dependence on the surrounding systems. Furthermore, if they fulfil specialized functions in a larger context, cells and organs should not be disturbed in their functioning by being affected by their environmental context or by being overburdened by pollution produced by man. This concerns, for example, the relationship between urban areas and the open countryside, woodland and grassland and so on.

Furthermore, at every level of the scale the corresponding cycle of materials should be kept to a minimum and remain a closed circuit. This means that society requires an intricately organized system for the collection and processing of goods parallel to the distribution system, so that there are no losses through leakage to higher levels of the scale resulting in an accumulation of polluting substances, while at the same time raw materials are being exhausted at source. Man must once again live within the ecological confines of the landscape, the river, the continent and the planet.

Where the wave of pollution produced by human activity exceeds the boundaries of the cells of landscapes and river basins in particularly specialized forms of processing, it will be necessary to set up a loop to return these processed products to their original source. As they occur at a higher level of scale, more weight should be given to preventive measures with respect to these problems. This means that one should not wait for the same degree of scientific certainty regarding effects in the approach to climatic change as is adopted with regard to insulating refuse dumped underground. With regard to changes in the climate, even fewer risks should be taken, as this can have an effect at every level of scale. Furthermore, the principle of free trade of goods, leading to unimpeded imports and exports of goods over ecological boundaries, should be moderated by a system of charges and duties aimed at controlling ecologically harmful trade.

This brief explanation will have to suffice here. However, I would like to examine in more detail one essential specific problem, the relationship between the Earth's population and its natural carrying capacity. The Earth's natural capacity is not sufficiently used as a starting point for environmental policy-making. However, Conclusion 29 of the Brundtland Commission Report clearly states: "Sustainable development can only be pursued if population size and growth are in harmony with the changing productive potential of the ecosystem."

Are there not too many people on Earth, and does some of the population not live too extravagantly? This question has been asked since the time of Thomas Malthus (1766–1834) with no consensus being reached about what is the optimum number.

Nevertheless, the demands of the Earth's inhabitants on Gaia's capacity is the most universal criterion for environmental planning and policy. It was the Club of Rome which first pointed out the limitations of the Earth's capacity.[6] However, the conclusions drawn from this were inadequate, and many people believe that technology will help us to increase the Earth's capacity. To some extent this is true. Waste matter which accumulates in the food chain can be recycled, and be assimilated by nature. However, the limits of what Gaia can survive move ever closer, and the cost of respecting these limits with a growing population are constantly increasing. The time seems to have come to establish objectives regarding the number of inhabitants the globe can support. In this respect the above–mentioned InterAction Council emphasizes "the paramount importance of adopting policies aimed at stabilizing global population at 8–10 billion." Resources allocated to international population assistance programmes for contraception should be doubled, accompanied by a programme of education on family planning.

It is not only in developing countries that it is important to introduce a policy on population, but also in the industrialized countries which are devouring the raw materials. While there are no agreements or policy measures regarding population size, it is at least necessary to adopt a policy on the basis of the maximum level of total pollution of the Earth, for example, by carbon dioxide. On this sort of basis, as well as the existing population figures, there is a possibility of reducing the standard of living instead of limiting the population, or of introducing accelerated technological innovations.

Controlling the size of the population is a controversial subject which governments prefer to avoid. Everyone hopes for a technological development which will allow a western standard of living for all of the ever-growing population of the world. However, this path is full of risks and uncertainties, and is quite impossible, given the current developments in technology.

On the other hand, there is a fear that children or minority groups could be eliminated or starved in order to achieve the prescribed population figures for every society, dictated from above. Furthermore, such a system is simply asking for fraud and evasion, added to which there are objections to human intervention in the incarnation possibilities of unborn children.

It is right that all these aspects should be borne in mind. The starting point must be that all people have a life of dignity. However, this does not detract from the fact that it will be necessary to make choices about population pressure on the basis of morality at different levels of scale, and at the individual level, for example, by stipulating the average number of children that parents should have. When more children are born, it will be necessary to indicate what consequences this will have for the demands they would be allowed to make on the scarce environmental resources.

Free choice will have to be safeguarded for man, but within the limitations which allow society to survive. As in other fields, such as abortion and euthanasia, man is forced to make conscious choices based on either materialism or moral responsibility.

If the size of the population is not controlled on the basis of education, measures to stimulate this, and voluntary restriction, there is a great danger that materialistic motives will eventually lead to a restriction imposed from above on the freedom of parents to choose how many children they decide to have.

Guaranteeing a minimum income in old age for all people could stop people in developing countries from having too many children. In industrialized countries, economic incentives and intensive educational campaigns, combined with other environmental measures, could be the approach to be adopted. Without international agreements and solidarity, it will be impossible to find a harmonious solution to the problem of population growth.

The essential role played by the population problem in solving the environmental problem is very depressing for many people. For decades attempts have been made in vain to limit the growth in population. There are no easy answers. The environmental question can lead to a new need and a broader capacity in order to make the leap to a stabilization of the population in the not too distant future. If that time is further away, more stringent measures will have to be taken, such as emission quotas, or even quotas on inhabitants per continent and per country. The introduction of quotas for inhabitants of the Earth will impoverish some rich countries and enrich some poor countries. Only the common threat of Gaia's decline will induce mankind to accept this. The question is: will this threat be recognized in good time? A gradual transition could take place because groups of people, cities and countries, continue to follow up some of these objectives. These may concern voluntary agreements between countries or small–scale experiments with a new social order. Governments should make these experiments possible within the old economic and social structures. Groups of consumers who are prepared to accept the goods and assume the financial risks will reduce dependence on the government. A great deal can be achieved by few, particularly if they feel supported by the inspiration which comes from spiritual hierarchies for the evolution of mankind. Sooner or later, opposition can be broken down in this way, as developments in South Africa and in Eastern Europe showed in 1990.

How could the right to create pollution, to burden the Earth with unhealthy substances and activities be expressed? Certainly the allotted amount of environmental pollution should entail the possibility of a common denominator with regard to the damage of various substances and activities. The permissible amount of environmental pollution should be based above all on pollution which is a threat to the health of planet Earth and of the globe. This concerns gases accumulating in the biosphere, such as carbon dioxide, nitrous oxides, chlorofluorocarbons and methane.

340

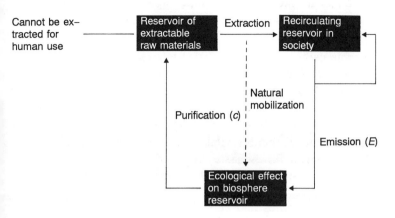

Table 11.5. The cycle of natural raw materials on Earth and those extracted by man.

Using the greenhouse effect as a guideline, alternative sources of heating also spring to mind on the basis of current knowledge.

Each person should only be allowed to make a particular contribution to the heating of the Earth. This would promote the use of harmless gases, and rich countries would still be able to develop alternatives to fossil fuels.

This sort of distribution of a maximum permissible level of environmental pollution per nation is an important step in the direction of the objectives of gaiasophy, which are to form the basis of the therapy to restore Gaia's health. Then the environmental pollution per inhabitant can be determined for a given number of inhabitants for each country. In this way, everyone in principle has an annual environmental credit from which deductions are made with every purchase of goods or services. The question whether an "environmental credit card" should really be introduced depends on whether simpler, but equivalent methods can be developed.

This sort of approach was also recommended by the Inter-Action Council. It proposed laying down an annual allocation of carbon dioxide emissions per country based on a worldwide restriction of carbon dioxide emissions and national populations. This allocation would have to be bought from an environmental agency to be established on an international basis. This system of leasable carbon–use permits is an interesting form of the inter-national allocation of scarce environmental resources.

Other forms of financial incentives, such as the abolition of subsidies which promote the consumption of raw materials, and the introduction of levies to stimulate an economic attitude to raw materials, are absolutely vital to achieve such global objectives. In this context, R.J. Schaele suggested introducing a worldwide environmental insurance which would make ecological preventive measures economically attractive.[7]

11.5 The basic law of sustainable development

Why has it taken so long for us to become aware of the environ-mental crisis? It is because there are natural reservoirs which are not immediately exhausted. These reservoirs of raw materials, the existence of a buffer to acid pollution, and particular types of organisms conceal the effects of our activities for a very long time. Decades passed before the acidity in the environment became apparent. Decades also passed before trichloroethylene appeared in the drinking water of ground water pumping stations. There is only one lesson to be learnt from history: at every level our activities will have to be aimed at harmonization with the natural cycles of raw materials. This means that we should not remove any more substances from nature than it can generate, and we should not add any more substances to it than it can process by breaking them down. Despite the reservoirs, which act as a buffer, our activities will have to be geared towards the ecological law of supply and demand: nature should not be required to maintain a higher level of purification than it can offer. This could be called the basic law of environmental policy, an environmental policy that is aimed at sustainable development. It is only on the basis of this basic ecological law that environ-mental policy can achieve its long–term objectives.

As a conclusion to this book, I should like to examine briefly the main points of this basic law of sustainable development. The starting point for sustainable development is that the purification we require of nature must be equal to what nature can offer us. This is logical, but not so easy to achieve. To do so, we have to understand what nature has to offer us, what the living Earth organism can tolerate in terms of the burden of civilization, and — even more important — how man and the Earth can achieve symbiosis. The Earth's natural wealth takes the form of supplies of raw materials, and the capacity to act as a buffer against the harmful effects of accumulated waste. I am assuming that this wealth serves to give us time to learn, and to provide us with capital in the form of natural resources which we can then constantly recycle. In this way, man creates his own dynamic wealth of raw materials, which does not lose more than nature can process, and to which no more can be added than nature can afford to lose.

To keep it simple, I will draw up a balance sheet aimed at permanence for the Earth's highest level, the planet. The formula for this reads:

$$E = c \qquad (1)$$

Here E is the total global emission of substances remaining after the extraction, production, consumption and recycling of

Year	World		Netherlands	
	Population $\times 10^9$	% urban area	Population $\times 10^6$	% urban area
1900	1.6	0.06%	6.0	2.3
1960	3.0	0.2	11.5	7.5
1985	4.8	0.9	14.4	14.2
2010	6.5	1.4	15.7	17.0
2050	9.5	2.5	15.6	17.3

* According to this definition, urbanized land is not land which is completely covered with asphalt, paving, concrete, etc., as indicated in Table 10.6.

Table 11.6. Land removed from vegetation by urbanization.

343

substances, on both natural and human levels, and c is nature's capacity for purifying emitted substances in such a way that they can be re–assimilated and again serve a useful function in the Earth organism.

Some of the substances which are emitted can be spread over the Earth's surface to such a degree that they can no longer be recycled, for example, when widely diluted in sediments (see Table 11.5). The emission (E) can also be replaced by other factors such as exhaustion of raw materials, or animals and plants becoming extinct. In this case, the capacity for purification or regeneration only applies on a very large time–scale. But this aspect is outside our present concern.

A more detailed analysis of the equation reveals the following comparison:

$$edp = rba \qquad (2)$$

Here, emission is equal to the product of e, the waste emission per tonne of manufactured product (kg/tonne); d, the production per inhabitant (tonnes product/inhabitant); and p, the population.

The planet's potential for purification is determined by the product of: r, the rate of purification per unit of weight of the natural biomass (kg/tonne); b, the density of biomass per unit of surface area (tonnes/km^2); a, the natural surface area (km^2).

If we restrict ourselves only to the surface area of the land, it is also important to correct the natural land area (150×10^6 km^2) for the surface area occupied by constructed infrastructure. If i is the infrastructure per inhabitant (m^2/inhabitant), equation (2) can now be written as follows:

$$edp = rb(a - ip) \qquad (3)$$

This simple equation for environmental management reveals some of the key elements of the sustainable development aimed at.

If the population grows, emission increases, and the natural purification capacity decreases. At a planetary level, the influence of urbanization is still relatively low but at the regional level of the Netherlands, this is certainly not the case.

The smaller the scale, the greater the effect of the pressure of

Use of land ($\times 10^6$ square km)	1900	1960	1985	2010	2050
Woodland	58	52	50	45	40
Grassland	63	63	63	60	56
Cultivated land	8	13	15	17	20
Desert/tundra	21	22	22	28	34
% vegetation	86%	85%	85%	81%	77%
% of 1900 woodland	100%	90%	86%	78%	70%
% of global b* in 1900	100%	90%	85%	73%	63%
% of Netherlands' b* in 1900	100%	94%	87%	86%	85%

* b is biomass density

Table 11.7. Change in vegetation and the use of land in the world, and the calculation of the biomass density (b).

population on nature's purification capacity. This is why the problem of overpopulation is a subject which plays an important role in discussions on environmental policy and sustainable development. Table 11.6 also shows that because of its lack of space, the Netherlands is in a sense one hundred and fifty years ahead of the rest of the world. The Netherlands can be viewed as a laboratory of world problems. Furthermore, the density of the natural biomass is considerably reduced by desertification and erosion, as shown in Table 11.7.

In the Netherlands the expected reduction in the density of the biomass *(b)* is much less dramatic than in the rest of the world because of the anticipated decline in the rate of growth of the population, and reforestation. The outlined levels of b are based on the product of the percentage of land with vegetation and the percentage of woodland, and they form a rough indication of the biomass density which can be further detailed by including grassland and cultivated land to a limited extent. This was not done here. Apart from the biomass density in the rest of nature, the vitality — or degree of poisoning of nature — is also important. As more poisonous substances are accumulated in a particular place, the rate of purification *(r)* of the biomass decreases. In our example it is assumed that this speed is declining more sharply in the Netherlands than, on average, elsewhere in the world, but that this decline will be stabilized by the year 2015, following rigorous environmental measures.

The factors in equation (3) also include the production per inhabitant and the waste emission per production unit.

As the level of welfare increases in a country, production and consumption increase per inhabitant, as well as the number of machines, energy consumption and the related flow of waste matter. In the example, the change in the per capita consumption of energy was used as a measure of welfare. Because of the increased savings in energy, this is no longer such a good standard for measuring the level of welfare, though the waste matter produced is.

Apart from the production per inhabitant, the emission factor plays an important role. Because of improvements in environmental technology, we shall be able to produce goods with ever smaller amounts of waste per tonne of product manufactured. This may be the result of cleaner production methods or measures to counter pollution. Rob Maas[8] points out that the prompt application of structurally cleaner production methods will eventually create highly economical conditions and considerably reduce the environmental crisis. Ideally the production of waste matter should be brought back to zero and everything should be recycled. It is conceivable that by the year 2050 this will be 99% successful in the Netherlands and 90% successful for the world as a whole. Table 11.8 shows a collection of the initial data. Table 11.9 shows the total range of the capacity for emission and purification. Table 11.10 shows the result, the relationship between E and c.

What does this picture show us? The outlook for the world is bleak; for the Netherlands sustainable development will be achieved before the middle of the next century (E is smaller than c). Sustainable development is possible only in a society which is prepared to recycle virtually all the raw materials extracted from the Earth. This must be done not only in the Netherlands, but throughout the world, for otherwise the resources of the global ecosystem (the so-called "resource base") could well be destroyed before the end of the next century. Sooner or later man

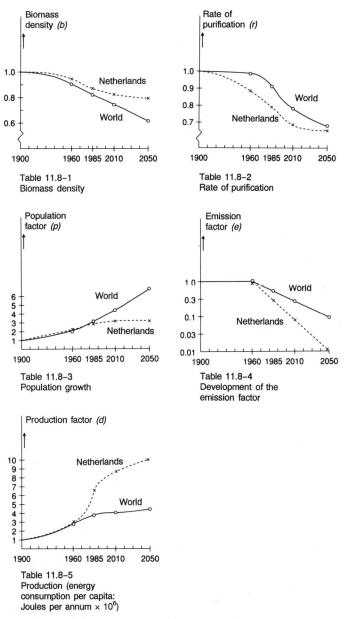

Table 11.8-1
Biomass density

Table 11.8-2
Rate of purification

Table 11.8-3
Population growth

Table 11.8-4
Development of the
emission factor

Table 11.8-5
Production (energy
consumption per capita:
Joules per annum × 10⁶)

*Table 11.8. Survey of initial data for calculating sustainable develop-
ment in the world and in the Netherlands for the period 1900–2050.*

347

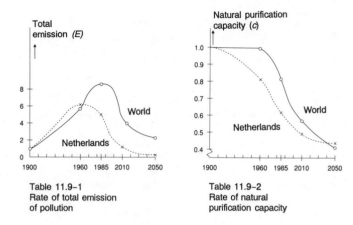

Table 11.9-1
Rate of total emission
of pollution

Table 11.9-2
Rate of natural
purification capacity

Table 11.9. Rate of total emission and purification capacity in the World and in the Netherlands in the period 1900–2050.

will have to accept that things cannot go on the way they are at the moment. Is this an unnecessarily pessimistic view? I do not think so. Let us take a sober look at the dangers and study the law of sustainable development:

$$edp = rb(a-ip) \qquad (4)$$

Which factors can be modified? The Earth's surface *(a)* is a constant factor, certainly at the global level. The infrastructure *(ip)* has a tendency not to become any smaller. Even if the population leaves, the infrastructure stays behind for a long time. Roman roads can still be found in the present system of roads in Europe. Moreover, energy is required to break down the old infrastructure. Nevertheless, it is important to make both *i* and *p* as small as possible by building compact cities which meet man's requirements as far as possible, require a minimum of connecting roads and allow for merging with nature as far as possible. Obviously it is vital to keep the biomass density *(b)* as large as possible. The main way of doing this is to avoid the land drying out, to prevent desertification and to implement programmes of reforestation. The poisoning of the biosphere and a decline in the rate of purification *(r)* is linked to the accumulation over time of toxic substances. The sooner a halt is made to the emission of these

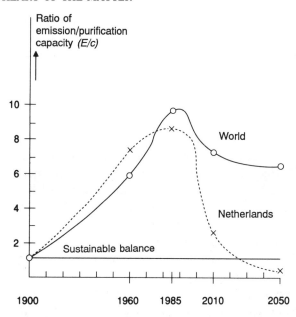

Table 11.10. Ratio of emission/purification capacity (E/c) 1900–2050.

substances, the less the rate of purification will be affected in the future.

It is not so much the level of welfare which will have to fall worldwide, for this is the motor for further development. The challenge facing environmental policy is to bring down the emission factor faster than the rise in production by establishing a recycling economy and improving the efficiency of the use of raw materials. A recycling economy at every level: for solid waste matter at the level of the landscape, for waste water in the river basin and the sea, for acid waste gases within continental boundaries, and for greenhouse gases in our planetary troposphere. It is not yet clear how this can be done, but it is clear that we do not have much time. The wealth of resources which delay the ecological effects is being exhausted.

We will go down in history as the generation of polluters. We cannot merely leave it at that. It is our responsibility to become pioneers of a new age of environmental management based on sustainable growth. This will make great demands on our imagination and energy. It is only by following this path that we will discover the unknown and help to create a new society which we can unashamedly pass on to succeeding generations.

11.6 The call of Europe

I have examined the significance of the fascinating views of our planet as seen both from the spiritual world and from the physical world which is dominated by the laws of economics. I have looked at the horror of technology which is increasingly disrupting the harmony of the Gaia organism. Standing on the wall which separates the two worlds, I will have to develop an innovatory approach. During my search I was inspired by theosophy and anthroposophy, and I have had many new insights. It is becoming increasingly clear that in my search everything centres on the heart area. The biosphere is the heart of planet Earth. The Gulf Stream and Europe are the heart of the biosphere. From Curaçao to Corinth — yes, throughout Europe — the same inspiration is being unveiled. Central Europe is the heart of the European continent. I feel as though there is a message for me which reads: "You are the heart." It is up to me — and up to us — in our divided Europe with its rich culture, to forge the link between west and east, technology and nature, natural science and spiritual science, between Gaia and Sophia. Science arose in seventeenth-century Europe, and spiritual science was stimulated in Europe at the end of the nineteenth century. Divisions will have to be conquered by means of the consciousness of the healing process in Europe, where all these traditions and all these languages are heard separately and together.[9] Europe — where two world wars tried to smother this attempt, where German national socialism transformed the highest spiritual inspiration into the blackest perversities and demonic inhumanity, where the European Community is in danger of being stranded in mutual one-upmanship and bureaucracy — this Europe nevertheless has a task in the United Nations. The unification of Germany is a sign of hope, although it also fills many people with fear inspired by the past. The hope which surrounds a unified Germany consists of the expectation that it will play a unifying, rather than a divisive role in the EEC and in the continent of Europe as a whole, which will be based on the highest spiritual ideals with which it was in contact in centuries gone by. Because of the great population density and the expansion of industry, it is necessary to adopt a vision in Europe first of all, allowing technology to be incorporated in the organizations of the living Earth. In the European continent it is countries like Switzerland, the Netherlands, Norway and Sweden which will first have to recognize that the landscapes and rivers of planet Earth are sick, and will have to be cured with man's help, for otherwise they will be lost. In Europe the future of Gaia will have to be considered first of all, and solutions will have to be advanced — if only for its own survival. There are some encouraging signs. Israel's reclamation and cultivation of the Negev Desert, the careful treatment of waste water in Switzerland, and the pioneering role of former West Germany and Sweden in combatting acid rain, are inspirations for the future. In addition, there is the artistic spirit of the French, who often build breathtakingly artistic constructions, the English organization of water achieved in most rivers, and learning to live with waste and with the wildness of the sea in the lowlands of the Netherlands. There are numerous other examples of initiatives which attempt to interweave harmoniously technology and nature at the level of the landscape or river basin. The prevention of large–scale unhealthy processes begins with combatting disease of the biosphere at the lowest level, in ourselves. Our own activities in our homes and in the town will have to coincide with the highest principles of gaiasophy if the Earth is to be cured.

Anyone who travels around the world will see with his own eyes that in Europe the idea that man must manage the land is evident everywhere. Every acre of land is planned. The soil has been cultivated for centuries, the landscape is always accessible. The whole continent is criss–crossed by roads, fields, dykes, ditches and canals. It is now a matter of translating the ties with the spiritual world which still formed a basis for the medieval peasant and the founders of modern science to relate to environmental and developmental problems on a planetary scale. It is only by means of a link with spiritual hierarchies that the healing spiritual force needed to neutralise the destructive tendency of all–pervading technology, can be developed. This requires a revolution in our inner selves and our social relationships, a revolution which is comparable to hopeful changes taking place in Eastern Europe since 1990. The realization that this broad social change will have to take place is reflected in the environmental policy aimed at "interiorization" introduced by the Dutch minister for the environment, Pieter Winsemius in 1985, and in Gro Harlem Brundtland, who concluded her speech in June 1988 as prime minister of Norway at the conference in Toronto on "The Changing Atmosphere" with the exhortation: "We must upgrade our civilization." Nevertheless, this does not indicate the far–reaching social change required to change the very essence of the causes of the growth economy and squandering of natural resources. The environmental movements, and to an even greater extent, the social and economic ideas of Rudolf Steiner, provide the building blocks and conditions for a true renewal of society. This clearly shows that there is a need for a different economic order in which energy and raw materials rather than labour are taxed, in which the value of money for exchange purposes is reassessed, as well as the right to interest, which leads to a constant growth in production. This gives rise to the question of how an economy based on taking can be transformed into an economy based on giving, an economy based on the brotherhood of man. This is an essential condition for the enormous changes required at a world level. Man will only be able to comply with this condition of the brotherhood of man if he feels in contact with the spiritual beings which have a visible effect on the Earth, and with the great evolutionary stages of mankind.

The world, Europe, and I myself, must wake up to the deadening effect of technology. It is only when man is fully aware, Europe is awake, and mankind has recovered from its spiritual crisis, that the heart and blood will be formed to cure the sick Earth.

References

Chapter 1
1. Heisenberg, W. (1962) p.139
2. Bohm, D. (1951)
3. Pribram, K. *Holonomy and Structure in the Organization of Perception,* in Nicholas J.M. (ed) (1977)
4. Capra, F. (1982) p.327
5. Bohm, D. (1951) p.48
6. Jantsch, E. (1980) p.75
7. Capra, F. (1982)
8. Daub, W., Capra, F. in *Jonas,* No.18 (1985) pp.11–13

Chapter 2
1. Krishnamurti, J., Bohm, D. (1985)
2. Steiner, R. (GA 13)
3. Sheldrake, R. (1981) p.201
4. Steiner, R. (GA 103)
5. Steiner, R. (GA 13)
6. Hazrat Inayat Khan (1948)
7. Steiner, R. (GA 207)
8. Steiner, R. (GA 103)
9. Steiner, R. (GA 103)
10. Hazrat Inayat Khan (1948)
11. Bailey, A.A. (1955) p.23
12. Steiner, R. (GA 2)
13. Hazrat Inayat Khan (1971)
14. Bailey, A.A. (1955) p.35
15. Steiner, R. (GA 207), (GA 10)
16. Hazrat Inayat Khan (1971)
17. Bailey, A.A. (1955)
18. Hazrat Inayat Khan (1948)
19. Plato, *Dialogues*
20. Steiner, R. (GA 2)
21. Steiner, R. (GA 10)
22. Steiner, R. (GA 99)
23. Ramala Centre (1978) p.163
24. Steiner, R. (GA 10)
25. Steiner, R. (GA 182)
26. Moolenburgh, H.C. (1984)
27. Steiner, R. (GA 11)

Chapter 3
1. Sheldrake, R. (1981) p.246
2. Murdin, P., Murdin, L. (1985)
3. Moody, R. (1980); Spinar, Z.V. (1972)
4. Walker, J.C.G. (1978)
5. Lovelock, J.E. (1979) p.16

Chapter 4
1. Steiner, R. (GA 13), (GA 11), (GA 230)
2. Steiner, R. (GA 110)
3. Steiner, R. (GA 230)
4. Steiner, R. (GA 99)
5. Steiner, R. (GA 110)
6. Julius, F.H. (1970) p.89
7. Spalding, B.T. (1924)
8. Ramala Centre (1978) p.43
9. Steiner, R. (GA 13) p.309
10. Steiner, R. (GA 99)
11. Hagemann, E. (1967) p.334
12. Steiner, R. (GA 11)
13. Steiner, R. (GA 103); (GA 106)
14. Cloos, W. (1986) p.44
15. Hagemann, E. (1967) p.251
16. Steiner, R. (GA 99); (GA 106)
17. Steiner, R. (GA 106)
18. Steiner, R. (GA 11)
19. Steiner, R. (GA 106)
20. Steiner, R. (GA 103)

21. Steiner, R. (GA 11)
22. Steiner, R. (GA 106)
23. Steiner, R. (GA 99)
24. Steiner, R. (GA 106)
25. Bock, E. (1978) p.33
26. Steiner, R. (GA 99); (GA 11)
27. Steiner, R. (GA 106)
28. Bock, E. (1978) p.35
29. Wachsmuth, G. (1950) p.52
30. Steiner, R. (GA 106)
31. Hagemann, E. (1967) p.236
32. Steiner, R. (GA 11); (GA 99); (GA 106)
33. Bock, E. (1978) p.37
34. Steiner, R. (GA 99)
35. Steiner, R. (GA 106)
36. Hagemann, E. (1967) p.251
37. Steiner, R. (GA 11)
38. Poppelbaum, H. (1956)
39. Cloos, W. (1983) p.56
40. Steiner, R. (GA 349); Hage-mann, E. (1967) p.236
41. Steiner, R. (GA 106)
42. Steiner, R. (GA 99)
43. Steiner, R. (GA 105)
44. Steiner, R. (GA 103)
45. Steiner, R. (GA 114)
46. Ramala Centre (1978) p.256
47. Hagemann, E. (1967) p.237
48. Steiner, R. (GA 11)
49. Steiner, R. (GA 11); (GA 99)
50. Steiner, R. (GA 234)
51. Hagemann, E. (1967) p.252
52. Steiner, R. (GA 103)
53. Steiner, R. (GA 106)
54. Steiner, R. (GA 194)
55. Steiner, R. (GA 99)
56. Steiner, R. (GA 11):25
57. Steiner, R. (GA 11)
58. Steiner, R. (GA 99)
59. Steiner, R. (GA 11)
60. Steiner, R. (GA 107); *see* Arenson, A. (1984) p.629
61. Steiner, R. (GA 99); (GA 103)
62. Urantia (1981) p.649
63. König, K. (1986); Poppelbaum, H. (1956)

Chapter 5

1. Schneider, H., Londer, R. (1984) p.4, p.8
2. Butcher, H. in *Nature,* 328 (1987) pp.127–31
3. Plato, *Myths*
4. Steiner, R. (GA 103)
5. Steiner, R. (GA 11)
6. Steiner, R. (GA 99)
7. Steiner, R. (GA 99)
8. Steiner, R. in *Vom Leben des Menschen und der Erde* (GA 349)
9. Steiner, R. (GA 349)
10. Steiner, R. (GA 349)
11. Bailey, A.A. (1972) p.32
12. Steiner, R. (GA 13) p.197
13. Steiner, R. (GA 120) p.218
14. Steiner, R. (GA 226)
15. Steiner, R. (GA 226)
16. Steiner, R. (GA 11) p.171
17. Steiner, R. (GA 207); (GA 194); (GA 157); Blavatsky, H.P. (1925), III.
18. Steiner, R. (GA 106)
19. Bailey, A.A. (1972)
20. Wachsmuth, G. (1950) p.77
21. Hagemann, E. (1967) p.233, p.242; Vreede, E. (1980) p.381
22. Vreede, E. (1980) p.393
23. Steiner, R. (GA 230)
24. Steiner, R. (GA 230)
25. Steiner, R. (GA 230)
26. Cloos, W. (1986) p.44
27. Poppelbaum, H. (1956)
28. Steiner, R. (GA 11)
29. Hagemann, E. (1967) p.233
30. Steiner, R. (GA 11)
31. Hagemann, E. (1967) p.233
32. Steiner, R. (GA 11)
33. Steiner, R. (GA 122)
34. Steiner, R. (GA 11)

35. Steiner, R. (GA 103); see Arenson, A. (1984) p.203
36. Steiner, R. (GA 11)
37. Steiner, R. (GA 103); see Arenson, A. (1984) p.203
38. Steiner, R. (GA 11)
39. Steiner, R. (GA 121) p.161
40. Poppelbaum, H. (1956)
41. Steiner, R. (GA 105)
42. Steiner, R. (GA 293)
43. Mees, L.F.C. (1984)
44. Cloos, W. (1986) p.42
45. Plato, *Timaeus*, p.121

Chapter 6

1. Steiner, R. (GA 110); (GA 136)
2. Bailey, A.A. (1972)
3. Blavatsky, H.P. (1925), III.
4. Steiner, R. (GA 103); (GA 106)
5. Bailey, A.A. (1972)
6. Hagemann, E. (1967) p.26
7. Steiner, R. (GA 105); (GA 110); (GA 137); see Arenson, A. (1984) p.513
8. Ramala Centre (1978) p.47
9. Steiner, R. (GA 136)
10. Steiner, R. (GA 99)
11. Ramala Centre (1978) p.43
12. Steiner, R. (GA 110); (GA 230); (GA 349); (GA 327); Ramala Centre (1978) p.43
13. Steiner, R. (GA 136)
14. Steiner, R. (GA 99)
15. Bailey, A.A. (1972)
16. Spalding, B.T. (1924)
17. Steiner, R. (GA 103)
18. Steiner, R. (GA 105)
19. Steiner, R. (GA 103); (GA 110); (GA 136); (GA 230)
20. Quoted in L. Günther: *Kepler und die Theologie*, Giessen, 1905.
21. Steiner, R. (GA 226)
22. Cloos, W. (1986) p.92
23. Steiner, R. (GA 349)
24. Steiner, R. (GA 103); (GA 136)
25. Wachsmuth, G. (1927) p.94
26. Steiner, R. (GA 121); see Arenson, A. (1984) p.918
27. Steiner, R. (GA 110); (GA 230); (GA 136)
28. Steiner, R. (GA 121)
29. Steiner, R. (GA 105)
30. Steiner, R. (GA 95); see Arenson, A. (1984) p.208

Chapter 7

1. Steiner, R. (GA 293)
2. Ramala Centre (1978) p.44
3. Steiner, R. (GA 155)
4. Steiner, R. (GA 120)
5. Steiner, R. (GA 230)
6. Ramala Centre (1978) p.46
7. Lovelock, J.E. (1979)
8. Lovelock, J.E. in *Atmos. Envir.* (1972); Margulis, L., Lovelock, J.E. *Icarus,* 21 (1974) pp.1–19
9. Redfield, A.C. in *American Scientist* (1958)
10. Schrödinger, E. (1945)
11. Postel, S. (1986)
12. Fenner, F. in *Austr. Ann. Med.* (1969) pp.351–60
13. Lovelock, J.E. in Dickenson, E. (Ed) (1987) p.19
14. Kerr, R. in *Science,* Vol. 240 (1988) p.393
15. Lovelock, J.E. (1988) p.204ff
16. Crowley, T.J. and North, G.R. in *Science,* Vol. 240 (1988) p.996ff; Russell, P. (1982)
17. Bartelink, G.J.M. (1978)
18. Steiner, R. (GA 113)
19. Steiner, R. (GA 113)
20. Iliad 8.14
21. Plato, *The Last Days of Socrates* p.173–78
22. Steiner, R. (GA 121)
23. Steiner, R. (GA 105); (GA 121)
24. Steiner, R. (GA 121)

Chapter 8
1. Steiner, R. (GA 136)
2. Hagemann, E. (1967) p.58
3. Steiner, R. (GA 293)
4. Uyldert. M. (1984) p.18
5. Steiner, R. (GA 350); (GA 354)
6. Steiner, R. (GA 293); (GA 23)
7. Steiner, R. (GA 354)
8. Steiner, R. (GA 170)
9. Steiner, R. (GA 202)
10. Steiner, R. (GA 352)
11. Steiner, R. (GA 202)
12. Steiner, R. (GA 293)
13. Steiner, R. (GA 95)
14. Steiner, R. (GA 121)
15. Von Gleich, S. (1983) pp.5, 19
16. Hagemann, E. (1967) p.29
17. Von Gleich, S. (1983) pp.19, 21, 32
18. Steiner, R. (GA 110) p.124
19. Wachsmuth, G. (1980) p.117
20. Steiner, R. (GA 105)
21. Wachsmuth, G. (1980) p.84
22. Romunde, R. van (1981) p.47
23. Wachsmuth, G. (1980) pp.84, 112
24. Romunde, R. van (1981) p.48
25. Wachsmuth, G. (1980) p.89
26. Wachsmuth, G. (1980) p.110
27. Romunde, R. van (1981) p.202
28. Yukutake, T. and Cain, J.C. in *J. Geomagn. Geoelectr.* 39 (1987) pp.19–46
29. Kamide, Y. in *J. Geomagn. Geoelectr.* 40 (1988) pp.131–55

Chapter 9
1. Ramala Centre (1978) p.65
2. Uyldert, M. (1984)
3. Steiner, R. (GA 230)
4. Hagemann, E. (1967) p.201
5. Wachsmuth, G. (1980) p.185
6. Reiter, E.R. (1967) p.84
7. Wachsmuth, G. (1980) p.197; Romunde, R. van (1981) p.90

8. Broecker, W.S. in *Nature,* 328 (1987) p.123
9. Boyle, E.A. and Keigwin, L. in *Nature,* 350 (1987) pp. 35–40; Crowley, T.J. and North, G.R. in *Science,* 240 (1988) pp.996–1002
10. Hagemann, E. (1967) p.206
11. Gribbin, J. (1982) p.167; Wollin, G., Ryan, W.B.F. and Ericson, D.B. in *Earth and Planetary Science Letters,* 41 (1978)
12. Steiner, R. (GA 354)
13. Steiner, R. (GA 230)
14. Steiner, R. (GA 230)
15. Wachsmuth, G. (1927) p.94
16. Steiner, R. (GA 230)
17. Walker, J.C.G. (1978) p.180
18. Hagemann, E. (1967) p.207
19. Bockemühl, J., Schad, W., Suchantke, A. (1978) p.60
20. Steiner, R. (GA 352)
21. Steiner, R. (GA 327)

Chapter 10
1. Steiner, R. (GA 293)
2. Wachsmuth, G. (1950) p.197
3. Jurriaanse, T. *Het bos,* Mededelingen van de Anthroposofische Vereniging in Nederland jg. 40, no.9 (1985) pp.245–53; Bockemühl, J. (1984) p.68
4. Steiner, R. (GA 348)
5. Schrödinger, E. (1945)
6. Tesla, N. in *Century Illustrated Monthly Magazine,* June issue (1900); Cheney, M. (1981) p.54
7. Uyldert, M. (1984) p.10
8. Correra, C. in *Vrij Nederland,* 28 March, 1987
9. Faasse, M. (1978)
10. Endlich, B. *et al.* (1985) p.230
11. Uyldert, M. (1984) p.124
12. Endlich, B. *et al.* (1985) p.233

REFERENCES

13. Endlich, B. *et al.* (1985) p.192
14. Steiner, R. (GA 327)
15. Endlich, B. *et al.* (1985) p.198
16. Steiner, R. (GA 327)
17. Lovelock, J.E., Margulis, L. in Rambler, M.B. (Ed) (1984)
18. Jurriaanse, T. *Het bos,* Mededelingen van de Anthroposofische Vereniging in Nederland jg. 40, no.9 (1985) p.248
19. Steiner, R. (GA 352)
20. RIVM Report *Zorgen voor Morgen,* (1988) p.84
21. Lovelock, J.E. (1979)
22. Bockemühl, J., Schad, W., Suchantke, A. (1978) p.66
23. Richards, P.W. (1964)
24. Bockemühl, J., Schad, W., Suchantke, A. (1978) p.25
25. Bockemühl, J., Schad, W., Suchantke, A. (1978) p.63
26. RIVM Report *Zorgen voor Morgen,* (1988) p.55
27. Clark, W.C., Munn, R.E. (Ed) (1986) p.30, p.104
28. Romunde, R. van (1981) pp.98ff
29. Clark, W.C., Munn, R.E. (Ed) (1986) pp.56–62
30. Clark, W.C., Munn, R.E. (Ed) (1986) p.264
31. Lovelock, J.E. (1979)
32. Steiner, R. (GA 350)
33. Schneider, H., Londer, R. (1984) p.242
34. Clark, W.C., Munn, R.E. (Ed) (1986) p.271
35. Wilson, R.C., Hudson, H.S., Frohlich, C., Brusa, R.W. in *Science,* 234 (1986) pp.1114–17
36. Crutzen, P.J., Birks, J.W. in *Ambio,* 11 (1982) pp.114–25; Turco, R.P., Toon,, D.B. *et al.* in *Science,* 222 (1983) p.1283
37. Mathews, J.T. in *Issues in Science and Technology,* Spring issue, (1987) pp.57–61
38. Clark, W.C., Munn, R.E. (Ed) (1986) p.229
39. Schoeberl, M.R. in *Nature,* 336 (1988) p.420
40. Gribbin, J. in *New Scientist,* 19 May (1988)
41. Paresche, F., Bowyer, S. in *Scientific American,* 255 (1986) No.3 p.84
42. Odum, E. (1953); Goldsmith, E. in *The Ecologist,* 18 (1988) No.2 pp.64–74
43. O'Neill c.s. (1986)
44. Reichle, D.E., O'Neill, R.V. *et al.* in Dobben, W.H. van, Lowe–McConnell, R.H. (Eds) (1975)
45. Moore, J.C., Hunt, H.W. in *Nature,* 33 (1988) pp.261–263
46. O'Neill c.s. (1986) p.95, p.184
47. Goldsmith, E. in *The Ecologist,* 18 (1988) No.2 pp.64–74
48. Goldsmith, E. in *The Ecologist,* 18 (1988) pp.160–85

Chapter 11
1. Galbraith, J.K. (1977)
2. Steiner, R. (GA 23)
3. Endenburg. G. (1982)
4. Thompson, W.L. (1987) p.198
5. Winsemius, P. (1986)
6. Meadows, D. (1972)
7. Schaele, R.J. in *De Volkskrant,* 9 November (1988)
8. Maas R.J.M. *A Choice of Technological Futures.* (Paper presented at VTT symposium on Non–Waste Technology, Espoo, Finland, June 1988); also in RIVM Report *Zorgen voor Morgen,* (1988) p.13
9. Steiner, R. (GA 353)

Bibliography

Arenson, A. (1984) *Leitfaden,* Verlag Freies Geistesleben, Stuttgart.
Bailey, A.A. (1955) *A Treatise on White Magic,* (6th ed) Lucis Press Ltd., London.
—— (1972) *Initiation, human and solar,* Lucis Press Ltd., London.
Bartelink, G.J.M. (1978) *Mythologisch Woordenboek,* Prisma 1346, Het Spectrum, Utrecht.
Bateson, G. (1972) *Steps to an ecology of Mind,* Ballantine, New York.
Blavatsky, H.P. (1925) *The Secret Doctrine,* edition of 1888, Theosophical Publishing Co., London.
Bock, E. (1978) *Urgeschichte,* Urachhaus, Stuttgart. Published in English as *Genesis,* Floris Books, Edinburgh, 1983.
Bockemühl, J. (1984) *Dying Forests,* Hawthorn Press, UK.
Bockemühl, J., Schad, W., Suchantke, A. (1978) *Mensch und Landschaft Afrikas,* Verlag Freies Geistesleben, Stuttgart.
Bohm, D. (1951) *Quantum Theory,* Prentice–Hall, New York.
Capra, F. (1982) *The Turning Point,* Wildwood House, London.
Cheney, M. (1981) *Tesla: Man out of Time,* Laurel, Dell Publishing, New York.
Clark, W.C., Munn, R.E. (Eds) (1986) *Sustainable development of the biosphere,* CUP, Cambridge.
Cloos, W. (1983) *Lebensstufen der Erde,* Verlag die Kommenden, Freiburg.
—— (1986) *Das Jahr der Erde, von der Alchemie der Jahreszeiten,* Urachhaus, Stuttgart.
Dickinson, E. (Ed) (1987) *The Geophysiology of Amazonia,* Wiley, New York.
Dobben, W.H. van, Lowe–McConnell, R.H. (Eds) (1975) *Unifying Concepts in Ecology,* W.Junk B.V., The Hague.
Endenburg. G. (1982) *Sociocratie,* Samsom, Alphen a/d Rijn.
Endlich, B. et al. (1985) *Der Organismus der Erde,* Verlag Freies Geistesleben, Stuttgart.
Faasse, M. (1978) *Karakteristiek Rotterdam,* Afstudeerverslag Afdeling Bouwkunde, Technical University of Delft.
Galbraith, J.K. (1977) *The Age of Uncertainty,* Deutsch/BBC, London.
Gleich, S.von (1983) *Die Umwandlung des Bösen,* Zbinden Verlag, Basel.
Gribbin, J. (1982) *Future Weather,* Penguin Books, UK.
Hagemann, E. (1967) *Vom Wesen des Lebendigen,* Görich–Weiershäuser, Marburg.

Haich, E. (1979) *Initiation*, Allen and Unwin.

Hazrat Inayat Khan (1948) *In an Eastern Rose-garden*, Sufi Movement, Geneva. Also as: *The Flower Garden of Inayat Khan*, East-West Publications, 1978.

—— (1971) *Mental Purification*, Sufi Movement, Geneva.

Heisenberg, W. (1962) *Physics and Philosophy*, Harper & Row, New York.

Jantsch, E. (1980) *The Self-organizing Universe*, Pergamon, New York.

Julius, F.H. (1970) *Das Tier zwi-schen Mensch und Kosmos*, Verlag Freies Geistesleben, Stuttgart.

König, K. (1986) *Embryologie und Weltentstehung*, Novalis Verlag, Schaffhausen.

Krishnamurti, J., Bohm, D. (1985) *The Ending of Time*, Gollancz, London.

Lovelock, J.E. (1979) *Gaia, a new look at life on earth*, OUP, Oxford.

—— (1988) *The Ages of Gaia*, OUP, Oxford. Paperback edition 1989.

Meadows, D. (1972) *The Limits to Growth*, Universe, New York.

Mees, L.F.C. (1984) *Dieren zijn wat mensen hebben*, Vrij Geestesleven, Zeist.

Moody, R. (1980) *Prehistoric World*, Hamlyn, London.

Moody, R.A. jr. (1978) *Reflections on Life after Life*, Corgi, London.

Moolenburgh, H.C. (1984) *Engelen*, Ankh-Hermes, Deventer.

Murdin, P., Murdin, L. (1985) *Supernovae*, CUP, Cambridge.

Nicholas, J.M. (Ed), (1977) *Images, Perception and Knowledge*, Reidel, Dordrecht.

O'Neill c.s. (1986) *A Hierarchical Concept of Ecosystems*, Princeton University Press.

Odum, E. (1953) *Fundamentals of Ecology*, Saunders, Philadelphia.

Plato, *The Last Days of Socrates*, Penguin Books, 1969.

—— *Timaeus*, Penguin Books, UK, 1965.

Poppelbaum, H. (1956) *Mensch und Tier*, Philosophisch-Anthroposophischer Verlag am Goetheanum, Dornach. Projected publication in English as *Man and Animal*, Hawthorn Press, UK, 1991.

Postel, S. (1986) *Altering the Earth's Chemistry: assessing the risks*, Worldwatch Paper 71.

Ramala Centre (1978) *The Revelation of Ramala*, Neville Spearman, Jersey.

Rambler, M.B. (Ed) (1984) *Global Ecology*, Jones and Bartlett Publishers.

Reiter, E.R. (1967) *Jet Streams*, Anchor Books, Garden City, New York.

Richards, P.W. (1964) *The Tropical Rain Forest*, Cambridge.

RIVM (Dutch National Institute for Public Health and Environmental Protection) Report published as: *Zorgen voor Morgen*, (1988)

Romunde, R. van (1981) *Materie en straling in ruimte en tijd 1: Materie en warmte*, Vrij Geestesleven, Zeist.

Russell, P. (1982) *The Awakening Earth*, Arkana, London.

Schneider,H., Londer, R. (1984) *The Coevolution of Climate and Life*, Sierra Club Books, San Francisco.

Schrödinger, E. (1945) *What is Life?* CUP, Cambridge.

BIBLIOGRAPHY

Schroeder, H.W. (1983) *Die himmlische Hierarchien,* Urachhaus, Stuttgart.

Sheldrake, R. (1981) *A New Science of Life,* J.P.Tarcher, Inc., Los Angeles.

Spalding, B.T. (1924) *Life and Teachings of the Masters of the Far East,* De Vorss, Los Angeles.

Spinar, Z.V. (1972) *Life before man,* Artia, Prague.

Steiner, R. (GA 2) *A Theory of Knowledge based on Goethe's World Conception,* Anthroposophic Press, New York.

—— (GA 10) *Knowledge of the Higher Worlds,* Steiner Press, London.

—— (GA 11) *Cosmic Memory,* Harper and Row, San Francisco, 1981.

—— (GA 13) *Occult Science — an outline,* Steiner Press, London, 1979.

—— (GA 23) *Towards Social Renewal,* Steiner Press, London.

—— (GA 95) *At the Gates of Spiritual Science,* Steiner Press, London.

—— (GA 99) *Theosophy of the Rosicrucians,* Steiner Press, London.

—— (GA 103) *The Gospel of St John,* (Hamburg) Anthroposophic Press, New York.

—— (GA 105) *Universe, Earth and Man,* Steiner Press, London.

—— (GA 106) *Egyptian Myths and Mysteries,* Anthroposophic Press, New York.

—— (GA 107) *Geisteswissenschaftliche Menschenkunde,* Steiner Verlag, Dornach

—— (GA 110) *The Spiritual Hierarchies and their Reflection in the Physical World,* Anthroposophic Press, New York, 1983.

—— (GA 113) *The East in the Light of the West,* Anthroposophic Press, New York.

—— (GA 114) *The Gospel of St Luke,* Steiner Press, London.

—— (GA 120) *Manifestations of Karma,* Steiner Press, London, 1976.

—— (GA 121) *The Mission of the Individual Folksouls,* Steiner Press, London, 1970.

—— (GA 122) *Genesis,* Anthroposophical Publishing, London.

—— (GA 136) *Spiritual Beings in the Heavenly Bodies and in the Kingdoms of Nature,* Steiner Press, London.

—— (GA 137) *Der Mensch im Lichte der von Okkultismus, Theosophie und Philosophie,* Steiner Verlag, Dornach.

—— (GA 157) *The Forming of Destiny and Life after Death,* Anthroposophical Publishing, London.

—— (GA 170) *Memory and Habit,* Anthroposophical Publishing, London.

—— (GA 182) *The Dead are with us; The Work of the Angels;* etc., Steiner Press, London.

—— (GA 194) *The Mission of the Archangel Michael; The Mysteries of Light;* etc., Anthroposophic Press, New York.

—— (GA 202) *Colour; The Soul's Progress;* etc., Steiner Press, London.

—— (GA 226) *Man's being, his destiny and World Evolution,* Anthroposophic Press, New York.

—— (GA 230) *Man as Symphony of the Creative Word,* Steiner Press, London.

—— (GA 234) *Anthroposophy, an introduction,* Anthroposophical Publishing Co., London.

—— (GA 293) *Study of Man,* Steiner Press, London.

——(GA 327)*Agriculture,* Bio–Dynamic Agriculture Association, London.

—— (GA 348) *Health and Illness.*

—— (GA 349) *Vom Leben des Menschen und der Erde,* Steiner Verlag, Dornach. Published in English as: *Cosmic Workings in Earth and Man,* Steiner Press, London.

—— (GA 350) *Rhythmen im Kosmos und im Menschenwesen,* Steiner Verlag, Dornach.

—— (GA 352) *Cosmic Workings in Earth and Man,* Rudolf Steiner Publishing Co., London.

—— (GA 353) *Birth of Christianity,* etc. Rudolf Steiner Publishing, London.

—— (GA 354) *The Creation of the World and of Man,* etc.

Thompson, W.I. (ed) (1987) *Gaia, a Way of Knowing,* Lindisfarne Press.

UN World Commission (Brundtland Commission) on Environment and Development (1987) *Our Common Future,* OUP, Oxford.

Urantia (1981) Urantia Foundation, Chicago, Illinois.

Uyldert, M. (1984) *Aarde's levend lichaam,* Die Driehoek, Amsterdam.

Vreede, E. (1980) *Astronomie und Anthroposophie,* Philosophisch–Anthroposophischer Verlag am Goetheanum, Dornach.

Wachsmuth, G. (1927) *Die ätherische Welt in Wissenschaft, Kunst und Religion,* Philosophisch–Anthroposophischer Verlag am Goetheanum, Dornach.

—— (1950) *Die Entwicklung der Erde,* Philosophisch–Anthroposophischer Verlag am Goetheanum, Dornach.

—— (1980) *Erde und Mensch,* (2nd ed) Philosophisch–Anthroposophischer Verlag am Goetheanum, Dornach.

Walker, J.C.G. (1978) *Earth History,* Scientific American, New York.

Winsemius, P. (1986) *Gast in eigen huis,* Samson H.D. Tjeenk Willink, Alphen aan de Rijn.

Index